These VVere

The Romans

Second Edition

G. I. F. Tingay, MA

J. Badcock, MA

DUCKWORTH

First published in 1972 by Hulton Educational Publications Ltd.

Second edition first published in 1989 by Dufour Editions, Inc.

Reprinted in 1998 by
Gerald Duckworth & Co. Ltd.
The Old Piano Factory
48 Hoxton Square, London N1 6PB
Tel: 0171 729 5986
Fax: 0171 729 0015

© 1972, 1989 by G.I.F. Tingay and J. Badcock

ISBN 0 7156 2851 8

A catalogue record for this book is available from the British Library.

Printed and bound in the United States of America

Contents

Preface

The Ancient World remains a subject of intense interest. Indeed, the further we move away from it in time, technology, and political or social conventions, the more we are drawn to a closer study and truer appreciation of its achievements. The Greeks and Romans have been the subject of many courses, both formal and informal, at all levels in schools and colleges, and this book will be particularly useful for such courses, though we hope it will also interest the general reader.

It has not always been very easy in the past to find books which offer broad and fully illustrated accounts of the Greeks and Romans. A companion volume, *These Were The Greeks*, has dealt with the Greek World. In this one, we have tried to describe the growth and development of Rome and its Empire, and to present a clear picture of what life was like for Romans of both sexes and all classes. Unfortunately history is rarely clear-cut or simple, and many historical problems have no certain answer. We thought it more profitable to choose what seemed to us the best solutions, and to omit the 'perhaps' or 'possibly' which ought to qualify so many statements, while discussing our doubts where that seemed useful. Wherever possible we have referred to contemporary inscriptions and archaeological evidence, and quoted the translated works of ancient writers (occasionally in shortened or simplified form), though we are aware that ancient literature usually represents the views and assumptions of the highly educated few in ancient society.

The many illustrations have been chosen with two aims: first, to make the readers familiar with the physical world of the Romans, as depicted by their artists, and second, to show that the representational evidence of coins, mosaics, wall-paintings, reliefs and statues is invaluable as a supplement to literary sources.

G.I.F. Tingay
J. Badcock

Introduction: What You Will Find in *These Were the Romans*

This is a book about Romans; about Romans as a whole people, and about individuals, famous or unknown, ordinary and extraordinary. It describes the growth of the people and their city from the earliest days, their quarrels and wars at home and abroad, their conquests and empire, and finally, after eleven centuries, their disintegration and decline.

Some chapters describe historical events, others deal more generally with Roman life and society. But they have one thing in common. On almost every page you will find direct evidence from the ancient world which helps us to create an accurate picture of the past.

First there is written evidence, which falls into two main categories:

- the writings of historians, philosophers, geographers and poets, speeches (written down by the public figures who delivered them), letters, biographies and encyclopaedias. Most of these writings, copied and recopied over the centuries, expressed the opinions and preserved the prejudices of their authors (who were almost invariably the wealthy and educated in Roman society), and may only give us one side of the story.

- inscriptions: some record official decrees and the actions of government, others commemorate events, or are carved on memorials or tombstones, and so preserve the names and family details of many ordinary Romans.

Secondly there is the evidence of pictures:

- photographs of buildings, bridges, streets, houses and everyday objects enable us to visualize much more clearly what the Roman world was like. They also show how the patient excavations of archaeologists often provide information which does not exist in written records.

- the pictures also show the ancient world through the eyes of its artists. The carvings, coins, mosaics, wall-paintings and portrait statues tell us how people looked, and provide thousands of examples of the everyday world of the Romans.

There are difficulties, however, in using all this evidence. Often the Roman writers will disagree when describing the character of a famous man or the details of an event; one grave may seem to show that the Romans cremated their dead, another that they buried them. Usually it would take too long in a book of this sort to explain the different arguments or to list the technical details: often we have had to choose what seemed to us the most sensible explanations put forward by modern scholars and experts, without even mentioning the doubts or disagreements. All the statements we have made have the support of other writers. But you may well think that a picture, for instance, suggests something different from what we say. If so, do not be afraid to disagree with us. A fact is not true just because a printed sentence in a book says so. Try to find out from other more specialized books what the evidence is, and then make up your own mind; you will then be doing what historians have always had to do in the past, and always will have to do in the future.

Acknowledgements

The authors and publishers are grateful to the following for permission to use previously published material:

Harrap Ltd for an extract from Apicius, *A Roman Cookery Book*, translated by B. Flower and E. Rosenbaum

Oxford University Press for extracts from Virgil, *Georgics* and *Aeneid*, translated by C. Day Lewis, 1966

Penguin Books Ltd for extracts from Juvenal, *Satires*, translated by Peter Green, 1967; and from *The Poems of Catullus*, translated by Peter Whigham, 1966

We would also like to thank the following for providing photographs and illustrations and/or granting permission to reproduce them:

Mansell Collection; Ministerio della Publica Instruzione, Rome; Fototeca Unione; Giraudon; BBC Hulton Picture Library; British Museum; British Library; Oscar Savio, Rome; Museo Nazionale, Naples; Landesmuseum, Trier; J. Allan Cash; Staatliche Antikensammlungen und Glyptothek, Munich; German Institute of Archaeology, Rome; Soprintendanza alle Antichita della Sicilia Orientale, Syracuse; Ashmolean Museum, Oxford; Biblioteca Apostolica Vaticana; Aerofilms Ltd; South Shields Public Libraries and Museums Committee; Grosvenor Museum, Chester; National Museum of Wales; Ny Carlsberg Glyptothek, Copenhagen; Reading Museum and Art Gallery; French Government Tourist Office; Verulamium Museum; Society of Antiquaries, London; Royal Commission on the Historical Monuments of England; Fotomas; The Ancient Art and Architecture Collection; Bemporad Marzocco, Florence; Sir Ian Richmond for the Inchtuthil Plan; U. E. Paoli, *Vita Romana*, Ed. Le Monnier, Firenze, 1968 for the Plans of the House of Faun and House of the Surgeon.

The authors are also grateful to Diana Badcock for her maps and diagrams.

CHAPTER ONE

The Growth of Rome

The Site

A traveller heading north along the west coast of Italy towards the land of the Etruscans in 600 BC had to cross the deep, fast-flowing waters of the River Tiber. About 16 miles from the sea the river threads through a ring of low hills, and here was the traveller's crossing point, for a small island divided the strong current, and the water was shallow and fordable.

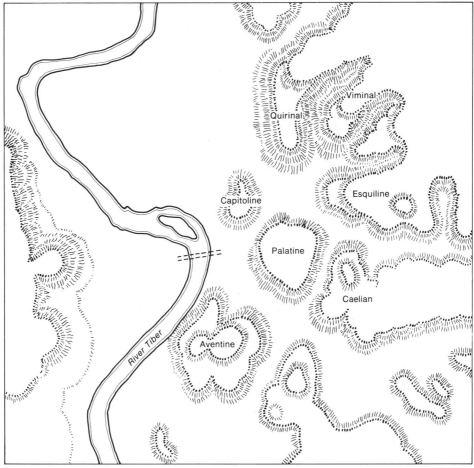

Rome: Tiber and hills

The site was inhabited, and the small hills had many lantern-shaped huts and some larger buildings on their slopes. The traveller's sharp eye was bound to notice the strength of the settlement's position: the hills themselves, surrounded by fertile agricultural land and grassy pastures, provided a natural stronghold and protection against attackers. One of the hills closest to the river bank was especially steep-sided, and formed an almost impregnable citadel. The river, too, made it risky to attack from the west, for the invading soldiers, struggling across the rapid waters, would be at the mercy of the defenders. For traders also the site had many advantages. Any merchant travelling overland along the west coast of Italy would be almost certain to cross the river at this point, and this was good for commerce. Merchants from the inland hills, making their way down to the sea, would also call at the settlement, and increase its prosperity.

Later Romans recognized that the Seven Hills provided a natural site for a city which controlled not only Italy but the whole of the Mediterranean world. Clearly the gods had inspired the choice of Romulus, the city's traditional founder:

> In choosing a site for the city, how could Romulus' inspired judgment have been improved on? For, by placing his city on the bank of a broad river which flows steadily into the sea all the year round he secured the advantages of a coastal town, and avoided its drawbacks. For the city can use its waterway for importing what it needs and for exporting its surpluses. . . . So it seems to me that even at this early stage Romulus predicted that the city would one day be the centre and heart of a mighty empire. For no other site in Italy would have enabled us to maintain our widespread dominion so easily.
>
> Furthermore, anyone with any powers of observation will have a clear impression of the natural strength of the city's defences. The line of its walls was cleverly planned by Romulus and his successors to run along steep and rugged hillsides for all its length, so that the single approach, between the Esquiline and Quirinal hills, was protected by a huge rampart and ditch, blocking an enemy advance. The city's citadel is so well-fortified by its surrounding precipices . . . that it remained safe and impregnable even during the terrifying onslaught of the Gauls. The site of Rome is well supplied with natural springs, and healthy, in spite of unhealthy neighbouring territory. For the hills channel the breezes, and provide shade for the valley.

> (Cicero, *De Republica* II, 5-6)

This is what Cicero, one of Rome's most distinguished citizens, wrote in 54 BC. But to the traveller almost six centuries earlier, the little community gave no hint of its later grandeur. There was nothing here to compare with the strongly-built hill-fortresses of the Etruscans, or with the elegant, well-planned cities of the Greeks. The Latin peoples, too, in their communities nearby, were poor and insignificant by comparison with the powerful Etruscan nation to the north, and the prosperous and sophisticated Greeks in the south.

Early Legends

But future generations of Romans, who looked back with pride to the early days of their city and its people, were not concerned with Etruscans and Greeks. In fact, the traditional accounts of early Rome make little mention of these powerful neighbours. According to tradition, the city was founded in 753 BC by Romulus, the first of a line of

2

seven kings. Titus Livius, in the first book of his massive 142-volume history of Rome, describes the events which led up to the foundation. Livy tells how Aeneas, escaping from the Greek sack of Troy at the end of the Trojan War, landed at Laurentum in Italy, formed an alliance with King Latinus of the Latins and married his daughter. Aeneas' son, Ascanius, then founded the city of Alba Longa, and was the first of a succession of kings to rule there. Thirteen generations later, Amulius, who had usurped the throne of Numitor, the rightful king, gave instructions to a servant to drown Numitor's twin grandchildren, Romulus and Remus. But the servant was too kind-hearted and left the twins on the river bank. There they were discovered by a she-wolf, who suckled them, until a shepherd found and brought them up. When the twins reached manhood, and had avenged themselves on Amulius, they decided to establish a city near the spot where they had been left to drown. Livy continues:

> Since the brothers were twins, and neither had seniority over the other, it was decided that the gods who kept watch over the site would choose by augury (the flight of birds) which brother should give the new city its name, and be its first king. So Romulus took the Palatine Hill for his observation point and Remus chose the Aventine. Remus is said to have seen the first augury – a flight of six vultures – but as soon as he had announced it, Romulus reported seeing twice that number. Each brother was accordingly saluted as king by his own followers, Remus on the grounds that he had seen the first heavenly sign, Romulus because his augury had been twice as big. Angry words followed, the two parties came to blows which led to bloodshed, and Remus himself was killed. But a more common version of the story is that Remus taunted Romulus by leaping over the newly-built city walls. At this Romulus, in a rage, killed his brother and added this threat:
>
> 'Death to anyone who leaps over my city walls.' In this way, Romulus gained sole power, and the city was founded and named after its founder.

(Livy I, 6)

Bronze wolf – a masterpiece probably by an Etruscan artist, about 500 BC. The figures of the children were added later during the Renaissance nearly 2,000 years later, but may have replaced original figures

3

Romulus was followed, according to the ancient tradition, by six more kings – Numa Pompilius, Tullus Hostilius, Ancus Martius, Tarquinius Priscus, Servius Tullius and Tarquinius Superbus. Tradition recorded the part that each king played in the growth and achievements of the new city. Numa Pompilius established Roman religion, Ancus Martius built a new port for the city at Ostia, at the Tiber's mouth. Servius Tullius surrounded the city with a wall, conducted a census and divided the citizens into classes, and the two Tarquins extended Rome's frontiers and carried out extensive building programmes.

Writing History

The legends give a detailed and colourful account of the early years of the city. But they are not history. Even Livy, to his credit, was sceptical about the accuracy of the time-honoured accounts in the early traditions. In the preface to his history he writes:

> I intend neither to confirm nor deny those traditions which describe events before and leading up to the foundation of the city. Such traditions are better suited to poetic fiction than to genuine records of historic fact. But a city with a long history is entitled to blur the distinction between the human and the supernatural in order to add dignity to its past. And if any nation deserves to be allowed to claim divine ancestry, surely Rome does.

(Livy, Preface)

Post holes which held the upright timbers of the primitive huts, dating from the eighth and seventh centuries BC. The grooves carried the water out of the huts, which measured about 14 metres in perimeter. Traces of the original hearths were clearly visible to the excavators in 1948

4

Historians in modern times echo Livy's doubts, but they are critical also of his account of the reigns of the first kings; for this too was often based on legends. But we may ask how a modern historian, writing 2,000 years after Livy, can hope to produce a more accurate version of Rome's origins. Part of the answer is that, unlike Livy, the twentieth-century historian is not trying to 'record the history of the greatest nation in the world' and so can be more critical of the legends and their heroes. Furthermore, historians now understand legends better: they see how they originate and develop, and can trace the different strands of Italian folklore and Greek myth which have become entangled in them. But most important of all, the contemporary historian has at his disposal a wealth of archaeological evidence which was not available to Livy. As the rebuilding of the city of Rome has continued during modern times, excavations have given scholars the opportunity to trace the development of the primitive community which first occupied the Seven Hills. The picture (opposite) shows some of the post-holes for the foundations of primitive houses which were discovered on the Palatine Hill in 1948. Evidence like this, and careful scientific analysis, helps us to piece together the fragments of history, and to produce a summary of Rome's early years.

From about 900 BC onwards the hills of Rome, particularly the Palatine and the Esquiline, attracted various separate settlements. These early inhabitants came from different tribes, with varying customs. But gradually a fusion took place until, about the middle of the eighth century, a single, unified community had emerged.

These hut-shaped urns, also eighth century BC, held cremated ashes. They help the archaeologist to reconstruct the primitive dwellings

Rome's First Years – the Kings

This primitive community was ruled by kings, as were most communities in Etruria and Latium, and though we cannot be certain about events in their individual reigns, we know that the two Tarquins in the traditional list are Etruscans, and that their presence in Rome indicates that Rome too had become part of the Etruscan dominion as this powerful nation pushed south down the west coast of Italy. Under Etruscan influence Rome grew and flourished, for the Etruscans at that time were one of the most advanced peoples in Italy. They lived in well-planned and well-fortified cities, carried out a wide range of industry – textiles, metal-work, farming, mining – and traded extensively with Greece and the Middle East. As a result, Etruscan civilization was more advanced and its culture more highly developed than that of its neighbours, and as they began to extend their influence north and south, Rome was bound to be affected.

Mounted warrior: part of the cover of an Etruscan urn

Etruscan warrior, wearing Greek armour

Under the two Tarquins, and Servius Tullius, (who was not himself an Etruscan) Rome developed fast. It ceased to be a settlement and became a city, surrounded by a defensive rampart, with temples and public buildings. Swamp land between the hills was reclaimed and a market area (*forum*) developed.

Tradition shows that Servius Tullius reorganized and reclassified the citizen body, and established many important political institutions: the *fasces*, (see p. 84), which were carried before Roman magistrates for centuries to come, made their appearance at this time. Under these last kings, Rome began to extend her influence over the nearby territory,

Etruscan bronze mirror and holder

and appears to have dominated much of the Tiber valley upstream and down to the sea, as well as some areas to the south, until her sphere of influence was larger than that of any other Latin city. Rome, in fact, was becoming a political centre of some importance, and when the Etruscans' hold on Latium began to weaken, the Romans were able to expel Tarquinius Superbus, and pursue an independent policy, as a republic. From this time 'king' was for the Romans a hated word.

Dating History

The Romans believed that the kings were expelled in the year 244 a.u.c. (*ab urbe condita*, 'from the foundation of the city'), in our terms 510 BC. Though we cannot be sure that this date is accurate, it cannot be far astray; Livy, who is our main written source for the early history of Rome, was writing roughly 30 BC–AD 17. *His* earliest written sources were the first historians of Rome writing (in Greek) soon after 250 BC and *their* sources were family records and personal memory passed from generation to generation. In dating events Livy is likely to be more accurate the closer these events were to his own times; but there were also more precise records he could consult, like the lists of annual consuls. Sometimes we can check his dates by confirming the dates of eclipses of the sun or moon which he mentions, and by corroboration from the histories of other nations like the Greeks and Egyptians. Thus any dates given in this book are likely to be roughly accurate down to 275 BC and hardly more than a year out at most from then on.

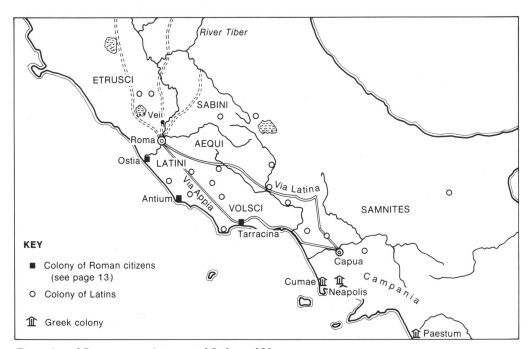

Expansion of Roman power into central Italy, to 300 BC

Respublica Romana

The new republic – the name given to their state by the Romans after the expulsion of the kings – now had to fend for itself, and other Latin cities were quick to challenge Rome's position. They formed an alliance whose forces fought a hard, but indecisive, battle against the Roman army at Lake Regillus early in the fifth century. As a result, Rome was forced to accept the status of equal partner in an alliance (the Treaty of Cassius – 493 BC) which provided for a common Latin defence against outside threats, and to abandon any claims to supremacy.

For the next hundred years the Romans were occupied in the defence of their territory, and repelling the invasions of the fierce mountain tribes – the Volsci, the Aequi and the Sabini (see map), who constantly threatened the fertile plains. Fierce fighting resulted, for Rome and the Latin cities were mainly agricultural communities, and were bound to resist any threats to their livelihood. The story of Cincinnatus (p. 18) summoned from his small farm to take command of Rome's forces as dictator in 458 BC, typifies the sturdy resistance of the tough farming people.

By 400 BC, through dogged fighting and resolute diplomacy, Rome came to dominate the surrounding territory and to exert a decisive influence in the alliance of Latin cities. Then a single disaster destroyed all she had achieved. In 390 BC a tribe of Gauls marauding from the north shattered a hastily collected Roman force in a battle at the River Allia, a few miles north of Rome, and advanced on the defenceless city. They found Rome deserted, except for a garrison on the Capitol, and the senators, who, according to Livy,

> . . . had gone home to await the arrival of the enemy, fearless in the face of death. Those who had held the highest positions of state wished to die dressed in the insignia of their rank, or wearing their decorations for distinguished service. So they put on the robes of civic dignitaries, or of generals who enter the city in triumph, and sat down on magisterial chairs in their courtyards . . .

The Gauls arrived in the Forum, but though the doors of the houses were open, they hesitated to enter.

> Awestruck, they looked in at the seated figures whose robes and decorations were more venerable than those of ordinary men and whose expressions, calm and majestic, made them look like gods. They might have been statues in some holy place. Then one of them, M. Papirius, when a Gaul tried to stroke his beard – for they grew beards in those days – struck him on the head with his ivory staff. That was the beginning. The barbarian killed him in a fury, and the other senators were butchered where they sat. From then on nothing was spared. Houses were ransacked and the empty shells set on fire.
>
> (Livy V, 41)

Only the Capitol held out, and after a long siege the garrison there surrendered. In return for 450 kilograms of gold the Gauls withdrew, leaving Rome (and most of its public records) burnt and ravaged. Archaeologists can still find the layers of ash and rubble. In a single disaster Rome had been devastated as a city and humbled as a state. Old enemies did not lose the opportunity to return to the attack.

9

Rome's Growing Power

Rome, however, did not give in. Under Camillus and other notable generals she regained the lost ground. Political and military reforms improved the leadership and made the army more efficient, until by the second half of the century Rome was strong enough to take the two steps necessary to dominate central Italy. In 338 BC she defeated the alliance of Latin cities and finally gained control over Latium. This was achieved with the help of the Samnites, a tough warlike people from the hill country of central

Samnite warrior, a bronze statuette from the sixth or fifth century BC. He would have originally carried a shield and a spear, with a crest on his helmet

southern Italy (see map, p. 8). It was against these allies that the Romans next turned. For some years Rome had been tightening its hold on the fertile and prosperous region of Campania, and a clash of interests in the area was inevitable. In a series of hard-fought campaigns, which lasted 40 years and on many occasions, as at the Caudine Forks in 321 BC, led almost to disaster for Rome, she at last defeated the Samnites, and gained control of their territory. By conquest and alliance Rome now dominated northern and central Italy. Only the Greek cities of the south stood apart, and Tarentum, by picking a quarrel with a Roman delegation, gave Rome the chance of completing the conquest.

This was no routine campaign, however. Lacking confidence in their own military resources the Tarentines secured the help of King Pyrrhus of Epirus, who landed in Italy in 280 BC with an army of highly trained mercenaries, and a contingent of elephants. The Roman force was thus faced by a commander and an army of international reputation, and Pyrrhus used his experience and his elephants to defeat the Romans twice in battle. But even in defeat the Roman legions were impressive. 'There is nothing barbarous about the military discipline of these barbarians,' said Pyrrhus, for his own losses were heavy. 'If we win one more victory against the Romans we shall be completely ruined.' And he withdrew to Greece. His garrison finally left Tarentum in 272 BC, and from then on Tarentum and the other Greek states accepted Roman domination.

Clay dish, showing a war-elephant carrying a battle-tower. Painted at about the time of Pyrrhus

The Reasons for Success

Rome now controlled Italy from the River Rubicon in the north to the southernmost tip, and international recognition followed immediately. Ptolemy Philadelphus, ruler of Egypt and one of the most powerful monarchs of the day, sent envoys to secure Rome's friendship. This was a proud moment for the Roman people: how had it been achieved?

11

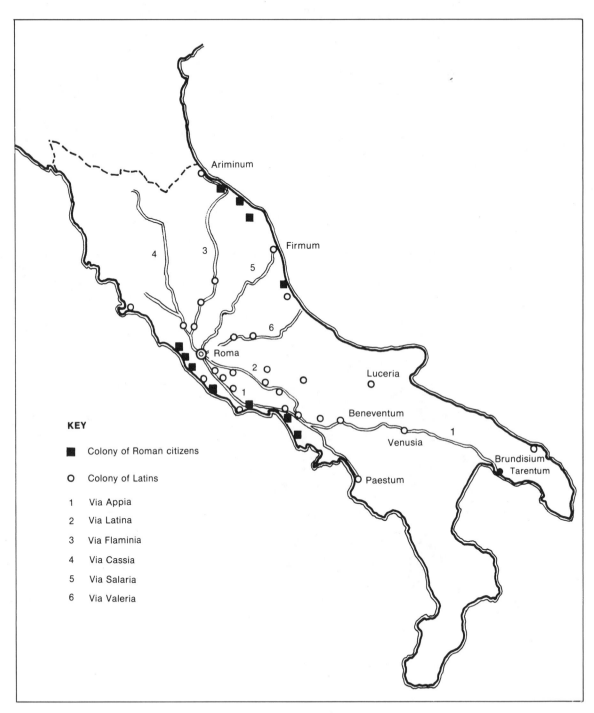

Rome and Italy, after Pyrrhus

Of course military success was the decisive factor. But fear of Rome's military power does not explain the loyalty of many allied cities who refused to open their gates to Pyrrhus as he marched towards Rome. Rome's strength lay in the nature of the policy which she adopted towards all the Italian peoples. Instead of conquest followed by ruthless oppression – the conqueror's traditional attitude to the conquered – Rome had created a political confederacy which came to include all the Italians. Each allied state was bound to Rome by a separate treaty, giving to each the status and degree of independence that the situation required. Some, like Tusculum in Latium, received full Roman citizenship, others a partial grant. Full citizens of an allied city had all the rights and privileges of a citizen at Rome, and in return paid taxes. Still more enjoyed 'Latin' rights, which involved some, not all, of the advantages of citizenship, while a third, less favoured group, although retaining domestic independence, had their foreign policies dictated by Rome. All allied cities were bound to provide troops for the Roman legions. In addition, by founding colonies of Roman citizens at key strategic points through Italy, Rome ensured the control and unification of the various tribes in the confederation, while by building roads and improving communications she bound Italy together as a nation. In this way, by a combination of ruthless military efficiency and fair and practical policy to the peoples who submitted, Rome became established as a world power. There was now almost unlimited manpower – which was going to be needed.

CHAPTER TWO

Peoples of Italy

It is now time to look more closely at these people – both the Italians and, more particularly, the Romans who led them. And there is no doubt that the Romans developed one unusual quality – the ability to win the loyal co-operation of allies and subjects alike. The federation of the peoples of central Italy that resisted Pyrrhus would have been vanquished at once if any of Rome's allies had defected; and they must have known that Pyrrhus would have welcomed them with open arms. Again, the union of all Italy south of the Rubicon, which was soon to take on the might of Carthage and the military genius of Hannibal, only survived because most of Rome's allies and subjects never wavered in their loyalty, despite great pressures and temptations to do so.

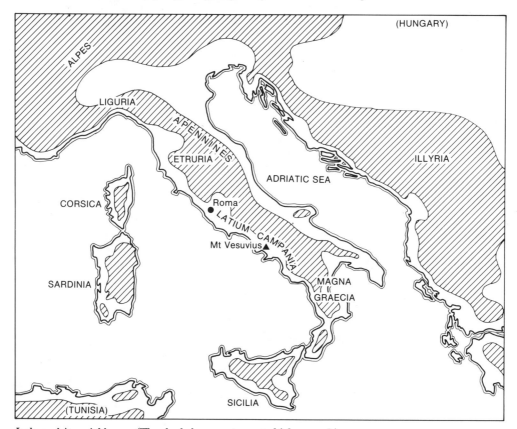

Italy and its neighbours. (The shaded area represents high ground.)

The Land

To some extent a people is shaped by the country it lives in; Italian history was largely determined by its geography.

Three-quarters of the land is hill-country, for the great northern plain between the Alps and Apennines was thought to be part of Gaul rather than Italy. The plain was only incorporated into the administration of Italy in the lifetime of Julius Caesar. It was cut off from the rest of Italy by the great ridge of the Apennines which here extend from the west coast to the east before turning southwards down the length of Italy. The mountainous character of the land, and the rigours of life which it brought, did much to mould the toughness, independence and tenacity of its inhabitants.

The central chain of the Apennines is so close to the Adriatic coast that the eastern shore has little fertile land until its windswept southern extremity, and few harbours. On the west coast, however, there are the two plains of Latium and Campania. They are not large, but their climate is warm and kind; the soil is fertile, enriched by the phosphates from the ash of volcanoes, active as recent as 1,000 BC, and watered by many streams.

Most of what we know of the earliest Italians has been discovered by archaeologists. In the last hundred years or so they have learnt how to interpret the evidence found in the burial grounds of these ancient people and in the layers of rubbish and rubble they left behind.

Immigrants Arrive

Successive waves of immigrants drifted over the Alps into the north of the country, each pushing its predecessors before it. First came Stone Age people, then pastoralists with copper tools, and next, from the Danube area, Bronze Age people, agriculturalists, who take their name from the alloy of copper and tin of which their tools were made. Around 1,000 BC, from the region of Hungary, came people with superior *iron* tools and weapons. Into the east of Italy came migrants from Illyria: from Tunisia, into the toe of Italy via Sicily, came the Siculi; and the south coast was so effectively occupied by colonies from the cities of Greece which soon grew into rich and strong trading communities, that the Romans later called this area 'Magna Graecia' – Great Greece. And on the west coast, in two groups north and south of Latium, were the Etruscans.

The origin of this strange people is still unknown, as is their language which is still to be seen on numerous inscriptions. But their elaborate cities of the dead, with their streets of tombs, have yielded a mass of evidence. The influence of Greece, and the Orient, is easy to see; it seems more likely that these influences came with the Etruscans when they migrated from overseas, but it is quite possible that they were acquired from traders and travellers. They probably came to Italy for the mineral wealth of the country, for copper and iron. They were a conquering aristocracy, vigorous and intelligent. Their grim religion may have led to human sacrifice; certainly they were able to contemplate without distress the massacre of their prisoners. They were morbidly fascinated by the future, divined by experts called *haruspices* from the entrails of the animals they sacrificed.

A street of Etruscan tombs at Orvieto in central Italy

We have other sources of information apart from archaeology. The names of the various tribes, their dialects and different alphabets tell us much. The Ligurians, far in the north-west, spoke an old tongue, for they were descended from the early Stone-Age inhabitants, driven by subsequent invaders into their inhospitable and remote country. Greek was spoken in the south, and the Etruscans had their own language as we have seen. But the tribes who came from the regions of Hungary along the ridge of the Apennines were divided into two groups, one speaking a language which developed into Latin, and the other a language later known as Oscan; it was spoken more in central

16

Italy and the south, and though it gradually gave way to Latin, it was still being used and written in Pompeii when the town was obliterated by the eruption of Vesuvius in AD 79. Both groups of people came into the plain of Latium and the surrounding hills: their remains, buried and cremated, have been found on the hills of Rome, and on the Alban Mount 12 miles away.

We have seen that at first small villages of herdsmen and shepherds grew on these hills: slowly the villages coalesced into one city, first recognized when a sacred boundary, called the *pomoerium*, was marked by a plough to indicate the area under the special protection of the city gods. Later an earthwork defence was built round tne city. This was probably not replaced by a stone wall until the fourth century.

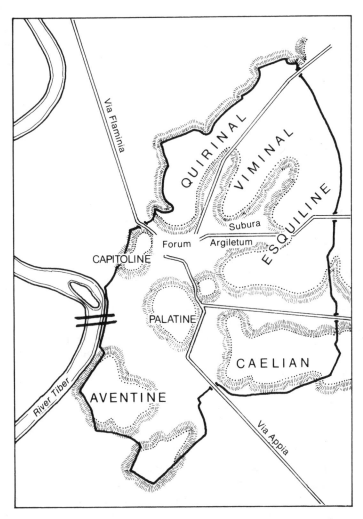

Rome in early days, showing the fourth century stone wall, known as the Servian Wall (see page 36)

17

Men of the Land

The existence of the city must not make us forget that by far the most important occupation of all the peoples of Italy was agriculture. The first settlers were probably shepherds, but soon they turned to the cultivation of the fields as well, going out to tend the sheep or cattle, or plough their land, and returning each evening to their houses in the city. The Romans first fought to defend their farms and, even when they ventured abroad to conquer and annex, they were no less anxious to get back to them.

The great Roman historian Livy, who filled the gaps in the early history of his country with a score of legends, constantly emphasizes the honest rustic lives of the early Romans. One story he tells us is of a desperate situation; a consul, Minucius, had allowed most of Rome's army to be trapped and encircled by an enemy force – their plight called for a dictator, a post specially created for such emergencies, and Lucius Cincinnatus was chosen.

> Cincinnatus was the people's only hope: he was cultivating his farm – a mere three acres; it was on the west of the Tiber, opposite the place where the docks are today, called the Quinctian fields. The messengers found him ditching, or ploughing perhaps, at any rate working on his land. After an exchange of greetings he was asked, together with a prayer for the success of himself and the state, to put on his toga and pay heed to the Senate's instructions. 'What's wrong?' he asked in surprise, and told his wife Racilia to run and get his toga from their cottage. Then wiping off the sweat and grime, he put the toga on. As he approached the envoys they congratulated him, saluted him as dictator and summoned him to Rome, explaining the terrible plight of the army.

> (Livy III, 26.8)

Within 15 days Cincinnatus had beaten the enemy, saved the army, resigned his dictatorship and returned to his farm.

Characters and Families

This was an exceptional achievement, but not without parallel. The Romans of later times certainly believed that their forefathers were distinguished by an excellence of character that was easily recognizable. This *mos maiorum* – ways of our ancestors – was something they were themselves always striving after; it rose from the frugal industry, the constant toil of farming and the resolute courage taught by their battles to survive and prosper. It is a combination of qualities easily intelligible in the original Latin – *gravitas, industria, diligentia, continentia, constantia, pietas, simplicitas, benevolentia,* and above all *virtus* – manliness.

There are many possible reasons for this respect for the past, and for the authority of the elders. The early settlers, together with the Etruscans by whom they were greatly influenced, had a great respect for their dead. Secondly, in societies with primitive standards of medicine and hygiene the mortality rate was extraordinarily high; many babies and their mothers died at birth – perhaps only a quarter survived into middle age, and the proportion of older people in the community was very much smaller than it is today. Again, the basis of Roman society was not the individual, but the family, with the *paterfamilias* at its head. (The *familia* was much wider than our 'family', and included the wife of the paterfamilias, his children, his sons' wives and their children and *all* their property.) When the paterfamilias died the family might split up, and the sons become heads of their own families, and so the numbers would increase. These families, even when the relationship was forgotten, were linked by their common name into a larger body, or clan, called a *gens*.

In each family the paterfamilias had absolute power over all the members of his family, including the right of life and death. And this was a real power: heads of families did decide to expose new-born children, and even on occasion to execute wives or sons – and since this right persisted in a limited form for hundreds of years we must presume that it was exercised justly. The paterfamilias was responsible for providing his children – the future citizens – with education, character training and religious upbringing. In these circumstances it is natural that the Romans should look with respect – even awe – on the authority of their fathers. And it is not surprising that these habits of respect and obedience should be transferred from family to state: heads of families themselves respected the heads of state chosen from the heads of the *gentes*; small wonder that the members of the governing body, the Senate, were themselves called *patres* or 'fathers'.

Part of the Ara Pacis (Altar of Peace), built by the Senate and dedicated in 9 BC in honour of Augustus. The altar and its surrounding wall-screen were covered in fine carvings, including this scene of a solemn procession, in which the emperor and his family were taking part

Patrons and Clients

Newcomers to Rome, such as merchants and craftsmen, ex-slaves, members of families who wanted to break away, anyone, in fact, who might be in difficulties without the legal protection of the family, might attach himself to a family. They were called *clientes*, their protectors *patroni*. It was the legal duty of the patron to give his client the same protection which a *paterfamilias* was obliged to give any member of his family. A poor client might expect to receive daily food, though this was often converted into money (*sportula*), or assistance in the law-courts. In return he was expected to help his patron in his political and private life. A freedman (ex-slave), for example, if required, had to provide the same service for his patron as he had been obliged to perform as a slave for his master. Clients might be asked to attend their patron in public as he moved through the forum, and their numbers gave him political prestige. They also showed him their respect by going to his house, formally dressed in the *toga*, to greet him in the morning (*salutatio*). The client/patron relationship persisted for many centuries, and helped to preserve the influence of the leading families.

Patricians and Plebians

There was another, much more important, split in Roman society: it was sharply divided between patricians and plebeians, or nobles and commons. The origins of the division are not certain: probably the *plebs* was formed from humble traders, or farmers who were unsuccessful because their lands, or their efforts on it, were inadequate. The *patricii*, however, formed the landowning aristocracy: only patricians entered the Senate and high offices of state, and controlled the religious institutions – and they aimed at social exclusiveness as well. In early Rome intermarriage between plebeian and patrician was forbidden by law.

Of course the plebs did not accept this situation happily, and within 15 years of the expulsion of the kings the common people began the struggle, lasting over 200 years, first to win protection from arrogant patrician officials, and later for complete equality. Their weapon was strike action: they threatened to leave Rome whenever they were most needed as soldiers. Livy tells us that they went on strike on five occasions. He says that after the first of these 'secessions', as they are called, in 494 BC, the plebeians were allowed every year to elect two 'tribunes of the people' – *tribuni plebis*; the plebs as a body swore to guard the lives of their tribunes, while the tribunes were champions of the plebs, and were officially recognized by the patricians.

After winning protection from the magistrates, the plebs then demanded that the laws be published, so that the magistrates might not interpret unwritten laws to their own advantage or to the harm of the plebs, and by 450 BC a code of laws was published on 'Twelve Tables' of stone: Roman schoolboys were still learning the words of these tablets some 400 years later. The plebs next sought the right to stand for official positions, and in 367 BC a law was enacted that one of the consuls should be a plebeian. The patricians retaliated by transferring some of the consul's powers to a new office – the praetorship – for which at first probably only patricians were eligible: but in 337 BC there was a plebeian praetor. Gradually the plebs were allowed to enter all official positions and all religious bodies. Final victory came in 287 BC when a law (the Lex Hortensia) was passed that all resolutions of the plebeian assembly, called *plebiscita*, should have the force of law, and be binding on the whole population.

This was a social revolution: but it is important to remember that it was a bloodless revolution. Only when it was completed did the united Rome begin the advance towards empire, with the long-delayed victory over Pyrrhus and the occupation of Magna Graecia.

CHAPTER THREE

Houses

Primitive Dwellings

When the first settlers came to the hills of Rome the houses they made for themselves
were very simple. Excavations on the Palatine Hill have revealed some of the remains.
Post-holes were cut into the solid rock, with channels to lead away the rain water (see p. 4).
The posts set in their holes in a ring about 14 or 15 feet across supported thatched roofs.
The walls were made from clay or mud daubed onto interlaced branches and strips of wood:
considerable fragments of walls of this type have been found – some very good examples
can be seen in the UK in the Verulam Museum at St Albans. The numerous hut-urns
found in the early graves of Latium and Etruria give us some idea of what the huts
looked like, and guided the artists who made the reconstruction of one.

Hearths were found in the centre of the huts, and traces of fires were clearly visible
when the huts were excavated. There was no chimney, and smoke from these fires found
its way out through a hole in the roof. An interesting survival from these primitive
conditions is found even in the luxuriously decorated stone and marble houses of the

*A modern model of an early hut, showing the frame and
covering*

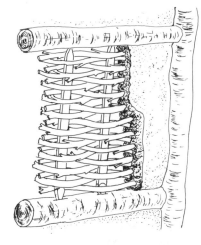

*A section of a wattle and daub wall. The mud and clay
daub hardens around the wooden framework
making an effective weatherproof surface*

rich aristocrats of the Empire, for the main living area of these houses is called the *atrium*. This name is derived from the Latin word *ater*, black, and recalls the gloomy, ill-lit huts with their smoke-blackened timbers.

No doubt, when stone, tile and plaster began to replace mud and thatch, houses of all shapes and sizes were built. But we can see from many excavations that town houses were usually variations on one basic plan, suitable for the warm climate of Italy. The large central *atrium* or living room was surrounded by a number of smaller rooms, bedrooms, kitchens, store-rooms, lavatories and so on, and at the side furthest from the entrance a small garden. Such a house looked something like this:

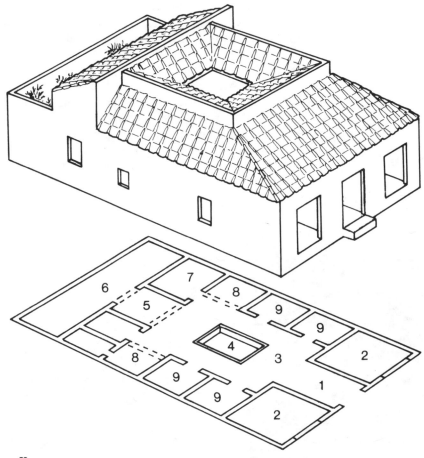

Key

1. *fauces*—entrance passage
2. *tabernae*—shops
3. *atrium*—hall
4. *impluvium*—rainwater basin
5. *tablinum*—passage room
6. *hortus*—garden
7. *triclinium*—dining room
8. *alae*—side-rooms
9. *cubiculum*—bedroom

The feature we may find most unusual is the elaborate opening, with its inward-sloping roof. Light and air entered by this *compluvium*, and rain-water collected in a pool below called the *impluvium*, corresponding in size and shape to the opening. Opening off the atrium were two open-sided rooms called *alae*: we cannot be sure of their purpose, but they are perhaps a traditional survival from more primitive houses in which the atrium had only a tiny smoke-hole, and light and air entered through window-spaces in the alae.

The compluvium *of the House of the Silver Wedding at Pompeii which admitted light and air into the atrium*

Greek Influences

As the Roman people grew more numerous and powerful over the years, their expansion brought two marked effects: first a great increase of wealth and spending power for a small section of the community, and secondly contact with the new ideas and cultured living of the Greeks in the towns of southern Italy. So it is hardly surprising that the rich wanted to build larger and more splendid houses, and that a composite house should develop, part Italian and part Greek; the parts of the older houses have Latin names – *vestibulum, atrium, alae, cubiculum* (bedroom), *hortus* (garden) – while the later additions have names derived from Greek – *triclinium, peristylium, exhedra, andron* and *oecus*. The Romans adopted the Greek habit of reclining to eat their meals, while formerly they had sat at table in the atrium, and special dining rooms were built containing three reclining places, hence *triclinium*; the *peristylium* was an elaborate garden, taking its name from the colonnade which surrounded it. The Greek word *andron* meant the men's quarters, and was mistakenly applied to the corridor joining the

Peristyle of the House of the Silver Wedding. When excavating, archaeologists identified pollen grains from the plants and bushes growing there before the eruption of Vesuvius. With modern equivalents planted in their place we can see what a Pompeian garden would have looked like

24

atrium and peristyle. The *exhedra* was a large room opening off the far side of the peristyle, and the *oecus*, derived from the Greek word for a house, was a sort of large communal dining room. The basic plan of these composite houses looked something like this:

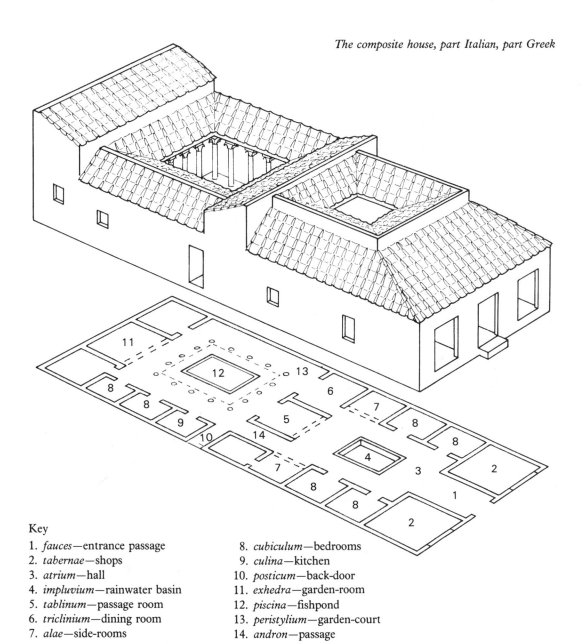

The composite house, part Italian, part Greek

Key

1. *fauces*—entrance passage
2. *tabernae*—shops
3. *atrium*—hall
4. *impluvium*—rainwater basin
5. *tablinum*—passage room
6. *triclinium*—dining room
7. *alae*—side-rooms
8. *cubiculum*—bedrooms
9. *culina*—kitchen
10. *posticum*—back-door
11. *exhedra*—garden-room
12. *piscina*—fishpond
13. *peristylium*—garden-court
14. *andron*—passage

Pompeian Houses

Most of our evidence, apart from literary allusions to individual rooms, and the elaborate descriptions of designs and proportions which survive in the *De Architectura* of Vitruvius, comes from the city of Pompeii, buried in volcanic ash in the eruption of Vesuvius in AD 79, and extensively excavated during the last hundred years or so. None of the houses there exactly follows either of the basic plans, but the 'House of the Surgeon', which took its name from the surgical instruments found in it, shows a simple house, while the 'House of the Faun' with its two atria and two peristyles shows the extent to which the simple plan could be elaborated by the very rich.

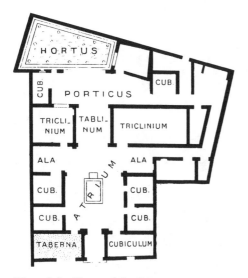

Plan of the House of the Surgeon

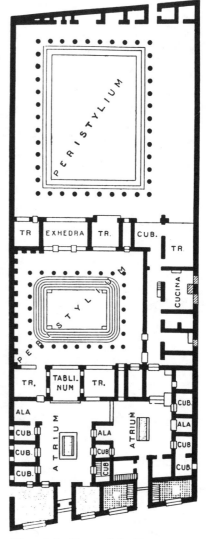

Plan of the House of the Faun

The walls of the rooms in the Pompeiian houses were painted in brilliant colours, and depicted scenes considered appropriate for the use of the room. There were hunting scenes, processions, paintings of architectural features, or cupid figures in various occupations in friezes only a few inches high. The floors were treated just as carefully, and there were many magnificent mosaics. These are pictures, or decorative patterns, formed from small cubes of stone of different colours set in a cement base. Many are rather clumsy and uninspiring, but others are superb works of art.

These houses are very different from ours. In particular the emphasis is on an open-air life in a warm country: it is noticeable that when the Romans built houses in the cooler northern provinces neither the open atrium nor the peristyle garden opening directly from the rest of the house are found. Another difference is that the Pompeiian house looked inwards: there are few windows in the outer walls, for light and air entered through the atrium and peristyle, the two main openings round which the smaller rooms were grouped. One great advantage of this plan in Roman towns was that the noise and uproar of busy streets was kept out. The outward appearance of these houses was unimportant: it was even quite common for the two rooms fronting onto the street at each side of the main entrance to be rented as shops, often perhaps for ex-slaves of the household to run. Normally these houses were of only one storey: when there was a second floor, the rooms were small and few.

City Houses

But these, of course, are the houses of the rich, and there were not many of them. Since land in towns was restricted and expensive, just as it is today, another solution was found for the poor and middle classes. Roman towns were planned methodically and divided by a grid of streets into rectangular areas known as *insulae*, islands. In these insulae were the public buildings, shops and houses. But also there were huge apartment buildings, which, since they took up the whole rectangle, came also to be called insulae. In a survey of the city of Rome carried out around AD 350 there were 1,790 private houses (*domus*) but 46,602 insulae, and each of these contained several families.

Our evidence for the apartment buildings comes mainly from the extensive remains of Ostia, the port of Rome, some 14 miles from the city. They were often four or five storeys high, and contained many small uncomfortable rooms overlooking the street or an inner courtyard. Ventilation and light came from outside, rather than from above as in the Pompeiian houses, and many windows and balconies were built in the outer walls for this purpose just as they are today. The outward appearance of these buildings was accordingly much more attractive than that of the richer houses.

Little else, however, was likely to be very attractive: life in the insulae could be unpleasant and even dangerous. Because early building techniques were uncertain the emperor Augustus issued a building regulation forbidding the construction of insulae over 21 metres (69 feet) high. But even that meant a laborious climb to the top floor, for there were no lifts or elevators: the poet Martial tells of a man who

> steals food, carries it to his house, up 200 stairs, then locks the door of his room, the greedy-guts, but sells it all on the next day.

(Martial VII, 20.20)

This insula with its balconies still surviving is at the old Roman port of Ostia

An insula looked something like this

28

Property developers were greedy as well, and did not waste an inch of space: when Martial had a room in an apartment block, he wrote:

> Novius is my neighbour – I can lean out of the window and touch him by the hand.

(Martial I, 86, 1–2)

The builders were no less unscrupulous. Augustus limited the height of the buildings because of the poor quality of the construction work. The ground floor might be solidly built of stone, which could be occupied by the owner of the property, or rented at high cost. More often, though, the construction was shoddier, and the ground floor was let off as small shops, *tabernae*. For the upper storeys a timber framework filled with rubble was used, which was often weak and dangerous. Plutarch explains that the financier Crassus made his fortune by buying up damaged property at a low price:

> He observed that every day in Rome buildings caught fire, or collapsed, because they were so large and close to each other.

(Plutarch, *Crassus*, III)

Crassus' contemporary Cicero, the famous orator and statesman, writes to his friend, complaining of the sorry state of an insula he owned as an investment:

> Two of the tabernae have fallen down, and the walls of the others have all cracked: my tenants are gone – and the mice as well!

(Cicero, *ad Att* XIV, 9.1)

Even under the Empire, when building regulations were much stricter, the poor in Rome still suffered. Tacitus tells of a disastrous year, when

> Unemployment and food shortages caused famine in the poorer classes, and the standing flood water sapped the foundations of the large tenement blocks, which collapsed as the river retreated.

(Tacitus I, 86)

And the satirist Juvenal, writing at about the same time, sums up the situation for us:

> We live in a city largely held up by slender props, for that is how the estate-agent holds up the tottering house, patching up gaping cracks in the old wall, and telling the occupants to sleep at ease, even though the roof is ready to tumble about their ears.

(Juvenal, 3.193)

The rooms were without heating, or even proper windows. Though central heating systems – hypocausts – became fairly common in the time of the emperors, they were reserved for the private houses of the rich, and for public buildings. Small stoke-holes were built at the side or basement of the main buildings: fires were lit, and hot air and smoke from these were allowed to circulate under the floors, which were supported on pillars, and passed up special flues in the walls. Though we have no evidence of any method of regulating the heat, apart from building up or damping down the fire, it seems highly unlikely that such a practical people as the Romans would not have devised some means of diverting or directing the hot air. In winter the poor man in his room in an

A Roman room-heater

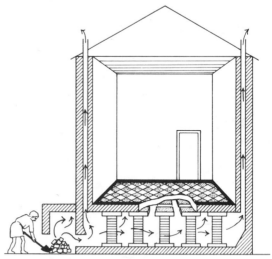

A hypocaust

insula had to burn charcoal in a brazier or stove – and stifled if he closed the wooden shutters, or shivered if he left them open.

The danger of fire in wooden buildings was, of course, enormous. There was no running water in the insulae, and accordingly no baths or lavatories. It is hardly surprising that the emperors built huge public baths, called *thermae*, containing libraries, rest-rooms and restaurants as well as bathing pools, and supplied heated public lavatories for their unhappy subjects!

Country Houses

The houses in the country were of many different kinds. There were the grim barracks housing the slave-gangs working the large estates or the state-owned mines, and simple farmhouses in which the pattern of farming determined whether there would be stables or sheep-pens, granaries or fruit-lofts. For the rich there were *villae*, comfortable houses which were often the centres of self-contained farming industries. The villas at Bignor and Chedworth in southern England are good examples of working villas. Some were of fantastic size and elegance, with countless rooms, private bath-houses, swimming pools and loggias. The younger Pliny owned two such villas, which he describes in detail, far too long to be recounted here. A model of one of them can be seen in the Ashmolean Museum in Oxford. An example of such a villa in Britain, obviously the property of a very rich aristocrat or official, can be seen at Fishbourne in Sussex, England.

Furniture

Rich and poor alike had, by modern standards, very little furniture. Beds were simple wooden frames across which were tacked leather straps, or webbing, in turn covered with mattresses stuffed with straw or wool. One or two plain woollen blankets formed the covering. There were few chairs, and these were reserved for honoured guests, the aged or womenfolk. Children, slaves or workmen used wooden stools, while men might recline on their beds which served as couches by day. Valuables were stored in boxes and chests of various sizes, and everyday objects were on shelves just as they are today. Rooms which lacked under-floor heating were warmed with portable braziers or stoves often elaborately decorated. Artificial lighting was very poor compared with ours, and supplied by small oil-burning lamps made of terracotta with simple wicks, which gave roughly as much light as a small candle. Elegant lampstands have been found, made of bronze, from which several small lamps hung by slender chains.

Tables were the most highly prized pieces of furniture in Roman houses, and were made of rare woods, bronze and silver, with inlays of wood or ivory or tortoiseshell. Those with a single central leg were particularly valuable, and Cicero spent 500,000 sesterces on one, enough to support a humble family in some comfort for a lifetime. The Romans were also prepared to spend large sums on statues and portrait busts to adorn their houses: we hear of shiploads being imported from Greece, and factories were set up to make 'reproductions' – copies of the many famous statues made by renowned Greek sculptors: many of these copies have survived.

It is clear in fact that the Romans regarded their homes much as we do, and did their best to decorate them and make them as attractive as possible. And they were, like us, secretly pleased if in doing so they went one better than their neighbours.

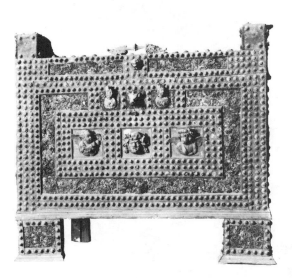

A typical storage chest

Ornamental lamp standards

31

CHAPTER FOUR

City

The First Stages

The city of Rome today is busy and modern, packed with over a million people and scoured by throbbing lines of insistent cars. The suburbs and business quarters, with their blocks of flats and offices, might belong anywhere in the world. But near the centre, scores of dazzling fountains and splendid churches set Rome apart from other capital cities. And at the very centre is the ancient Forum – empty spaces, a few broken buildings, a couple of arches and a single road – filled with a constant throng of tourists, all trying hard to conjure the glories of the past from the disappointing stones around them. This is all that can be done. Rome of Republican times disappeared beneath the

The Roman Forum

concrete and marble of the Empire, which in turn fed the lime-kilns and palaces of mediaeval nobles and churchmen. We have to build our pictures from the scanty reports of Roman authors, the foundations uncovered by patient archaeologists and the few more or less complete structures that remain to tantalize us. There was more to be seen a few hundred years ago, as the engravings and paintings of the time show us, and there are some superb models and reconstructions in modern museums, but the sightseer standing in the Forum has to rely almost entirely on his or her imagination.

But the Forum was once very different from its present ruins, as a story from Livy and a few lines from Ovid will show:

> Mettius Curtius . . . had driven the Romans in flight over the space where the Forum now is. Romulus charged him with a band of his toughest men. Mettius was fighting on horseback, and was easily driven away. But when the shouts of his pursuers terrified his horse he galloped into a swamp. When the Sabines saw their hero's plight they turned towards him: they shouted and beckoned, and encouraged by their support he fought his way out. . . . In memory of the battle the spot where his horse first brought Curtius out of the deep swamp on to dry land was called the Lacus Curtius.

> (Livy VII, 6.5)

> Dense swamp covered the ground where the Forum now is: a ditch would be filled up by water seeping back from the river. This is the Lacus Curtius – dry altars now rise from it, the soil is dry, but once it really was a lake.

> (Ovid, *Fasti*, 6.403)

A relief showing the story of Mettius. This carving was found in the Forum in the sixteenth century

33

The swampland was reclaimed by the Etruscan king Tarquinius Superbus, with a feat of engineering remarkable for the time. He drained the swamp by means of a huge underground channel, at first covered with planks, but later vaulted over with stone. It collected all the standing water and carried it away to the Tiber. The outlet of this great sewer, the *Cloaca Maxima*, can still be seen.

The outlet of the Cloaca Maxima, under the Ponte Palatino crossing the Tiber. The human figure makes it plain how large it is

The arches, now dry, of the Cloaca Maxima

The same Tarquin also built a great temple to Jupiter Optimus Maximus – Jupiter Best and Greatest – on the Capitol, making it the hill most honoured by the Romans. As well as a religious centre it was their citadel, an invincible stronghold like the keep of a mighty castle. It was from this hill that a beleaguered garrison watched with anguish when, in 390 BC, a host of Gauls reduced Rome to a heap of smouldering ruins. Then the dictator Camillus saved the city twice over. First he defeated and butchered the Gauls: secondly he persuaded the Romans not to leave their ruined city and move 12 miles away to Veii. This was a fine town they had recently captured undamaged. Instead they followed Camillus' advice and demolished Veii to rebuild Rome. Livy tells the story:

> The proposal [to move to Veii] was defeated, and the rebuilding of the city began, without any planning at all. Tiles were supplied at government expense. A law allowed any man to take stone or timber from wherever he wanted, provided he gave a pledge that building should be finished within the year. In their haste they took no care in laying out the streets: since all property boundaries had disappeared they were building, so to speak, in empty land. This explains why the old sewers, which formerly ran under publicly owned land, now frequently pass beneath private houses, and why Rome looks more like some haphazard setttlement than a properly planned city.

(Livy V, 55, 2–5)

35

Street Plans

The planning which Livy talks of is the 'grid-iron' pattern of straight streets crossing each other at right angles which the Romans copied from the Greeks and Etruscans. The same plan was adopted by the Roman army when camps were built, and there is a strong similarity between civil and military planning. The effect of the Roman town patterns is still very evident in a great number of European cities.

For some years after the sack of their city the Romans were kept busy in recovering their leadership over the neighbouring towns, which had naturally taken advantage of Rome's weakness to break away from the league which she had dominated. But, around 380 BC, they found time and energy to replace the earthwork defences of the city with a wall of smoothed and finished stone, the so-called Servian Wall (see p. 17). They also took the opportunity to enlarge the city: the ancient pomoerium had included 180 hectares (445 acres), the new wall embraced 280 (692 acres).

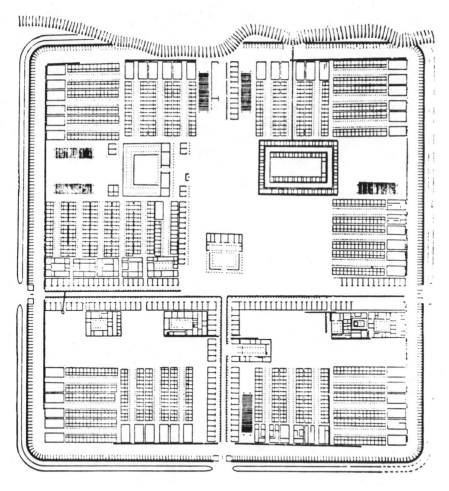

The plan of Rome's most northerly legionary camp, at Inchtuthil, in Perthshire, Scotland

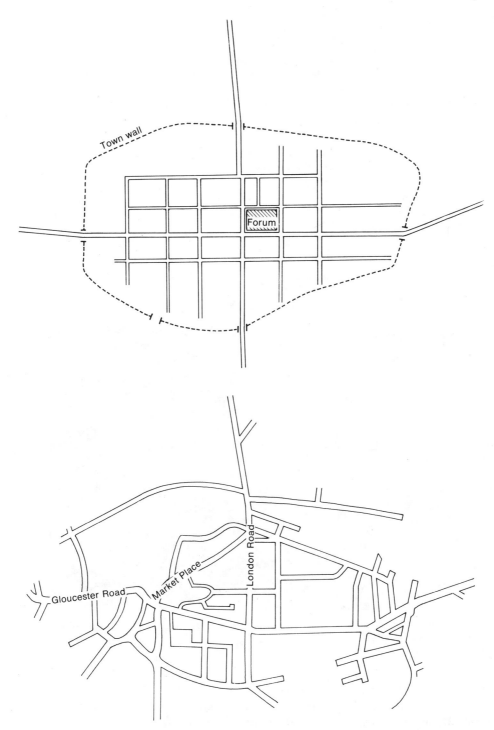

You can see from these diagrams how the planning of the Roman town has affected the street plan of modern Cirencester in southern England

Growth and Change

As Rome's conquests in Italy continued, and her territory spread wider, war booty was carried back into the city to be sold: successful generals built temples with the money they had won to fulfil vows made hopefully before battle. The Via Appia and the Via Latina were also built from the proceeds: at first they were military roads; soon they encouraged trade and traders to Rome. The city continued to grow, even outside the walls, and as the population increased, further demands were made upon municipal organization. The Appius who built the road also gave his name to the first aqueduct, constructed in the same year: it was an underground channel, barely a mile long. Within 30 years another was needed: this time the Anio Vetus stretched for 40 miles to bring clear fresh water from the Sabine hills: this too was a channel, but the Aqua Marcia, built 144–140 BC was a high level aqueduct, supported where necessary on arches of stone marching across the fields. When Frontinus wrote his treatise on aqueducts in AD 97 there were nine major aqueducts supplying the city: their total length was about 264 miles, and it has been calculated that they delivered 1,000,000,000 litres (260,000,000 US gallons) every 24 hours.

A few surviving arches of the Aqua Claudia which carried water into Rome. Built in AD 47, it brought water 43 miles (69 kilometres) into the city

When the war with Hannibal began in 218 BC Rome had become by far the largest city in Italy, comparable perhaps with Antioch and Alexandria, the great cities of the eastern Mediterranean. But the wars with Carthage and the vast sums of money they consumed, put an end to this expansion, and for a time building had to stop. Hannibal was to march within sight of Rome, and gaze at the walls, but he never attacked the city: if he had done so, and had broken into the centre and stood in the Forum, what would he have seen? There were lines of shops and houses, for the only public buildings were the Curia Hostilia, a cramped and antiquated building where the Senate met, and a few ancient temples. These included the round temple of Vesta, wooden till 241 BC when it was burnt down and rebuilt entirely in brick; the temple of Janus, whose doors were only closed in time of peace, and the temple of Castor, simple and primitive. On the Capitol hill was the temple of Jupiter, and on its slopes were the temple of Saturn and the Roman mint housed in the temple of Juno Moneta. All these were in the Etruscan style, for Greek fashions had only just begun to be felt.

Turning his back on the Capitol, Hannibal would have seen a closely packed mass of narrow streets, humble houses, and a bustling market: behind this, and to his left, rose the Esquiline, hardly inhabited as yet, and covered with grass and scrub. To his right the Palatine hill held the politicians' houses, still simple and small, though in the years to come the mob was to tear down Cicero's house, only to see it rebuilt at enormous cost.

In the next two centuries, as the wealth of the provinces poured into Rome, building and re-building continually changed the face of the city. In the Forum, crowded from dawn to dusk with chattering citizens, public buildings replaced the shops and houses. Greek influence was apparent in the new *basilicae* or public halls, which served as markets, offices and law courts. The shops were moved together into the Macellum, a provision market near the Subura, the bustling working-class district, or westward towards the Tiber. Here on the banks of the river, wharves were built, and warehouses and granaries arose as goods from all over the world were brought in to Ostia, transferred to barges, and brought up the Tiber. Here too was the Forum Boarium, or meat market, the Forum Cuppedinis for luxury goods, and the huge Velabrum, the general provision market, which the poet Horace called 'the stomach of Rome'. Nearby a great mound of broken pots and jugs grew higher and higher, the Mons Testaceus, as big as the slag heaps which loom over the coal-mining towns of today.

In 179 BC the foundations of the first stone bridge over the Tiber were laid by Aemilius Lepidus to supplement the wooden trestles of the Pons Sublicius which up until then had carried all Rome's traffic over the river. The old streets of gravel and mud were paved with flags of lava, and lined with the apartment buildings of the poor and the great houses of the rich. The Via Sacra, running through the Forum, was the only road of any size, and nothing was done to widen or straighten the others. The dark and narrow lanes of the Subura were still squalid, stinking and noisy as citizen and slave jostled their way into the shops for anything from cabbages to shoes, and sweltered in the blacksmith's forge or chatted in the barber shops.

But the feverish activity of the Forum, the airless heat of narrow streets, could soon be left behind. The magnificent Gardens of Sallust to the north were laid out from the spoils pilfered from Numidia by its unscrupulous governor, whom we know better for the histories he wrote of the war against Jugurtha, a former king of Numidia, and of the conspiracy of Catiline to overthrow the state which was suppressed by Cicero.

The green fields of the Campus Martius between the Forum and the river were not covered with buildings until the time of Augustus. And Maecenas, Augustus' Minister of the Arts, then took care to replace them; he converted the gloomy cemeteries of the Esquiline into a large park whose beauty attracted the spacious villas and palaces of the rich.

Public Amenities

In the last days of the Republic there was an increasing awareness of the importance and dignity of the city as the centre of an empire, and a genuine determination to improve its amenities. Julius Caesar spent vast sums on a new forum – Pliny says the site alone cost him 100,000,000 sesterces – and a new basilica on the site of the old one. Under one of his decrees the owners of property in the city became responsible for the maintenance of the roads that ran by their property to the satisfaction of the aediles, who were also given precise instructions about repairing and cleansing the roads. Another decree forbidding wheeled traffic in the city during the hours of daylight, with the exception of builders' wagons clearing rubble or carrying building material, has interesting modern parallels, as we too find the sheer number of vehicles bringing traffic to a standstill. Caesar intended a massive replanning of Rome, but 'death overtook him in the midst of these projects and plans', as Suetonius says.

For public entertainment there were two circuses, one in the Campus Martius, another behind the Palatine, called the Circus Maximus. Tarquinius Superbus had laid out the latter in the distant past, and its size was increased on several occasions till it held nearly 250,000 people, a quarter of Rome's population. One such enlargement was due to Julius Caesar, for the celebrations to honour his final victory in the Civil War:

> For the races the Circus was lengthened at each end, and a sunken roadway was dug all round it: young men from the best families drove two-horse and four-horse chariots, and rode

A view of the Republican circus showing a beast fight in progress. The seven eggs in the background are lap markers for chariot races (see page 148). The circus was used for both chariot races and beast fights until the Colosseum was built

pairs of horses, leaping from one to the other. The 'Troy Game' was played by two teams, one of older, one of younger, boys. Wild-beast fights were put on for five successive days. Last of all a battle was staged between two armies, each with 500 infantry, 20 elephants and 30 horsemen.

(Suetonius, *Julius Caesar*, 39)

In contrast to the two arenas for physical sport and recreation there was, until Augustus' time, only one permanent theatre. This had been built of stone in 55 BC from the spoils of the eastern provinces won by Pompey the Great. Until then Rome had been content with temporary stages of wood erected for special performances and then dismantled.

A modern model of Pompey's theatre

Augustus' Building Programme

The greatest changes to the appearance of Rome were made by Augustus. In the *Res Gestae* – a proud catalogue of his achievements which was inscribed on bronze and stone and set up in Rome and throughout the Empire – the list of his building-work is staggering:

I built the Senate House and the Chalcidicum next to it, the temple of Apollo on the Palatine with its porticoes, the temple to the deified Julius, the Lupercal, the portico at the Circus Flaminius – I allowed this to be called the Octavian Portico after the man who built the previous portico on the same site – the temples on the Capitol of Jupiter Feretrius and Jupiter the Thunderer, the temple of Quirinus, and on the Aventine the temples of Minerva, Queen Juno, and Jupiter Libertas, the temple of the Lares at the top of the Sacred Way, the temple of the Di Penates on the Velia, the temple of Youth and the temple of the Great Mother on the Palatine.

41

I restored the Capitol and the Theatre of Pompey, both these works at great expense, and I did not inscribe my name on either. I restored the channels of the aqueducts which in a number of places were crumbling away through age, and doubled the supply of the Aqua Marcia by directing a new spring into its waters. I completed the Forum Julium and the basilica between the temples of Castor and Saturn, works which my father (Julius Caesar) had begun and almost finished; when the same basilica was burnt down I enlarged its site and began to rebuild it in the name of my sons, and gave orders for it to be completed by my heirs if I did not live to do so. On the authority of the Senate, in my sixth consulship I restored 82 temples of the gods in the city, neglecting none that needed repair at that time. In my seventh consulship I repaired the Via Flaminia from Rome to Ariminum, and all the bridges except the Mulvian and Minucian.

From the proceeds of war booty I built on private ground the temple of Mars the Avenger and the Forum Augustum. I built the theatre next to the temple of Apollo on ground for the most part bought from private owners, to be called the Theatre of Marcellus, after my son-in-law.

(Augustus, *Res Gestae*, 19-21)

This was a colossal achievement, and is aptly summed up in the words of Suetonius, the biographer of the first 12 emperors:

Since the city was not as splendid as the dignity of the Empire demanded, and was subject to flood and fire, he made it so beautiful that he could justly claim to have found it made of brick, and left it made of marble.

(Suetonius, *Augustus*, 28)

CHAPTER FIVE

The History of the Success and Failure of the Republic

Hannibal and the Threat to Rome

While Roman armies had been fighting to win control of the Italian peninsula, the political battle at home had been equally fierce. Although the long-standing feud between patricians and plebeians was over before 300 BC, the right of the assembly of the people to make law was only established, as we have seen, in 287 BC, by the Lex Hortensia.

But events in the Mediterranean moved too fast to allow the people to gain much advantage from their new power. Barely ten years after Tarentum submitted, Rome was drawn into conflict with Carthage, the prosperous North African trading city which dominated the sea and coasts of the Western Mediterranean. The clash of interests arose over Sicily in 261 BC and hard fighting continued on land and sea for more than 20 years before victory enabled Rome to annex the island. Sicily became the first Roman 'province'. During the war, faced by the powerful Carthaginian fleet, the Romans had been forced to build a navy, using a captured Carthaginian vessel as a model for all her new ships. Two huge fleets were lost, and only the third, fashioned with enormous determination and courage, won the final victory. Rome could now transport its army to all parts of the Mediterranean, and with Carthage still weak after defeat, Rome snatched the island of Sardinia (239 BC).

But Rome's strength still lay in the land army. Highly drilled and well organized, the Roman legions, man for man, appeared a match for any army in the world. The fact, too, that the legionaries were Roman citizens and allies, fighting, as the historian Polybius says, 'for their country and children' often gave them the edge over the paid (mercenary) forces of the other Mediterranean powers. Numerically the Roman land army was formidable. A census taken in 220 BC revealed that the total number of Romans and allies able to bear arms was more than 700,000 foot soldiers and 70,000 cavalry.

But these numbers did not deter Hannibal, the brilliant Carthaginian general. Carthage had occupied Spain to replace the island possessions it had lost, and in 218 BC to revenge his country on Rome, Hannibal led his army over the Pyrenees, and then fought his way over the snow-covered Alps. It was his tactical brilliance, and the inexperience of plebeian generals, rather than a superior army, that brought him his great victories. Roman forces were defeated at the River Trebia and at Lake Trasimene: then at Cannae, in 216 BC, an entire army was annihilated. Their enormous losses left the Romans momentarily without any army at all, and at his mercy. But the Senate kept its nerve and refused to give in: they decreed that the city walls should be manned by slaves, boys and old men. Hannibal did not even dare make any attack on the city. Strengthened by the unshaken loyalty of the allies in central Italy, and by the determination of magistrates and people alike, the Senate fought on.

A strategy was adopted – to avoid pitched battles, and to gain time to re-organize their resources and to allow a new army to grow up. Able generals, Fabius Maximus (the Delayer) in particular, carried out the Senate's instructions to the letter. Rome fought back. Then an army under Cornelius Scipio landed in Spain and drove out the Carthaginians. Scipio then took his legions to Africa, and the threat to Carthage itself forced Hannibal to leave Italy. In 202 BC Scipio challenged Hannibal to battle at Zama, and won a great and final victory.

Hannibal. A Carthaginian coin portrait

The Recovery of the Senate

Scipio, now Scipio Africanus, was the hero of the hour, but everyone knew that the Senate had master-minded the conduct of the war. Senatorial policy had succeeded: it was only right that the Senate should remain at the controls. Her victory over Carthage made Rome a world power, with immense diplomatic influence. Delegations began to arrive from all over the Mediterranean, to ask for rulings on provincial boundaries, treaty obligations and territorial rights. Most of these questions were too complex to be debated in the People's Assembly, and only the Senate had the necessary experience to deal with them. And so the Senate's authority grew at home as quickly as Rome's influence spread abroad.

The Republican Constitution

But the constitution itself remained unchanged, and Senate, magistrates and People kept their traditional powers. Polybius, one of the greatest historians to write about Rome, was certain that Rome owed her success to the way in which the separate elements in her constitution balanced and combined with each other. Writing about it in 150 BC he describes the powers of the consuls, the Senate and the People:

> The consuls have authority over all public business. All other magistrates, except the tribunes, are under them and take their orders. They consult the Senate on matters of urgency, and carry out the Senate's decrees. . . . They summon assemblies of the People, bring

proposals before them, and carry out what the majority decrees. In the preparations for war they can appoint military tribunes, levy soldiers, and select those who are fittest for service. . . . They can spend as much public money as they choose, and have a financial officer (*quaestor*) to act on their instructions.

The Senate controls the Treasury, and regulates all revenue and expenditure. Except for payments made to the consuls, financial officers are not allowed to draw on public money unless the Senate gives permission by decree. Even the grant to the censors for expenditure on public works is under senatorial control. The Senate hears cases of treason, conspiracy, poisoning and assassination (for these require public investigation) and acts as arbitrator in private disputes. It is responsible for sending ambassadors abroad to settle differences, to give advice, to make demands, to receive submission or to declare war. The Senate too receives all foreign delegations, and decides what answer to give them. . . .

But there is a role, and a very important one, left for the People. The People have the sole right to confer honours and inflict punishment. They are the only court to decide matters of life and death. . . . It is the People, too, who by their votes, bestow honours on those who deserve them. They have the right to accept or reject laws, and, most important of all, they debate questions of war and peace. And in the case of alliances, armistices or treaties the People can ratify or cancel them. . . .

Each of these three groups can have its power counteracted by another group, and none has absolute control. Even the Senate is unable to put any of its resolutions into effect if one of the tribunes of the People uses his veto, and in fact a tribune's veto can prevent the Senate from meeting altogether. And those tribunes are always obliged to act as the People decree, and to fall in with their wishes.

(Polybius, 6.11.11. with omissions)

This, in theory, was the successful constitutional blend. In practice, as we have seen, the Senate, because of its great experience and the victory over Hannibal, was firmly in control of the Roman state during the first half of the second century. Senators maintained their status and dignity through family alliances and the client system (see Chapter 2). Although rival senatorial groups, centred on the great families, fought bitter political battles about domestic and foreign policies, the Senate as a whole held firmly to its controlling position. The Scipios might be denounced in the Senate house by an angry Cato, who rejected their views on foreign affairs, and their attitude to Greece in particular, but to the outside world the Senate showed itself a strong and united ruling council. By their personal influence the old and famous families controlled the elections and the magistrates; nearly all the consuls from 200–146 BC came from distinguished families which had produced consuls in the past, and it was extremely difficult for a senator without these connections to reach the highest office. Even the tribunes – 'the People's representatives', according to Polybius – were usually ambitious young politicians, anxious not to offend the powerful consular families who could smooth their path to the consulship.

Crisis on the Land

Nothing seemed to threaten the Senate's secure position. But the war with Hannibal, which had given the Senate the chance to control the constitution, had other unforeseen effects on Rome and the Italians. For 15 years Hannibal had marched over the farmlands of Italy, and the legionaries who fought and finally defeated him were mostly Italian farmers. Neglect and devastation had left their farms in ruins, and the farmers, returned from the war, could not usually afford to repair the damage. And so their smallholdings were bought up, and large areas of state land were leased by wealthy landowners, while the dispossessed soldier-farmers drifted to the towns and cities. Another historian, Appian, describes what happened:

> The rich took possession of the greater part of the state lands, and, as time went by, became confident that no one would ever take this land away from them. They then absorbed the adjoining strips of land, and the smallholdings of their poor neighbours, sometimes by buying them out, sometimes by force, and in this way began to cultivate vast tracts instead of single estates. They used slaves (who came onto the market in their thousands as a result of Rome's overseas conquests) as agricultural labourers and herdsmen, because a free labourer might be conscripted into the army at a moment's notice. In this way, some powerful men became extremely rich, and slaves, who were exempt from military service, increased in number, while the people of Italy, weighed down by poverty, taxes and military service, grew fewer and fewer. And even if they managed to escape these hardships, they idled away their time, because the rich owned the land, and slaves, not freemen, cultivated it.

(Appian, *Civil War*, I, 7)

Farms became larger and more efficient. Flocks, herds, olives and vines on a large scale replaced the tiny farmsteads. And in the cities the displaced peasants and the veterans returned from the wars swelled the numbers of unemployed, without property or prospects. But Rome needed soldiers, and only property owners were eligible for service in the legions. If the army was to be kept up to strength it was necessary to help the small farmer get back to his holding on the land. This, in turn, would mean reclaiming the state-leased public land.

The Reformers

Some senators saw that reform was essential, but many, especially the rich landowners who occupied large areas of public land, were bitterly opposed to any change. But their opposition to reform had a result which none of them expected. In 133 BC a tribune, Tiberius Gracchus, proposed that the public land should be redistributed, and the small-holders restored to the land. His proposal surprised no one. But the Senate was astonished when, sensing opposition from the landowning senators, Tiberius introduced his proposal to the Assembly of the People. The Assembly, without consulting the Senate, used its powers under the Lex Hortensia (see p. 20), to make the proposal law and to grant funds to a land commission to carry it out. With one stroke the delicate balance of power inside the constitution was destroyed. For, although the Senate quickly regained the upper hand, by eliminating Tiberius – he was clubbed to death by some over-zealous senators – the damage was done. The way was clear for tribunes in the future; and the People, who after so many years had tasted real power, were eager to repeat the experience.

They did not have to wait long. Gaius Gracchus, Tiberius' younger brother, within ten years gave another jolt to the wavering balance. Determined to secure a fairer deal for Rome's Italian allies he appealed for the support of an increasingly important class of citizens, the Knights (*equites*). These were wealthy Romans outside the senatorial order, who ran businesses and the finance companies which were growing more and more prosperous and important as the Empire increased. By law Roman senators were not allowed to take part in business activities, and the Knights, who through banking, money-lending, trading, contracting and tax-collecting, were becoming increasingly influential, welcomed the chance of gaining political power. Passing laws through the plebeian assembly, Gaius took the control of the law courts from the Senate, and gave it to the Knights, and in this way added another counter-weight to senatorial influence in the constitution.

Procession of Knights. The equites, *who in Rome's early history had provided horses and formed cavalry, were still reviewed every year, even under the Empire, in traditional fashion, as this scene shows*

For almost a century there followed a struggle for power between magistrates, Senate, Knights and People. One of the main results was the disintegration of the Senate. Senators no longer combined in the face of a threat from outside, but factions and individuals within the Senate looked for support wherever they could find it. Some senators, who wished to see senatorial control re-established as it had been after the wars with Carthage, fiercely resisted any changes. Others, equally ambitious, but more independent, bid for the support of the People and the Knights, in order to reach the highest positions in the state. In particular, provincial governors at the head of their armies could no longer be expected to be loyal to the government at home. Tribunes, too, because of their power to veto 'senatorial discussion' and their ability to influence the People, became extremely powerful officials. Personal and political rivalry was bitter and intense, and government was often disrupted by social disorder and civil wars.

The army reforms of C. Marius in 107 BC gave new strength to the magistrates and ex-magistrates who commanded Rome's legions. By these reforms, Roman citizens with no property of their own (*proletarii*) became eligible for military service, and generals could now count on the loyalty of soldiers who joined the army to escape from the poverty and uncertainty of life in the cities and country towns. As they had no property, the legionaries relied on their general to find them a small-holding or settlement when they reached the end of their service, and so were prepared to follow him wherever he led – even against Rome itself.

Portrait generally believed to be Gaius MARIUS (157–86 BC), seven times consul

Ambition and the Generals

The history of the final 50 years of the Republic is the story of distinguished generals, and the power that their armies gave them. Marius himself, whose reforms created that power, beat back the vast hordes of barbarians from Italy's northern frontier, and held the consulship, exceptionally, for five consecutive years as commander-in-chief of the Roman armies. L. Cornelius Sulla, his younger rival, in the confused years which followed the rebellion of many of Rome's Italian allies (91 BC) twice marched on Rome with his army. In 82 BC he was nominated dictator and charged with the task of rebuilding the constitution he had helped to shatter. His methods were straightforward: he slaughtered his political opponents, and restored supreme power in the state to his reconstituted Senate, taking the courts from the Knights, and checking the power of the tribunes. Among many well-intentioned judicial reforms he created a new treason court, to prevent any ex-magistrate from leading an army out of his province without the Senate's permission. No one, if Sulla had his way, would come to power as Sulla had.

Lucius Cornelius SULLA (138–78 BC)

But this 'new' Senate could not survive and was quickly undermined, in particular by Cn. Pompeius Magnus (Pompey the Great), who had helped Sulla capture Rome, and, at the head of a privately raised army, was already recognized as a brilliant general. Returning from a victorious campaign in Spain (71 BC) he joined M. Crassus in defeating the slave rebellion of Spartacus and was elected consul with Crassus for 70 BC. As consuls they justified the support given them by Knights and People by sweeping away the conservative parts of Sulla's constitution, and restoring full powers to the tribunes. The Senate's last chance to dominate the state had gone.

So the struggle was renewed between rival army commanders and the small group of diehard but influential senatorial families, whose political experience and control of the elections through their clients and supporters gave them a decisive voice in the Senate's policies. Mob violence was commonplace. Catiline's conspiracy aimed to overthrow the state itself. The Senate House was burnt down, and even a consul could be pelted with refuse in the Forum by a hostile crowd. Political and personal loyalties shifted and changed. Pompey, Crassus and Julius Caesar combined together in an alliance which had the support of the legions, the Knights and the People: the Senate was powerless. M. Cicero who proposed that all moderate men from all classes should join together to

Gnaeus POMPEIUS Magnus (106–48 BC), the most distinguished Roman of his generation, until his defeat at Pharsalus by Julius Caesar. A talented general and unrivalled administrator, Pompey secured the eastern provinces for Roman rule, and almost doubled the Empire's revenues

Gaius Julius CAESAR (100–44 BC), one of Rome's most brilliant sons. Among the finest generals in history, he grew intolerant of the restrictions and inefficiency of the Republican constitution. His conquest of Gaul (58–51 BC) opened up Western Europe to Mediterranean civilization, and laid the foundations of modern France

50

prevent the state from being overthrown, went unsupported. Cato, the spokesman of the small group of extremist conservatives in the Senate, could do nothing while Caesar and Pompey remained allies. But eventually Pompey agreed to become sole consul and to co-operate with the Senate in restoring order in Rome, and the extremists quickly drove a wedge between Pompey and Caesar, who was completing his conquest of Gaul. Rome's two most brilliant generals were now on different sides. Moderate senators voted overwhelmingly for disarmament and a peaceful settlement, but the extremists, confident in Pompey's military skill, forced the absent Caesar to choose between accepting humiliation by his opponents, and armed conflict. Caesar chose to fight, and civil war began again.

Gaius Julius CAESAR. Portrait from a coin struck after his appointment as 'Dictator for life' in the year of his assassination 44 BC

The Civil Wars

Against all the odds, Caesar won. By speed of movement and brilliant generalship he was successful in a series of major battles against the forces of Pompey and the Senate, in Spain (49 BC), Greece (48 BC) where he defeated Pompey himself at Pharsalus, the Middle East (47 BC) where he met Cleopatra, Africa (46 BC) and Spain again in 45 BC. Though he was appointed dictator first in 49 BC Caesar made only short visits to Rome until 45 BC when he was made dictator for life. In the brief intervals between campaigns he began a series of reforms designed to relieve hardship, improve administration throughout Rome and Italy and unify the Empire. His reformed calendar (modified only slightly in AD 1582) is still the basis of our present calendar. As dictator he was more powerful than the ordinary magistrates, and immune from the tribunes' veto. The Senate, which he had enlarged and filled with his own clients, supported his programme, as did the Knights and People. The Roman state had come a long way from Polybius' ideal.

But some senators resented Caesar's power and the way he used it, and saw his perpetual dictatorship as a threat to the republican state, which had lasted for five centuries. No magistrate should be permanently above the constitution. A conspiracy was formed by C. Cassius, with M. Brutus as the figurehead, and Caesar was murdered on 15 March 44 BC – the Ides of March. Shakespeare's tragedy *Julius Caesar* is based on this dramatic assassination.

Marcus Junius Brutus (c.85–42 BC). Leading conspirator at the Ides of March

Reverse of the same coin, showing the Cap of Liberty between two daggers

But Caesar's violent death solved nothing. In his will the dictator left the bulk of his estate to his young nephew, Octavianus, and bequeathed his gardens across the Tiber to the Roman people. But his most important legacy was the example of his own career – the way he had gained and then kept supreme power. M. Antonius (his lieutenant) and Octavian quickly showed that the lesson was well learned. They renewed the Civil War, and once again the Senate was helpless against generals at the head of their armies. Anthony, Octavian and Lepidus established a triple-dictatorship (Triumvirate), purged the opposition and overwhelmed the army of the conspirators and republicans at Philippi (42 BC). But, as had happened with Caesar and Pompey, jealousy and ambition forced the triumvirs apart, until in the last great battle of the Civil War, at Actium 31 BC, Octavian defeated Anthony and drove him and his ally, Cleopatra, to suicide. Caesar's heir had come into his inheritance.

Marcus ANTONIUS (c.82–30 BC). Triumvir

Cleopatra

Gaius Julius Caesar Octavianus AUGUSTUS (63 BC–AD 14), depicted as Imperator, *addressing his troops. The elaborately carved breastplane shows Augustus, hand outstretched, receiving from a representative of the Parthians a legionary standard, captured from the Romans at the battle of Carrhae in 53 BC. To lose a battle standard was a great disgrace for Roman armies, and this breastplate celebrates Augustus' success in recovering the standard*

Peace at Last

Octavian's task was immense, for he had to repair and restore the shattered Empire, and bring back peace and stability to Rome and Italy. In particular, he had to devise a form of government which though resembling the old constitution avoided the weaknesses of the Republic, without resorting to the despotic dictatorship of Sulla or Caesar. Octavian's own version of the way he achieved this has been preserved on stone in a temple in modern Turkey (the *Monumentum Ancyranum* or *Res Gestae*).

> In my sixth and seventh consulships I put out the flames of civil war, and although I was in complete control of affairs with everybody's agreement, I transferred the Republic from my power to the charge of the Senate and the Roman People. For this service I was named Augustus, by the Senate's decree, the door-posts of my house were publicly wreathed with bay leaves, a civic crown fixed over my door, and a golden shield set up in the Senate House. Its inscription commemorates my courage, mercy, justice and piety. From this time I excelled everyone in influence, although I possessed no more official power than the others who were my colleagues in the various magistracies.
>
> (Augustus, *Res Gestae*, 34)

The normal machinery of the Republic began to work again. Magistrates were elected by the people, and once elected, undertook their usual duties. Ex-magistrates were appointed to govern the provinces – except for the enlarged province, comprising Spain, Gaul and Syria which Augustus controlled through his legates. In 23 BC Augustus ceased to hold the consulship every year – some senators objected to the way he monopolized the highest office. In return he received the powers of a tribune, with all its rights and privileges, and supreme power over all the provinces of the Empire. At Rome, where it mattered, there was little outward difference between the new Republic and the old, except for the many signs of respect and deference towards the 'first citizen', or 'Princeps' as Augustus was frequently called. But no one who stopped to think where the real power lay was deceived for a moment. Augustus' enlarged province contained almost all Rome's legions, and though the Princeps displayed his tribune's power at Rome for all to see, his real strength lay in his provincial armies encircling Italy.

Polybius' balanced constitution had disappeared for ever. Although Augustus used his powers with great tact, his supreme position created a precedent which his successors were bound to follow. Slowly, but inevitably, the Princeps accumulated power and responsibility. He commanded the armies, who swore an oath of loyalty to him. He virtually controlled foreign policy. Much of the administration of Rome and Italy was in his hands. Finance, the courts, legislation – all came into his sphere of interest, and he was entitled to appoint a successor. After five hundred years, Rome had become a monarchy again in everything but name.

CHAPTER SIX

Imperium: How Rome Acquired and Governed Its Empire

Rome's Early Empire

We have seen how Hannibal's vengeful attack on Rome led to the eclipse of the Carthaginian power in the western Mediterranean, and the loss of all her overseas possessions. In the struggle to survive Rome had unwittingly acquired an instant empire, but how was it to be governed? Rome's previous treatment of conquered peoples, in Italy, had been fair-minded and practical (see Chapter 1), and the network of alliances she set up was designed to unify the whole country. But this sort of alliance was not suitable for the vast area of the new Empire. For although Rome could, and did, give favourable terms to some cities in the conquered territories, in general it was necessary to bring the whole country under the control, or *provincia*, of a Roman magistrate with military power. So Sicily, Sardinia, Corsica and Spain became provinces (Spain in fact was divided into two separate provinces) and charters were drawn up to set out the boundaries of the provinces, details of local government, taxation districts, and the administration of justice. Because a 'province' was governed by a magistrate with military power, it was thought of as a military district. As a result the governor, like a commander-in-chief, had complete control of his province, and was solely responsible for everything that happened there. This made him an extremely powerful man, and we shall see shortly that he sometimes abused his power.

Part of a sculptured frieze, showing a Roman warship with a detachment of legionaries aboard. First century BC

55

Victory over Carthage focused attention on Rome. With prestige came influence and responsibility. Smaller states asked for alliances and settlements of disputes, and begged for Rome's help when they were threatened. Major powers like Macedon and Syria to the east tried at once to strengthen their position in the face of this fast-growing empire to the west, and Rome soon became involved in wars in Greece and the eastern Mediterranean. Fifty years of diplomatic activity and fierce fighting followed, and the Senate finally decided that only harsh, even brutal, settlements could guarantee stability in the conquered lands. In 146 BC Corinth was utterly destroyed, and Macedonia and Greece came under the control of one Roman governor. Carthage was razed to the ground in the same year, and the province of Africa formed.

Publius Cornelius SCIPIO AFRICANUS (236–184 BC). Renowned both for his military achievements and as a champion of Greek culture at Rome

Expansion

The maps illustrate the growth of the Empire during the next century. In the east, King Attalus of Pergamum bequeathed his kingdom to Rome, and this became the province of Asia in 133 BC. In the north and west Roman legions subdued most of the inland regions of Spain and the territory north and south of the Alps. Gaul-across-the-Alps (Transalpine Gaul) appeared in 120 BC and Gaul-this-side-of-the-Alps (Cisalpine) was formally added to the Empire in 81 BC. Bithynia and Pontus, Syria, Cyrene and Crete became provinces after Rome's eastern campaigns 75–64 BC (the future peace and prosperity of this region was largely due to the sensible re-organization imposed upon it by Pompey the Great 64–62 BC), joining Cilicia which had already been annexed in 102 BC. Caesar's victories north of the Alps extended Transalpine Gaul to the English Channel, 52 BC, and Augustus, who had annexed Egypt, 31 BC, fixed the northern frontier of the Empire along the line of the Danube. After this, apart from the transformation into provinces of some dependent kingdoms, and the alteration of provincial boundaries, the Empire changed comparatively little. Claudius annexed Britain in AD 43 and the emperor Trajan conquered Dacia, across the Danube. You can still see the monuments which both emperors set up to commemorate their success.

It would be wrong, however, to think that the Romans in the second century BC deliberately set out to grasp as much territory as possible, and that their only aim was to enrich themselves at the expense of these territories. Rome's reasons for conquest were complex and varied. She was certainly over-anxious about the security of the frontiers, and too quick to imagine a threat from neighbouring states. Individual Romans, too, were glad of the opportunity to combine military glory with the spoils of war. But for the most part the Empire was acquired as much by accident as by design, though it is impossible to tell how much effect the voices of individual senators, or the wishes of individual cities, may have had on the decisions of the central government. The Senate was usually reluctant to take over more territory, because it recognized that provinces had to be administered, and the expense that this involved was not always balanced by the taxes the provincials paid.

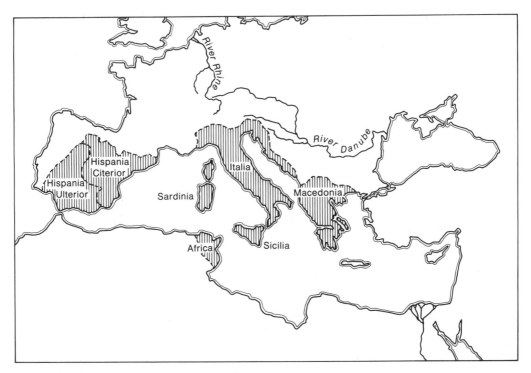

Territories under Rome's control 146 BC

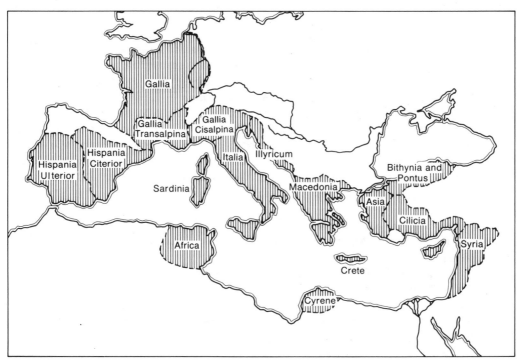

Territories under Rome's control 50 BC

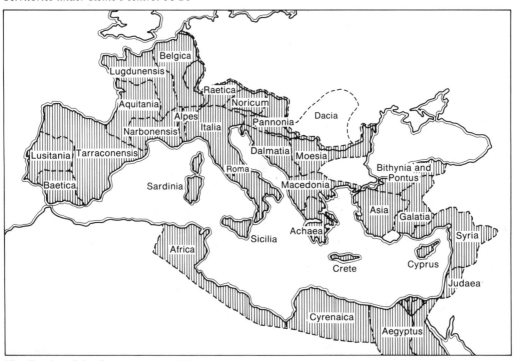

The Empire of the first emperor AD 14

58

Part of a triumphal procession, from a relief carving on a temple to Apollo. Chained prisoners crouch under the victory trophy. Trumpeters and sacrificial oxen approach from the right

But one thing is certain. As Rome's Empire grew larger, the methods of conquest became harsher and more ruthless. After the sack of the cities of Epirus, in north-west Greece in 167 BC 150,000 people were made slaves. Twenty years later, when Corinth was razed to the ground, its male population was slaughtered and the women and children enslaved. Most of the citizens of Carthage were killed when their city was destroyed the same year. In his Gallic campaigns, almost a century later, Caesar did not hesitate to enslave or massacre whole tribes. But it would be unfair to judge the Romans by standards which were not accepted in the ancient world. War was savage, victory often led to massacre, and the victor was entitled to his loot. Slaves, treasure, and works of art passed into his hands for distribution; a defeated nation did not expect mercy. Perhaps we should not judge too harshly. Caesar was said to have killed one million people during his Gallic campaigns. The figure is exaggerated, but even that fearsome total is considerably less than the number of French soldiers killed in World War I (1,400,000). In World War II Russia lost 7,500,000 troops. Civilian deaths were double that amount. Romans would doubtless have defended the destruction of Carthage as the Allies in World War II justified the obliteration of Hiroshima, on military grounds.

Oppression

But if the brutality of Roman conquest was in keeping with the savagery of the times, there is less excuse for the way in which the Romans exploited the conquered peoples. By their organization of the Italian confederacy they had shown their administrative ability, and their fair-mindedness. But while they usually called provincials 'allies' they more often than not treated them as subjects. The governor himself was often to blame for this state of affairs. Because he was so far away, it was very difficult for central government to check on his activities, with the result that incompetence and injustice

59

were commonplace. The unscrupulous governor, in fact, had unlimited opportunities for lining his own pockets, and those of his staff. Listen to the prosecutor, as a corrupt governor faces the Extortion Court at Rome:

> . . . and I maintain that you exported from Syracuse a great weight of gold, silver, ivory and purple fabrics, an immense quantity of Maltese cloth and tapestries, a collection of Delian pottery, a large number of Corinthian vases, vast amounts of grain and huge quantities of honey. Nor is there any record of export tax on these goods. . . .
>
> Now I am not asking you where you got all these items from. What I am asking is what you wanted them for. Forget about the honey. But why so much Maltese cloth, as if you wanted to dress even your friends' wives, and why so many couches, as if you wanted to furnish all their country houses? And this list of exports covers a mere three months: Verres' governorship, gentlemen of the jury, lasted three whole years. . . . In these few short months, therefore, he exported contraband goods worth 1,200,000 sesterces from one port alone. Now as the country concerned is Sicily – an island with ports all round its coast – calculate the amount of contraband you think will have been exported from all the other harbours.

> (Cicero, *In Verrem* II 2.72, 74, 75 with omissions)

Cicero was the prosecutor, and the trial that of Verres, the notorious ex-governor of Sicily. For three years he had plundered his province, stripping temples of their treasures, robbing the islanders of their money and works of art, and even crucifying

Romans fighting barbarians. A carved relief from a sarcophagus (stone coffin) showing the Romans, on horseback and on foot, overwhelming their disordered enemy, who are probably Gauls

Roman citizens who opposed his wishes. Hardly the sort of conduct to make the Empire popular, thought Cicero, on another occasion:

> Words cannot express, gentlemen, how bitterly we are hated among foreign nations because of the outrageous behaviour of the men whom we have recently sent to govern them. Have these governors considered any temple sacred? Is any state safe from attack? Are locked doors enough to protect a home against men like these? Why, they look around for a rich and prosperous city, so that they can find an excuse to attack it and gratify their lust for loot.

(Cicero, *Pro Lege Manilia*, 22, 65)

Cicero himself had a clear idea of a governor's duties. He wrote to give advice to his brother, who was governor of Asia.

> Briefly, the entire province must come to realise that your whole concern is for the welfare, the children, the reputation and the possessions of the people you are governing, . . . for it is my personal opinion that provincial governors must judge everything they do by this one standard – the greatest possible happiness of the governed.

(Cicero, *Epist. ad Q.* f. I. 1, 13, 24)

Taxes

But there were difficulties. Cicero himself mentions them in the same letter.

> But however sympathetic and conscientious you may be in all you do, there is one serious obstacle – the tax gatherers. If we oppose them, we will antagonise a class of people that deserves our support, and has come to play an increasingly important part in the state. On the other hand, if we make concessions to them all the time, we shall be allowing the provincials, whose interests it is our duty to protect, to be utterly ruined. . . . So your assignment is to satisfy the tax gatherers while at the same time not allowing the provincials to be ruined.

(Cicero, *Epist. ad Q.* f. I., 1, 32, 33)

In other words, he had to square the circle. The Romans had no Imperial Revenue Department to collect the taxes from the distant provinces. Instead they auctioned the right to tax a particular area to finance companies. Employees of the companies (the *publicani*, or tax gatherers mentioned above – St. Matthew was one of them) were responsible for the collection of taxes on the spot. The companies themselves were owned and directed by an increasingly important class, the *equites*, or Knights (see p. 47). They were business men, who had no position in the Senate, but were rich and influential, and always on the lookout for opportunities to increase their business. Once a company had bought the right to tax an area, it set about recouping its expenditure by taxing the inhabitants very heavily. The heavier the taxes, the greater the profits, and it is not surprising that many of the provincials complained. Many of them could not afford to pay all that the publicans demanded, and had to borrow money from these same companies, at high interest rates – sometimes up to 50 per cent compound. The governor himself often co-operated with the companies to make sure that nothing prevented them from making a handsome profit, and in return the financiers contributed generously to the governor's private bank balance. The governor himself usually needed money. He had his election expenses to recoup, his own future to safeguard and he might have to bribe a judge and jury if, like Verres, he was prosecuted for extortion when he returned to Rome.

Millions of provincials suffered in this way, and honest governors were the exception in the last century BC. But there were compensations. Under Roman rule peace was more widespread, and most of the provinces enjoyed internal security. Many communities were self-governing in local affairs, and the Romans encouraged the building of roads, bridges and harbours to improve communications. After the seas had been cleared of pirates, trade became easier and more profitable. Most important of all, although justice was often imperfectly administered, Roman rule did establish a framework of law in the conquered territories, and this was the basis of stability and good order through the Empire.

It was not until the time of Augustus, however, that most of the abuses we have mentioned disappeared. The administrative system under the emperors became more streamlined – fast, just and effective. Injustices occasionally came to light. But the complaints of provincials were quickly heard by the central government, and offenders were punished without delay. The settled conditions brought great prosperity and increasing wealth. This, coupled with the benefits of security, and firm, fair government, seemed to most provincials adequate compensation for the loss of their liberty. It is however worth remembering that the evidence we have comes from the Romans, who were naturally prejudiced, and that we rarely hear anything from the provincials. When early emperors sought to extend the frontiers, the peoples on the fringes of the empire did often fight to preserve their independence. In the third century AD two parts of the empire did, for short periods, break away. But it is significant that many of the later troubles were caused by barbarians trying to get *into* the empire, not by provincials trying to get *out*.

CHAPTER SEVEN

Roads

We saw in Chapter 1 that as Rome's power spread and town after town acknowledged Rome's leadership, first in Latium and then further afield, roads stretched north, east and south to the subject peoples in Italy. When the legions marched into the new provinces they extended the network of roads beyond Italy to the boundaries of empire, through Gaul and Spain, along the coast of Africa, deep into Syria and north to the hills of Scotland. They were built so that troops could move easily and quickly about their business, and so that supplies of food and wine, new boots and bags of nails, paymasters and recruits, could reach the great forts that protected the frontiers. Then merchants followed the soldiers, first to sell to the troops, and later to the native inhabitants of the new territories: and raw materials, wood, leather, ivory, tin, iron and even gold, flowed back from the provinces to swell the wealth of Rome.

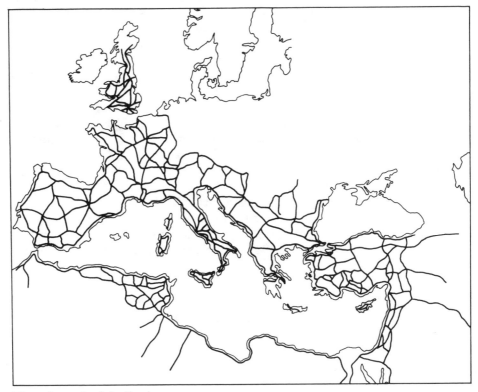

The main roads of the Empire

Construction Methods

In time there were over 53,000 miles of major roads in the Empire: but the first road of all was built in 312 BC, and stretched the 132 miles from Rome to Capua: it was called the Via Appia, after its builder, the blind censor Appius Claudius. Nearly 900 years later the historian Procopius saw it, and recorded his impressions:

> The Appian Way is a five-day journey long, if you are travelling light, for it stretches from Rome to Capua. It is wide enough for two wagons to pass, if they meet each other: it is one of the famous sights of the world. All the stone is hard – the sort of rock used for millstones: Appius had it quarried a long way off and transported to the road, for it is not found locally. He had the stones made smooth and level, and squared off so that they fitted snugly without concrete or anything else in between. They fit together so securely and closely that when one looks at them they appear to have grown together rather than to have been fitted together. Though such a long time has passed, though great numbers of wagons and animals of every sort have crossed them every day, they have not separated at all at the joints, nor has any of the stones been destroyed or even worn thin – they haven't even lost their polish. That is what the Appian Way is like.

(Procopius, *History of the Wars of Justinian*, V, xiv 6–11)

The secret of the permanence and strength of this and every Roman road is not the surface, which was repaired again and again, but the foundations. Usually a trench was dug, about one metre (three feet) deep, and filled with large stones, wedged tightly together. On top was a layer of smaller stones, sometimes bound by cement. Finally came the surface. Often this was gravel or small flints rammed tight; where plenty of stone was available then slabs of this were laid, as on the Via Appia. Local materials were used: in the Weald of Kent, in south-east England, for example the slag from the iron mines was spread over the road and rusted into an incredibly hard surface. Sometimes instead of a trench, earth from pits or ditches was piled up into a mound, and the foundation stones laid on top of this. The *agger* – archaeologists still use this Latin word for the name of these embankments – was sometimes enormous: it is 12 or 15 metres (39 or 49 feet) wide and 1 to $1\frac{1}{2}$ metres (3 to 5 feet) high in places along Ermine Street, the Roman road running north 141 miles from London to Lincoln; elsewhere it is hardly visible. There seems no obvious reason why the size of the agger should vary, except for the whim of the man in charge of the construction of each length.

The engineers knew that good drainage was essential to prevent water lying in puddles: ditches were dug alongside the roads for this purpose. For the same reason there is usually a considerable camber, with a fall of as much as 1 in 8 from the centre to

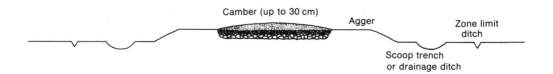

Cross-section of a Roman road

the sides of the road. Sometimes traces of smaller ditches parallel with the roads but further away can be seen. Since they are almost always 28 or 21 metres (91 or 68 feet) apart they seem to indicate a division into major or minor roads: they might also have defined the official area of the road zone in which all trees were cleared so that there might be no hiding-places for enemy or animals.

Roman roads are famed for their straightness, but of course they are far from completely straight. They have to wind round impassable obstructions, or move across the sides of a valley to make the slope less steep: but once the obstacle is passed they usually resume the original line. The roads are in fact made up of short straight lengths with small, but often abrupt, turns on high points. It is by sightings made from one high point to the next that the surveyors determined the general line of the road. In flat or wooded country their men lit fires and the surveyors watched for the rising smoke, giving orders for intermediate points to be shifted this way or that till the line was straight and the shortest practicable route was marked.

Bridge Building

Where the route came to rivers, or valleys that were too steep for men or mules to climb, bridges, causeways or viaducts had to be built. Many of them can still be seen; many are still in use, from the small but elegant Pons Fabricius in Rome, to the majestic Pont du Gard in Provence, or the great half-mile long bridge over the Guadiana river in Spain, with no less than 60 arches. In Spain, too, is the great Alcantara, 183 metres (600 feet) long, with six huge arches rising to 45 metres (148 feet) above the river bed. The inscription on it survives – *Pontem perfeci mansurum in saecula* – 'I have built a bridge that shall endure for centuries': since the bridge was erected in AD 105, its builder spoke nothing but the truth.

Alcantara – a famous Roman bridge in Spain

The Pont du Gard – a magnificent Roman aqueduct in southern France

In Romania, at Turnu-Severin, we can still see the piers of the bridge built by the emperor Trajan to enable him to support the Romans he had settled north of the Danube after his great campaigns in Dacia. The historian Dio Cassius had this to say about it:

> Trajan made a bridge of stone over the Danube, and I cannot say adequately how greatly I admire him for it. His other achievements are remarkable enough, but this surpasses them. There are twenty piers of squared stone, 45 metres (148 feet) high above the foundations, and eighteen (59 feet) wide: they are 51 metres (167 feet) apart, and are joined by arches. The cost was extraordinary: so was the construction, for each pier was made in a deep river, with the water raging in whirlpools, and on a muddy bottom, and it was impossible to divert the current.

(Dio Cassius, LXVIII, vi, xiii)

And 20 miles away to the west the following words are cut into a cliff:

The Emperor Caesar Nerva TRAJAN Augustus Germanicus, son of the deified Nerva, *pontifex maximus*, holding the tribunician power for the third time, father of his country, three times consul, made this road by cutting through mountains and eliminating the curves.

(C.I.L. vol. 3, no. 8267)

The *pontifex maximus* was the leading religious official in the state, but the word pontifex, from which our word pontiff comes, means 'bridgemaker', though we cannot be certain how the word became associated with religion.

Travel and Transport

These massive feats of civil engineering were one of the benefits conferred on the provinces by membership of a powerful empire. They could not have been contemplated without its huge financial and technical resources, and required the far-sighted but ruthless direction of autocratic emperors to see them completed. They have fired the imagination of people of all times and types: the poet Statius, writing in the time of Domitian, chose the building of the Via Domitiana, which linked the Via Appia to Naples, as the rather unlikely subject of one of his poems. In a few lines he combines awareness of the benevolent concern of authority for the welfare of the people, understanding of the difficulties involved, and an astonishingly accurate account of roadbuilding methods!

Dismayed at the travelling conditions of his people, and at the open plains that slow down every journey, Domitian is removing the long detours, and laying a new paving over the clinging sands.

Here, in the past, our traveller, late, riding in his two-wheeled cab, tossed back and forth as his yoke-pole swung down and the quicksands sucked in his wheels – the people of Latium were afraid of seasickness even in the middle of the country: no carriage could move swiftly as the muddy ruts hindered and slowed their passage, while the exhausted oxen, groaning at the weight, inched forward beneath the great yoke.

But now, a journey that used up a solid day, barely takes two hours: birds on their outstretched wings fly no more swiftly through the air, nor ships through the sea. The first task was to mark out the furrows, and cut the edge of the road, and to dig a trench deep into the earth; the next to fill in the ditch they had dug with other material, and on top of this to prepare a foundation, so that the soil should not give way, in case a weak foundation should give a weak bed for the rocks pounded into it; then to bind it with kerbstones driven in at either side, and with many pegs. What great gangs of men are working side by side! Some cut down the woods, and clear the mountain sides; others are chiselling smooth the timbers and stones; others are bonding the rocks together with lava dust and cement and surfacing the work, or bailing dry the pools, and diverting the smaller streams.

(Statius, *Silvae*, IV iii)

The names of many of the various types of Roman horse-drawn vehicles are known to us, and there are many illustrations of them in mosaics and wallpaintings, and carved in stone: unfortunately it is often difficult to be sure which name should be applied to which vehicle. The *cisium* was a light two-wheeled cab holding one or two people which could cover up to 25 miles in comfort in a day. The *carpentum* also had two wheels, but was a more formal carriage, used mainly in towns. A larger travelling coach or wagon was the *raeda* with four wheels, which a man on the road with his family and baggage would use. The *carruca* was even larger, and could be used as a sleeping carriage: Pliny employed one of these for his journeys over the Roman Empire, and he would dictate to his secretary, poor man, while they were moving. There were goods wagons, too, of every kind, from small carts drawn by a single horse, to great solid-wheeled wagons pulled by teams of lumbering oxen. On all these the wheels were rimmed with iron; little wonder that the roads had to be firmly built and solidly paved. Obviously the roads were in constant need of repair, just as ours are, and a special board of traffic control was set up by the Senate, called *curatores viarum*, to look after the roads.

One of the four-wheeled covered coaches used in the cursus publicus

They had other problems too. Traffic in Rome became so busy that the streets were clogged with carriages and wagons: Julius Caesar went so far as to forbid wheeled vehicles from entering the city between sunrise and sunset, with the exception of those carrying building materials. An unfortunate consequence was the din of iron wheels rattling over the paved streets all night long. Juvenal, an unhappy poet writing bitter satires in Rome nearly 150 years after Caesar's decree, found worse dangers on the roads:

> Here comes a dray with a long fir tree on it, quivering, and wagon after wagon carrying pines, their ends waving about high in the air and threatening the people below. If an axle

carrying a load of Ligurian marble breaks, and the mountain of stone overturns and falls on the crowds, what's left of their bodies? Not a limb or a bone is to be found: every corpse is ground to pieces and disappears like their souls.

(Juvenal, III, 254)

There is an obvious parallel with the appalling accidents of today when huge vehicles run out of control and crash. But, just as today, the benefits far outweighed the perils. As the roads spread through Italy and the provinces, so buildings of many sorts appeared alongside them. There were the *cursus publici* – posting stations between six and 16 miles apart where the official messengers of the Empire could rest or change horses, and upwards of a dozen horses would be kept at some of them for these official postmen. Private travellers stayed at *mansiones*, built every 15 miles or so, and maintained by taxes levied on the local community: they were state controlled, and travellers could not be refused service at them. But they were not always very elegant or clean, and rich families preferred to stay at the villas of their friends, or if they made frequent journeys even to buy small houses for themselves along the way.

Near many of the mansiones were *tabernae* – our word 'tavern' is of course derived from the Latin – where wine and food were sold to local farmers, postmen, muleteers and wagon drivers. And round these tabernae towns often developed, for blacksmiths, butchers, bakers and grocers found them convenient centres to sell their wares. Cologne and Vienna are examples of such towns, and London owes its size and importance to the roads that lead from it to every corner of the country as well as to its river, as merchants and their goods went to and fro in ever growing numbers.

The Impact of Roads

It is clear how important the roads were in the development of the Roman Empire, as they helped first the conquest, and then the 'Romanization' of the provinces. And after hundreds of years of splendid service, when the Empire collapsed, and the *curatores viarum* no longer cared for the roads, when bridges fell down and paving was ruined by potholes, the influence of the road system still survived. A comparison of a map of the roads of Roman Britain, for example, with a map of the modern transportation routes reveals at once that the transport system, road and rail, is based on the Roman. And when the Saxons came to England they found the agger still rising above the surrounding fields, and naturally they called it the 'high way'. They gave the name 'streat' to the stretches of stone paving that still remained in many places, and these are the origins of 'High Street', and 'highway'. All over the Empire, in Spain and Africa, Syria and Yugoslavia, modern engineers have followed their Roman predecessors, and laid tarmac and concrete where the men of the legions dug their long trenches and rammed in load after load of stone.

CHAPTER EIGHT

Growing Up

The Toga of Manhood

In the Roman calendar, 17 March was marked as a public holiday, for the celebration of the festival of *Liberalia* (in honour of the god of fertility). On a public holiday, when public and legal business was not transacted, the Forum was quieter than usual, and an observer in mid-March would have been almost certain to witness a series of short private ceremonies. Small groups of people entered the Forum, each escorting a boy, aged about 15, who was the central figure at the ceremony. The boy, looking dignified and perhaps a little nervous, wore a new plain white toga. His retinue was composed of relatives and family friends – some may have been magistrates or people of influence, who would themselves normally expect to be accompanied as they came down to the Forum. Passers-by saluted and called out greetings to the boy, and some shook his hand.

A bulla. You can see two children wearing bullae on page 19

For the boy this was the most important day of his life so far. For formal occasions, until now, he had worn the 'toga of youth' (*toga praetexta*), which carried a purple hem like that worn by the senior magistrates. But at home that morning he had put on the plain white 'toga of manhood' (*toga virilis*), and had dedicated to the household gods his old toga and the lucky charm (*bulla*) which he had worn round his neck since the day he had been given his name, nine days after he was born. Then he set out, with his father, uncles and friends, for the Forum, to be registered as a full citizen, and to have his name placed on the roll of his tribe. From there the party moved to the Capitol, to offer a sacrifice, and then home again for a family celebration. Boyhood had been left behind, and another Roman had entered public life as a young man.

70

Relief on a sarcophagus, representing the various stages of childhood

Schools and Education

Equally important for the youth who had just come of age was the fact that at this time he had just finished his course at the school of the *grammaticus*. A son from a wealthy Roman family was carefully brought up and thoroughly educated. As a child he was looked after by a nurse, under the supervision of his mother, but as he grew older his father took a greater interest in his development, his skill at riding and games, and his willingness to stand up for himself. From his father, too, he learnt a great deal about the achievements of his ancestors: Rome, it seemed, would not have been the same without them. Just before he began to attend school, at seven, a boy was entrusted to a Greek slave as a personal attendant (*paedagogus*). The *paedagogus*, who became his constant companion, was responsible for his behaviour and appearance, and began to teach him to speak Greek. Sometimes he acted as a personal tutor, and taught his pupil to read, write and do simple arithmetic. However, many young Romans of good family went to an elementary school (*ludus*) of their parents' choice, where they were taught these same subjects by a schoolmaster (*ludi magister*).

Few schoolboys will have looked back with any pleasure on their first five years in school. They probably envied those of their friends who had been given private tuition at home. Almost any room served as a classroom – some were open to the street at one end, and the noise from outside was a constant distraction. The pupils sat on wooden benches, without desks, holding their wax writing-tablets on their knees. From dawn to mid-afternoon, with a break for lunch, they were compelled to practise writing, and to recite the names of letters, chanting the alphabet backwards and forwards, and singing out their multiplication tables for hours on end.

There were good teachers and bad. The bad ones, not surprisingly, made a splendid target for the satirists:

> You rascally schoolmaster, hated by the girls and boys in your class, why do you disturb your neighbours? Though the cock has not yet crowed, you shatter the silence with your savage threats and cruel blows.

(Martial, *Epigrams*, 9.68)

71

That was what Martial thought, while Horace nicknamed his teacher 'the swiper'. But perhaps it was unreasonable, as a wiser Roman once remarked, to expect perfection from a schoolmaster when he was paid for one year what a successful charioteer could earn in an afternoon.

After elementary school came the school of the *grammaticus*. Many children left school before this secondary stage, which involved the study of grammar and literature. The work was hard and demanding, and must often have been unbearably tedious. The great works of Greek and Latin literature were read and carefully analysed, details of grammar and idiom and figures of speech studied and understood. The student was frequently required to read aloud, to answer questions on style, metre and content, and to learn long passages by heart. So great was the concentration on literary studies that there was little room in the curriculum for history, mathematics or finding out about other lands and peoples. But enthusiastic pupils could at least find a challenge in the exercises in speech-making which formed the final part of the *grammaticus'* course. These, at any rate, were of practical value for the future.

A school scene. A pupil arrives to find his classmates already at work. Most children in fact sat on benches – not these rather comfortable looking chairs

With the first two stages of his education completed, the young Roman had a reasonable command of the Latin and Greek languages and literature. He would also have made many friends, and this compensated for the monotony of his schooldays. In the future, doubtless, he would look back on his schoolboy experiences as some of the most carefree days of his life, and would maintain that a sound beating, when it was needed, could do no harm. Like most Romans, he would believe in firm discipline for its own sake, and would not think of doubting whether Roman education was the best form of training. Rome had few educational theorists.

One exception was a schoolmaster of the first century AD, Quintilian, who laid down certain educational principles in his textbook on *The Education of an Orator*:

72

I think that a father should have the highest possible hopes for his son, and so will take more trouble over his education from the start. . . . He should make sure that the child's nurse speaks correctly . . . for although it is important that the nurse is a good person, she should speak correctly too, for it is her words and diction that the child hears first, and he will try to imitate her way of speaking. . . . His *paedagogus* should either be a fully educated man or should, at least, be aware of his limitations.

A boy should begin his schooling by learning Greek, because he will pick up Latin, which is in general use, whether we like it or not. . . . Shortly afterwards, Latin should be studied, and should rapidly come to play an equal part in his lessons.

Then the teacher should consider how to handle the developing intellect of his pupil. There are some boys who are idle, unless they are pushed along, others who dislike being ordered about; some who can be held in check by fear, others who are paralysed by it; some need continuous practice to develop their minds, others improve most with short periods of intense concentration. But every pupil needs some kind of relaxation, because no one can stand the strain of continuous effort. In any case, learning depends on the enthusiasm of the student, and this cannot be achieved by compulsion. So, fresh after a break he will be sharper and more energetic in his studies.

I strongly disapprove of beating, although it is common practice, for the following reasons. First, because it is an uncivilized form of punishment more appropriate for slaves, and an insult. Second, if a boy is so set in his ways that words cannot hold him in check, he will merely become hardened to beatings.

(Quintilian, *Inst. Or.* I, 1.1, 4–5, 8, 12, 14; I, 3.6, 8, 13–14)

Higher Education

After the *grammaticus* the young Roman faced the final period of his education, and he would know what to expect. He was now to study rhetoric – the art of public speaking – under the guidance of a *rhetor*. He would know, too, some of the details of the syllabus, and the exercises which would give him practice in composition; writing speeches, for example, in praise of famous men, or of characters in history, composing attacks on Rome's enemies past or present, arguing for or against a particular point of view. He would have to learn how to write a speech, how to research and arrange his subject matter, and how to deliver a speech – what tone of voice and diction to use and what gestures to make. When his training was completed he would be able to undertake simple cases in the courts, or to deliver a speech on a public occasion.

This third stage in a young Roman's education had no fixed length. The conscientious and enthusiastic student could spend years improving his technique, and gaining invaluable practical experience as Cicero's account of his early training shows.

When I was about 16, I used to listen as carefully as I could every day to the most distinguished speakers in Rome, and to write, read and compose speeches. But I had other interests beside these oratorical exercises. The following year I studied civil law under Q. Scaevola, who, though not a teacher, gave legal opinions to those who consulted him. At 18 I listened daily to the speeches of the tribune P. Sulpicius, and got to know his style thoroughly, while at the same time, because of my tremendous interest in philosophy, I became a devoted pupil of Philo, head of the Athens Academy, who had fled to Rome.

For the next three years I spent my days and nights in study of every kind. I studied with Diodotus, the Stoic, who came to live at my home. But although I concentrated on his teaching and on all the subjects he was an authority on, I never let a day go by without some exercises in oratory . . . often in Latin, but more frequently in Greek.

By the time I was 25 I began to undertake cases in the civil and criminal courts, and at this time too I began to study under Molo, the famous orator and teacher from the island of Rhodes, who happened to come to Rome as a member of a delegation of Rhodians. . . . In those days I was very thin and frail physically, the sort of person who everyone thinks is running a great risk if he works hard and puts his lungs and voice under strain. . . . My friends and doctors begged me to stop speaking in the courts altogether, but I was determined to accept any risk rather than give up my ambition to be a famous barrister. But I decided that a more relaxed manner and better voice control would lessen the risk to my health and give me a smoother speaking style, and so I left for Asia.

On my way there, I spent six months at Athens with Antiochus as my guide and teacher, and caught up on my study of philosophy, but at the same time, I continued my oratorical studies under the supervision of Demetrius. Afterwards I travelled through the whole of Asia Minor visiting all the distinguished orators of the area . . . but not content with this I went to Rhodes and studied with Molo, whom I had already heard at Rome. So, after an absence of two years. I came back to Rome better trained and changed almost out of recognition.

(Cicero, *Brutus*, 89, 90, 91 with omissions)

Cicero was nearly 30 when he got home, and though not every ambitious young Roman would be prepared to give so much time to his studies, most spent at least as long as a modern university course in training to become public speakers. Athens was a favourite centre for study, because many of the most famous teachers lived there, but only the sons of wealthy families could afford the expense involved. Cicero's son, Marcus, was costing his father 80,000 sesterces a year during his course of studies at Athens, and still seemed reluctant to work. His anxious father complained

I will never consider it a good report when your tutor merely writes 'Still the same'.

(Cicero, *ad Att*, XIV, 16.3)

The education of their daughters caused Roman fathers less anxiety. After all, it was not necessary for them to distinguish themselves in public life. But most girls from good families attended elementary school with the boys, under the supervision of a nursemaid. When they could read and write well enough, their education was continued at home by a tutor, who gave them a good grounding in Greek and Roman literature. They also learnt needlework, and to dance, to sing and play the lyre, while at the same time gaining experience in the running of a home, directing the household slaves and supervising the kitchens.

Marriage and Weddings

About the age of 14 a girl was considered eligible for marriage. In wealthy families marriages were usually arranged, and the father chose a husband for his daughter after consultation with her mother. When both families had agreed to a marriage, the engagement took place, and an informal contract was drawn up before witnesses. Gifts were exchanged, in particular a ring which the bride-to-be wore on the third finger of her left hand. A party (*sponsalia*) was held to celebrate the arrangement, and both families would list the advantages of the new relationship. No one, of course, would think of mentioning that as the engagement had been made for social, business or even political purposes, it could quickly be broken off for the same reasons. Augustus himself had been engaged three times before his first marriage.

The wedding day was chosen with care, because of the many ill-omened days on the Roman calendar. Best suited was the second half of June, and then there was a rush of weddings. There were many different kinds of ceremony from which to choose. In the older, traditional ceremonies, which contained many strange and elaborate rituals, the bride passed into the family and the power of the husband. As women became more emancipated, however, and played a more influential part in society, an alternative form of marriage was generally used. In this, the wife remained technically in the power of her own family: this way she could keep her own property and be much more independent.

Mother, son and daughter. A portrait in gold leaf on glass, third century AD

On the day before her wedding the bride-to-be dedicated her childhood toys to the household god and changed her girl's clothes for the bridal gown. For the wedding day itself, the house was decorated with wreaths of flowers, branches of evergreen and coloured ribbons. Meanwhile the bride prepared for the ceremony. First, her hair was made ready. Helpers, using a bent iron spearhead, parted it into six locks held together by woollen ribbons, creating a cone shaped arrangement. Her head-dress was made of flowers, while the wedding veil was flame coloured, to match the colour of her shoes. The dress itself was a plain white tunic, full length, and fastened at the waist with a belt, tied in a special knot.

The guests now assembled, and at last the bridegroom arrived. The ceremony began with a sacrifice, followed by the signing of the marriage contract, before witnesses. Then the bride was led foward by her bridesmaid (*pronuba*) who joined the right hands of the bride and groom (see illustration). When the formalities were over, the guests called out 'Good luck', and the wedding feast began. The celebrations continued until the evening, when the groom led the bride, who at first pretended to resist, to his own house, in a procession. Torch-bearers and flute players led the way, and the bride, who carried a distaff and spindle, was escorted by three young boys, one carrying a hawthorn torch. Spectators shouted good wishes, and children scrambled for the small coins and nuts which the groom scattered as he walked. When the procession reached the bridegroom's house the bride smeared fat on the door posts, and was then carried over the threshold.

Wedding ceremony. Cupid appears between the bride and groom. The pronuba *is in the background and the husband holds the marriage contract. The joining of the right hands of the bride and groom (*dextrarum iunctio) *was the most solemn moment of the ceremony, and was often commemorated, as here, on the coffin of one of the marriage partners*

The ceremony in this form did not take place at every wedding. Second or subsequent marriages were quieter, and many families did not want, or could not afford, the expense involved. But it is interesting to compare the Roman rituals with modern weddings, and see how many modern customs have their parallels, and perhaps origins, in the Roman ceremony.

Names

The Roman marriage contract, like modern marriage services, gave the raising of a family as the reason for marriage, and from the time of Augustus, a man was entitled to certain privileges if he had three or more children. A naming ceremony was held nine days after the birth of a boy (eight for a girl) and the baby was given a lucky charm. He was also given his name. If his family was noble, he would in fact receive three names: first his personal name (e.g. Marcus), then, most important, his clan name (e.g. Junius, i.e. the clan of Junii) and lastly his family name (Brutus). A girl would be named from her clan name – Julia from the Julii, Caesar's clan, or Tullia, the daughter of Marcus Tullius Cicero.

Deaths and Funerals

Inevitably, because of the primitive nature of medical science, many children died either at birth, or shortly afterwards. Only a small proportion, in all classes, survived infancy. Roman families, of course, were hardened to losses of this kind, but vast numbers of inscriptions on tombs testify to the grief and affection of bereaved parents. A funeral for a dead child took place at night. At night, too, the poor were buried or cremated, with the minimum of ceremony. During the day the body had been washed, and laid out in the hall of the house. A branch of pine or cypress placed in front of the house warned passers-by of the death inside. Provided that enough money had been saved to meet the expense, the simple funeral took place the following evening.

Tombstone of Lucius Vibius, his wife Vecilia Hila, and their son. Note the family likeness

77

For the noble families, however, the death of a distinguished person required solemn and complicated rituals. The funeral was publicized by a herald, who announced the time and place of the ceremony. On the appointed day, a grand procession took place, which included pipers, flute and horn players, torch-bearers, hired mourners and the family of the dead person. Polybius describes the impression made by such funerals:

> Whenever a distinguished man dies, he is carried, during the course of the funeral, into the Forum, to the public speakers' platform: the corpse is sometimes conspicuous in an upright position, and more rarely reclined. When the people have gathered, an adult son, or some other relative, mounts the platform and makes a speech on the dead man's virtues and the successful achievements of his lifetime. As a result when the deeds are recalled to their minds and brought before their eyes these spectators are moved to such sympathy that the death seems to be not a private affair for the mourners, but a public loss, affecting everyone. Next, after the body has been buried, they place the image of the dead man in a most conspicuous place in the house, in a wooden shrine. The image is a mask which resembles the deceased very closely, both in features and complexion. These images are displayed at public sacrifices, and when any important member of the family dies, they are carried in the funeral procession, and are worn by men who seem to bear the closest resemblance to the original in build and appearance. These mask-carriers put on togas with a purple border, if the mask's original was a consul or a praetor, an all-purple toga if he was a censor, and a toga embroidered with gold if he had celebrated a triumph. The mask-carriers ride in chariots in the funeral procession with all the trappings and insignia to which the rank of the original entitles them, and when they arrive at the Forum they sit down, in order of rank, on ivory chairs. There could hardly be a more inspiring spectacle . . . for who would not be stirred by the sight of images of men, renowned for their excellence, all together and seeming to be alive and breathing?

> (Polybius, 6.53.1. ff.)

A funeral scene, from a sarcophagus. Musicians, pall-bearers and mourners are all clearly shown

The distinguished families buried their dead in the large expensive tombs, whose monuments lined the roads leading into the city. The ashes of the poorer citizens were placed in small niches in specially constructed buildings, while the bodies of the poorest and the slaves were thrown into communal pits. From the personal details carved on monuments, archaeologists can learn a great deal about the events and conditions of the time. Perhaps more important, we can begin to understand the ordinary people from an epitaph like this:

> Stranger, my message is short. Stand here and read it through. Here is the ugly tomb of a lovely woman. Her parents named her Claudia. She loved her husband with all her heart. She bore two sons. One of these she leaves on earth, the other she has buried under the earth. She was charming in conversation, yet gentle in manner. She kept house, she made wool. That is all I have to say. Go your way.

(C.I.L., vol. VI, 15 346)

A Roman with the busts of his ancestors

A Politician's Progress

Marcus Tullius CICERO (106–43 BC)

We learned in Chapter 8 that Roman education aimed to make the young Roman an accomplished public speaker. As Cicero's reminiscences showed, it could take years for a young man to acquire the oratorical skills he needed if he was to be a success in public life. But the length and the expense of the training did not deter distinguished or ambitious Roman families from giving their sons this opportunity. Most would have agreed with Cicero that an able and well-educated Roman was an asset to the Republic, and that he, in turn, had a duty to serve the state by entering politics. As Cicero told his son Marcus:

> Those who by nature have the ability to assist in their country's government should not hesitate – they should seek election to the magistracies, and play their part in the administration of the Republic. This is the only way that the state can be governed, and the only way that a man can prove his exceptional qualities of mind.

> (Cicero, *de Off.*, I, 72)

Cicero's own career reflects this approach. The biographer Plutarch (AD 46–126) in his 'Life of Cicero', confirms the details of his long and thorough training as an orator, and shows how profitably Cicero used his great talent for public speaking. In these extracts from the biography you will see how closely success as a barrister was linked to success in politics and public life – a link which the Romans took for granted, because many lawsuits were inspired by political rivalries, and a trial was held in the open Forum, so that the electorate could watch, and listen to those taking part.

The Early Steps

Cicero started life as a member of the equestrian order, whose family came from the small Italian town of Arpinum, 60 miles south-east of Rome. None of his ancestors had ever held high office in the capital. His public career began dramatically against the threatening background of Sulla's dictatorship. His first criminal brief was to defend Sextus Roscius, the innocent victim of one of Sulla's agents, and thus risk offending the dictator himself. Plutarch takes up the story – notice how Cicero's activities in the courts run parallel with his election by the People to the various offices of state.

> Because Sulla was quick to take offence, lawyers fought shy of Roscius' case, and no one would take it on. Abandoned in this way, the young man turned to Cicero, whose friends encouraged him to accept the brief, pointing out that there was no better publicised or more honourable way for him to begin to make his reputation. So Cicero undertook the defence, and when he won the case he was much admired for his success. But he was still afraid of Sulla's reaction, and went abroad to Greece, on the pretext that he was travelling for health reasons. . . .
>
> But when the news came (78 BC) that Sulla was dead . . . Cicero's friends at Rome wrote to him, and begged him to return and involve himself in politics. Cicero therefore put the final touches to his oratorical equipment and roused his political spirit. . . . But during the first part of his time in Rome he moved cautiously, and because he did not thrust himself forward as a candidate for office, his claims were overlooked. But he was ambitious by temperament, and at the prompting of his father and friends he devoted himself to his work as a barrister. In this way he quickly reached the top of his profession, and earned himself a brilliant reputation, far outdistancing his rivals in the courts. . . .
>
> In 75 BC he was elected quaestor, during a grain shortage. The province of Sicily was allotted to him and at first he made himself unpopular with the people there by forcing them to send grain to Rome. But afterwards they found him thorough, just and good-natured, and honoured him more than any of his predecessors. . . . When his quaestorship was over, he began to involve himself more seriously with politics . . . and for this reason he trained himself to remember not only the names of his fellow-citizens, but also whereabouts in the city every important person lived, where his estates were, who were his friends, and who his neighbours. And so, wherever Cicero travelled in Italy, he could easily point out the estates and country houses of his friends.

(Plutarch, *Cicero*, 3, 4, 6)

Cicero Speaks for the Sicilians

In 70 BC Verres, who as ex-praetor had governed Sicily in a scandalously corrupt and tyrannical way was prosecuted by the Sicilians. Cicero, bound by ties of friendship with the islanders, led the prosecution, and his brilliantly successful handling of the case in the face of much opposition increased his reputation. Plutarch continues:

The Sicilians were grateful to Cicero, and when he was aedile (in 69 BC) they brought him all sorts of produce and livestock from the island. Cicero made no profit from these, but used the generosity of the Sicilians to lower food prices at Rome. . . . He himself lived in a house near the Palatine Hill, so that those who came to call on him in the morning should not have far to walk. As many daily visitors called on Cicero as called on Crassus for his wealth, or on Pompey because of his military influence; Pompey and Crassus were, in fact, the two most powerful and admired men in Rome at the time. Pompey himself used to call on Cicero, and owed much of his reputation and power to Cicero's efforts on his behalf.

Although a number of well-connected candidates stood for the praetorship (in 67 BC) Cicero topped the poll. During his term of office it was thought that he handled the legal cases which came before him fairly and honestly.

(Plutarch, *Cicero*, 8, 9)

Consul Cicero

The next step in Cicero's political career was the most important, and the most difficult. Because none of his ancestors had ever been consul, Cicero knew that his chances of reaching the consulship were limited. As always a small number of noble families jealously guarded the privilege of the highest office. But luck and his own ability were on his side. One of the rival candidates was Catiline, whose revolutionary schemes were causing the nobility great anxiety.

Catiline, wishing to begin his operations from a position of strength, stood for the consulship. He had great hopes that his colleague as consul would be Gaius Antonius, a man with no aptitude for leadership in any direction. He was, however, capable of using his power in support of another's lead. Almost every responsible citizen recognized this threat, and supported Cicero for the consulship. The common people approved of this, and Cicero and C. Antonius were elected consuls; Catiline was defeated. And all this in spite of the fact that Cicero was the only candidate whose father was an equestrian, and not a senator.

(Plutarch, *Cicero*, 11)

So a New Man (*novus homo* – a senator with no ancestral claim to the consulship) had reached the top of the ladder of office (*cursus honorum*) which every politically ambitious Roman had to climb. According to the regulations which Sulla had enforced, the *cursus* began with the quaestorship. A candidate for this office (there were 20 posts in all) had to be 30 years old, and would often have served for a number of years in the army, as a military tribune. As a quaestor's duties were primarily financial, a successful candidate would either be sent to a province as financial officer on a governor's staff (as Cicero was), or be attached to one of the departments of state at Rome. Most important, a quaestor automatically became a senator, eligible to stand for the praetorship, after an interval of eight years. In the meantime he might become a tribune of the People, with the chance to increase his popularity by political action on the People's behalf, or an aedile, whose control of the public games allowed him to make a name with the voters by providing magnificent shows. Cicero's largesse with the gifts of the Sicilians, though on a smaller scale, had the same end in view.

Bronze statue of an orator, from the first century BC. Cicero would have looked like this as he held the attention of the crowds in the Forum and Senate House

Lictors (attendants of senior magistrates) carrying fasces, *bundles of rods and an axe, symbols of the traditional power of the magistrate to flog or execute. Praetors were preceded by two lictors, consuls by 12. The rods and axe were often combined into a single bundle*

Electioneering Advice

As one of the eight praetors, the politician served as a judge in one of Rome's courts, and his year as magistrate was often followed by his appointment to a provincial governorship. On his return, he would involve himself completely in his candidacy for the consulship, which he was allowed to hold three years after the praetorship. As there were only two consuls, the competition was intense. Rivals often brought lawsuits against one another, and the candidates spared no effort or expense to increase the number and influence of their supporters. The powerful families in the Senate, calling up all their resources of political patronage and family alliances, mobilized support for their favourite candidate; almost invariably such a candidate was one of their own inner circle. Bribery was lavish and commonplace. Much was at stake, as Cicero's brother Quintus, in a piece of hard-headed advice, reminded Cicero during his candidacy in 64 BC.

> Take these three things into account: what state this is, what you are aiming for, and who you are. Then, as you make your way to the Forum every day, say to yourself, 'I am a New Man, I am a candidate for the consulship, and this is Rome'. Your great reputation as a speaker will compensate for your lack of magisterial ancestors, for oratory has always carried with it the highest distinction. A man who is considered worthy to defend ex-consuls in the courts must be thought worthy of the consulship. . . .

Make sure that you secure the votes of people in every section of the voting assembly through the number and variety of your friends. The first and most obvious step is to canvass senators and equestrians, and the active and influential men of the other classes of society. There are many hard-working city men and freedmen engaged in business who are popular and energetic. Some of these you can ask for support in person, others through mutual friends. Make sure that they are enthusiastic for your cause, work hard, seek them out, assure them that they will be doing you the greatest service. Next, review the whole city, all the guilds and political clubs, the districts and neighbourhoods. If you can win over the leading men in these, you will easily gain the support of the rank and file. After that, keep before your mind a map of all Italy, divided and catalogued by tribes. Learn it by heart, so that there is no municipality, no colony, no prefecture – in a word no place at all in Italy – where you do not have sufficient support. . . .

Now for those who attend you about the city. You must take care to receive large numbers every day of every class and rank. . . . Such supporters fall into three categories. The first consists of the morning callers who come to your house. These supporters, as is normal practice nowadays, come in great numbers. But you must contrive to make them believe that you value even this slight service very highly. . . . The second group is of those who escort you to the Forum. Since this is a greater service than a morning call, make it clear to them that you are so much the more grateful for their attention – for this numerous daily escort produces a splendid impression and confers great distinction. The third group comprises those who regularly accompany you as you canvass for votes. See to it that those who do so voluntarily understand that they are placing you in their perpetual debt by their kindness . . . I think that it is extremely important that you should always be surrounded by a throng of supporters. . . . Lastly, take care that your campaign is full of pomp, brilliant, sparkling and pleasing to the People, and gives the impression of the utmost dignity and magnificence. Ensure, too, that if possible some new scandal is stirred up against your competitors, for crime or loose-living, or corruption, as is appropriate for the particular character. Above all, in this election you must make sure that the public have confidence in you, and think you honourable. Do not engage in political argument in the Senate or in public meetings for the moment: while you are a candidate you must hold back, so that the Senate may judge you to be a defender of its authority because you have been until now; so that the equestrians and responsible and wealthy citizens in general may judge from your past behaviour that you are a lover of peace and tranquillity; so that the People shall remember your speeches for popular causes, at public meetings and in the courts, and judge that you will not be hostile to their interests!

(Quintus Cicero, *Comm. Pet.*, 2, 8, 9, 13)

A coin showing citizens voting. Voters walked along narrow gangways and dropped their ballot into an urn at the end (right)

85

The Senate House (Curia), which stands near the west end of the Forum Romanum. Julius Caesar had it rebuilt on its earlier foundations after it had been destroyed by fire. In its present form it dates from about AD 300

The Summit of Ambition

When his year of consulship was over, the ex-consul usually went as governor to one of the more important provinces, where if he was fortunate, he might win military distinction, and if unscrupulous, amass a considerable fortune. But an eminent ex-consul might seek other honours – the office of censor, for example, to which two ex-consuls were elected every five years. The censor's duty was to review the list of senators and to keep a close check on the registration and classification of citizens. Another title of honour which an ex-consul might acquire, if he had not done so already, was membership of one of the colleges of priests (see Chapter 17). Such an office was mainly political in influence: saintliness was not a qualification, as Julius Caesar proved by becoming Chief Priest in 63 BC.

Senators and priests in solemn procession. The priests have their heads covered. The assistant on the left carries a box of incense. Another scene from the Ara Pacis

But perhaps the most sought-after distinction which a consul or ex-consul was best placed to achieve was to be awarded a triumph for a victorious campaign against Rome's enemies. This honour was coveted by peace-loving and warmongering senators alike, and provided one of Rome's most memorable spectacles, here described by a Byzantine scholar:

> When a general had achieved a conspicuous success, which deserved a Triumph, he was immediately hailed as *Imperator* by his men. Then he tied sprigs of laurel to his *fasces*, and handed them to the messengers who announced the victory to the City. When he himself

The emperor Marcus Aurelius (AD 121–80) in a triumphal chariot. In the background is a triumphal arch

arrived home he convened the Senate, and asked them to vote him a Triumph. If they agreed, and both Senate and People voted for the honour, his title of *Imperator* was confirmed. . . . Then, dressed in the triumphal robe (*toga picta*) and wearing armlets to ward off evil spirits, with a laurel crown on his head and holding a branch in his right hand, the victorious general called the People together. In their presence he praised the troops who had fought with him, both collectively and as individuals, and presented them with money, and various decorations of honour. To some he gave special armlets, to others ceremonial spears with the heads removed, to others he gave crowns, sometimes of gold, sometimes silver, bearing the name of each man and a representation of his deeds of valour. . . . A large part of the campaign booty was divided among those soldiers who had taken part in the campaign; but some victorious generals even distributed the spoils among the whole city population . . . and if anything was left over, they spent it on temples, porticoes or some other public benefaction.

When these ceremonies were completed, the triumphant general climbed into his chariot – this was a special turret-shaped vehicle, quite unlike the chariots used in races or in battle. . . . Alongside him in the chariot rode a public slave, who held over the general's head a crown of gold, with jewels set in it. The slave continually repeated 'Look behind you' (or as most sources suggest 'Remember that you are mortal'. Both commands warned the *Imperator* of the dangers of pride). . . . In this way they entered the city. In the front of the procession were carried the spoils and trophies, as well as images representing captured forts, cities, mountains, rivers, lakes and seas – everything that had been captured and conquered. If the exhibition of the spoils and images took more than a day, the celebrations might last two or even three days. After the parade, the victorious general was driven to the Forum, where he gave instructions for some of the prisoners to be led to prison and executed. Then he rode up to the Capitol, to perform rituals and make sacrifices before dining in the porticoes there. When evening approached he made his way home, to the sound of flutes and pipes. This is what a Triumph was like in ancient times.

(Zonaras, *Epitome*, 7.21)

With prizes like this to be won, it is not surprising that young men of ability and ambition aimed at a senatorial career, with all its perils, and spurned the easy affluence of the equestrian order. As Cicero states, a successful senator could expect

position in society, authority, a magnificent home, reputation and influence among foreign peoples, the purple-rimmed toga of high office, the *curule* chair, insignia of distinction, the *fasces*, command of armies, executive power and provincial governorship.

(Cicero, *Pro Cluentio*, 154)

Rewards like these were worth all the risks.

CHAPTER TEN

Writing and Writers

Books and Publishing

The Argiletum was one of the streets which led north from the Forum (see map on p. 17). It was a shopping street, like many of those in the neighbourhood, where stallholders and shopkeepers competed with one another to attract the attention of passers-by. In Caesar's day, the Argiletum was already well known for its bookshops, and posters stuck to the columns of the porticoes advertised the publishers' wares. Under the portico, the bookseller himself arranged his latest and most attractive volumes on the counter, while behind him, in the dim interior, it was possible to see tiers of shelving and pigeon holes holding row after row of scrolls.

If a particular volume was selling well – in the first days of publication, for instance – the publisher would estimate the likely demand, and if necessary instruct his staff of copiers to begin work on the next edition. The copiers would then set to work. The sheets of papyrus had already been prepared: thin strips from the Egyptian papyrus reed had been placed side by side horizontally, then a second layer vertically. The two layers had been glued and pressed firmly together, and the resulting 'two ply' papyrus had been smoothed and polished to make writing easy. Each of the scribes was given a portion of the author's manuscript to copy, and worked with a pen (*stilus*), and ink (*atramentum*) made from resin and soot.

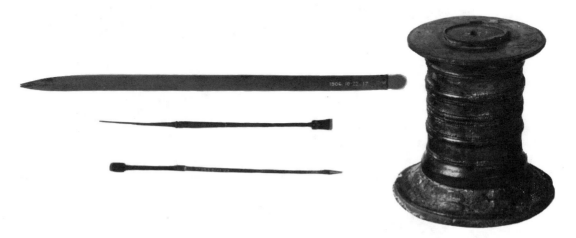

Pens and ink pot. The calamus *or reed pen was dipped in ink. The two* stili *(below) were used for writing on wax tablets, with the squared end for rubbing out mistakes*

Wall painting from Pompeii, showing hinged wax tablets (left), ink pots (centre) and a volumen *(right)*

When the separate sheets were completed they were joined together, edge to edge, in the correct order, to make a continuous strip which was rolled into a cylindrical scroll (*volumen*). The edges of the scroll were smoothed off with pumice stone, and tinted black and finally a central rod, often with ornamental ends, was inserted into the roll as a sort of spine. More expensive scrolls were sometimes given a cover of parchment for protection, and to make them look elegant. But although only the wealthier Roman could afford the highly decorated copies of books, the simpler versions were not too expensive.

Naturally, the publisher hoped the work he was publishing would receive favourable comment in literary circles, and perhaps be read at recitations and to entertain guests after dinner parties. In this way a book became widely known, and its success was assured.

Reading a volumen. *Clearly as awkward for the listeners as for the reader. Scene from a casket for sacred relics*

Catullus

News of a literary success spread quickly through Rome's fashionable society, and so it did not take long for the young poet C. Valerius Catullus to make a considerable reputation. He had come to Rome in 62 BC from his home in Verona. His family was rich, and he was quickly accepted by fashionable circles in the city. Many distinguished Romans became his friends, and the attractive young man-about-town found many subjects for his poems in the restless, varied life of the Capital. He was observant, witty, and quick to point out quirks of character and behaviour in his friends and enemies. For example he abused Egnatius, a Spaniard who prided himself on the whiteness of his teeth, for breaking into a beaming smile at the most inappropriate moments; 'Even when a mother weeps at the funeral of her only son, he flashes his teeth at everyone.' Another acquaintance always added 'H' to words beginning with a vowel, so that an 'ambush' became a 'hambush' and advantage 'hadvantage'. Rufus' armpits smelled as though a goat lived under them. Catullus' poems make no attempt to conceal his likes and dislikes. To Cicero he writes a most complimentary piece, while his references to Caesar and his subordinate Mamurra are abusive and contemptuous. His real friends were the younger orators, poets and literary personalities of the day. Time spent in their company was delightful and Catullus did not hesitate to record his own pleasure at being with them. Like them, Catullus found his lifestyle expensive. Two country houses and a yacht were a drain on his finances, and his purse was often 'full of cobwebs'. Once when he invited a friend to a meal he even had to ask him to bring his own food with him. Even his trip to Bithynia on the staff of a provincial governor, Memmius, failed to produce the financial rewards expected. But it did enable him to visit the tomb of his brother, who was buried near the ancient site of Troy. His poem to his dead brother, short, affectionate and final is a masterpiece which highlights Catullus' ability to express powerful emotions in a few words.

> Journeying over many seas and through many countries
> I come dear brother to this pitiful leave-taking
> the last gestures by your graveside
> the futility of words over your quiet ashes.
> Life cleft us from each other
> pointlessly depriving brother of brother.
> Accept then, in our parents' custom,
> these offerings, this leave-taking
> echoing for ever, brother, through a brother's tears.
> 'Hail and Farewell'.

(Catullus, 101)

Catullus was a highly gifted poet, and his poetry gives us a clear insight into the life of a wealthy, talented young man at the time when Caesar and Pompey dominated politics at Rome. But his most admired poetry springs from his relationship with Lesbia – the name he gives in his poems to the woman he loves. She was an aristocrat, attractive, temperamental and fascinating, and she quickly bewitched Catullus. His poems cover the whole course of the affair, from the first tender advances of an admirer to the embittered desperation of a rejected lover. Every stage, every crisis is reflected in a poem and Catullus describes his most personal feelings with complete openness and directness. His passion, his doubts, and finally his despair, expressed in simple, beautiful Latin, are as vivid today as they must have been to readers at the time.

The Philosopher Poet

Everyone in Roman society would know of Catullus, even if they had not met him. Only a few would know of T. Lucretius Carus, and even fewer would have read his major poem, which was published when Catullus' poetry was all the rage. Lucretius dedicated his poem 'On the nature of the Universe' (*de rerum natura*) to the same Memmius whom Catullus accompanied to Bithynia. But the two poets had little in common. Lucretius lived away from Rome, and played no part in the frantic activity of the city. Withdrawn and remote, he watched the political struggles and the armed conflict of the Republic.

> How pleasant it is, when the sea is lashed and churned by gales, to watch from the shore while someone at sea struggles to keep afloat. This is not because I derive any pleasure from someone else's sufferings, but because it is delightful to realise that I have no similar problems. Equally, it is pleasant to look down on two great armies facing one another on the battlefield when you yourself are in no danger. But nothing is more delightful than to be high up in Reason's calm temple, protected by the teaching of wise men, and to look down and see other men wandering about, searching vainly for a way of life. They fight for superiority by every possible means, claiming precedence, exerting all their efforts, by day and night to join the ranks of the rich and powerful.

> (Lucretius, *de rerum natura* II, 1–13)

But Lucretius was more than an observer. His poem was a philosophical textbook, whose purpose was to convert Memmius and others to the philosophy of Epicurus, a Greek who had lived three centuries earlier. Epicurus believed that in order to obtain peace of mind, a man had to free himself from superstition and the fear of death. He could only do this by learning to understand the universe and the laws of Nature. According to Epicurus all matter – earth, rocks, water, animals and men themselves – is composed of atoms which move about in space, and come together in chance formations. Even the human mind, our soul, thoughts and emotions are the products of infinitely small atoms. But just as all material objects decay, leaves wither and rocks crumble, so man's body and his mind must decay and die and the atoms they are made of disperse once again. From this it follows that death is inevitable and final, and there can be no life after death. For this reason, says Lucretius, it is wrong to fear death, and foolish to believe that the gods, even if they exist, can help us to overcome it. The superstitious belief (*religio*) that we can alter fate by prayer and sacrifice is merely wishful thinking. So Lucretius' advice to Memmius is to keep to himself and to steer clear of politics. Only then will he find real peace of mind, and be rid of superstition, the fear of death, and the greed and ambition which follow from them.

All this is unusual subject matter for a poem. But Lucretius was an inspired poet. Though his long poem had to contain much technical detail about atoms and the universe, Lucretius' sensitive descriptions of nature in all forms and of human society, with all its weaknesses, reveal his eye for detail and his poetic genius.

Cicero, Master of Prose Style

But it was not easy to withdraw from politics in the late Republic. Most Romans felt compelled to take sides in the upheavals which led to the civil war. M. Tullius Cicero the distinguished orator and statesman, who had been consul in 63 BC, was one of the first to read Lucretius' poem. But although he was impressed by much of the poetry, he could not accept Lucretius' advice to steer clear of politics, or to withdraw from society. Cicero had worked hard for his prominent position through his brave and brilliant speeches in the law-courts and his powerful support of Pompey in the Senate House and the Forum. Politics, the art of government and the principles by which men lived and were ruled were his keenest interest, and this is reflected through the whole range of his writings and speeches.

From his first speech as a young barrister and throughout his career, Cicero's writing displays two remarkable qualities. The first is his prose style, which was admired by critics in the ancient world, and influenced the writing of Latin and other languages for centuries afterwards. Cicero wrote in a style which few modern writers imitate. Instead of the short, direct sentences which popular journalism has made so familiar, his sentences were long and fluent, with a wealth of subordinate clauses. But his speeches did not lose impact because of the length of his sentences. By his control of the rhythms of the language, and his mastery of the subordinate clauses in each 'period' or sentence, his supreme descriptive powers and his use of wit and pathos, he could hold his hearers spellbound. The second quality was his mastery of his subject. Anyone reading his six speeches against Verres (only one of which was needed to drive Verres into voluntary exile) will be impressed by the way Cicero collects and presents evidence, the skill of his arguments and the conclusiveness of his proofs. The total effect of Cicero's speeches was overwhelming. As Quintilian, who wrote a textbook on the training of an orator, put it:

> What orator can inform his hearers with greater thoroughness, or stir their emotions more deeply? What speaker ever had more charm than Cicero? The result is that when he wrings a concession from the opposition by ruthless argument, you feel that it has been granted as a favour. And when he compels a member of the jury to change his mind by the sheer force of his argument, the juryman does not seem to be swept away, but rather to follow of his own free will. There is such authority in everything he says that his listeners feel ashamed to disagree with him. . . . All these excellent qualities (any one of which is beyond the reach of an ordinary person) are fused into his speeches with no apparent effort on Cicero's part, and his whole style (unparalleled in its excellence) has a most delightful fluency.

(Quintilian, *Inst. Or.* X 1. 110–12)

But his speeches, which were written to be read as well as heard, were only one part of Cicero's vast literary output. He wrote treatises on the techniques and training of orators, and many books on a variety of subjects – government, law, friendship, duty, old age.

Letters

Best known of all, and most valuable to the historian are his letters, written to relatives and friends, in particular to Atticus, an equestrian, whose close friendship with Cicero led to a continuous correspondence. We still possess the texts of over 800 of Cicero's letters (together with some of the replies), and from them historians can learn a great deal about the social and political situation of the time, in far closer detail than other sources supply. From the correspondence, too, we know more about Cicero than about any other person in the ancient world, for most of the letters were not intended for publication, and give a frank and authentic picture of their author. Here is Cicero's account for Atticus of a security-conscious visit to his villa by Julius Caesar.

> What a guest to entertain: yet I don't regret it! In fact everything went off most pleasantly. But when he reached Philippus' villa, the evening before he was due here, the place was so full of soldiers that there was hardly room on the couch where Caesar was to have his dinner. Two thousand troops in all. Believe me, I was very alarmed about what would happen the next day, but fortunately my neighbour Barba Cassius came to the rescue and lent me some guards. A camp was pitched on my estate, and my villa sealed off. Caesar stayed at Philippus' house until early afternoon and allowed no one to see him . . . after that he went for a walk by the sea. An hour later he had a bath . . . and had an oil massage, and then sat down to dinner at my house. As he was taking a course of emetics he ate and drank without restraint, and enjoyed himself. The dinner itself was lavish and beautifully served. . . . Meanwhile his staff and bodyguard were given everything they could want in three other dining rooms. . . .
>
> In other words, we ate together like human beings. But he is not the sort of guest to whom you would say 'I would be delighted if you would come to stay on your return journey'. Once is enough!

> (Cicero, *ad Att.* 13.52)

Sending a letter was, of course, the usual way to get in touch with someone who was away on business, on a campaign, or in one of the provinces. But although Rome controlled a vast Empire, no reliable postal service existed until the first century AD, and in Cicero's time a letter had to be entrusted to a courier or a traveller. Cicero often complains that it is difficult to find a reliable courier; 'Most couriers will try to make their load lighter by reading the messages they are carrying,' he tells Atticus. But a good courier could travel fast, and Cicero, while he was governor of Cilicia in 51–50 BC, received a stream of letters from friends in Rome telling him the latest news, and asking him to bring back presents from his province.

Although short messages could be written on wax tablets which could be cleaned and used for the return message, most letters were written on papyrus, and looked like a *volumen*. A letter was rolled up, tied with a cord and then sealed, often with the recipient's name on the outside. If a courier was employed, and his journey was uneventful, the letter could be expected to travel about 50 miles per day (though progress in winter would always be slower). Cicero received two letters from Caesar which he wrote while campaigning in Britain. These took 26 and 28 days respectively to reach Cicero at Rome.

Other Writers

In the literary sphere, Cicero and Julius Caesar had much in common, though they were usually on opposite sides politically. Both were outstanding orators, both were widely read and cultured men with a taste for literature and both wrote polished and elegant prose, though their styles differed. But Caesar's continuous political and military

A Pompeian mural depicts Paquius Proculus and his wife holding a volumen *and a wax tablet*

activity gave him little time to match Cicero's remarkable output. His surviving writings, however, are full of interest and significance. Best known are his commentaries on the Gallic War (*de bello gallico*), in seven books – each book written after a campaigning season to describe the events of the previous year. Many students will have read Caesar's account of the invasions of Britain, and will remember his matter-of-fact, direct style of writing. He did not exaggerate or over-dramatize situations, but wrote simply, clearly and with great control, and let events speak for themselves. Later Caesar began an account of the Civil War, but he had completed only three books before he was killed by the conspirators (44 BC).

The same year C. Sallustius Crispus, one of Caesar's supporters, began to write his vivid and highly dramatic accounts of two incidents in Rome's recent history – the war against Jugurtha, in Africa 112–105 BC, and the conspiracy of Catiline, which Cicero as consul had helped to suppress in 63 BC.

Perhaps it is surprising that in a period of social upheaval and civil war so many great poets and prose writers should come to prominence within a few years of each other. In fact the last years of the Republic and the first years of Augustus' principate formed the background for a remarkable burst of literary activity known as 'The Golden Age of Latin Literature'. By comparison with Greece, Romans had come late to the literary scene, but contact with the Greeks, in Sicily especially, and throughout the second century BC, had led to the rapid development of Latin literature. All classes of people were affected. The nobility read the works of the historians and the autobiographies of distinguished citizens, the epics of Ennius (d. 169 BC) and the satires of Lucilius (d. 102 BC) while everyone enjoyed the comedies of Plautus (d. 184 BC) and Terence (d. 159 BC) and wept at the tragedies of Ennius and Accius (d. 86 BC).

Audiences in Cicero's day laughed and wept at these same plays, for the theatre was very popular. But in the fields of oratory, history and poetry, the writers mentioned in this chapter reached new standards of excellence. The achievements of Cicero, Caesar, Sallust, Catullus and Lucretius led on naturally to the writings of Virgil, Horace, Ovid and Livy under Augustus (see Chapter 16), so that in the history of world literature, Rome can stand comparison with Athens in the fifth century BC and Elizabethan England.

A writer of comedies examines an actor's mask. His comic muse looks on. Greek sculptured relief, third century BC

CHAPTER ELEVEN

The First Emperors

Heirs of Augustus

When Cornelius Tacitus wrote the history of the years AD 14–69 the prefatory chapters of *The Annals* included this short sketch of Augustus' reign:

> He won over the soldiers with gifts of money, and civilians with cheap food: both alike were beguiled by the delights of peace. His powers grew step by step as he took over the functions of the Senate, the public officials and even the laws. No one stood in his way, as his boldest opponents had been wiped out by war or execution. As for the other aristocrats, the more slavish their obedience, the greater the riches and honours bestowed upon them. The revolution had brought them prosperity, so they preferred the safety of the new government to the dangers of the old one. The provinces accepted the situation, for they mistrusted the régime of Senate and People, as they had found no safeguard against the struggles of rival power-groups or the greed of officials in the laws, which were overruled by force, intrigue or bribery.

(Tacitus, *Annals* I, ii)

Augustus dressed as a priest

Tacitus' dislike of Augustus cannot conceal the benefits his rule had brought. Personal liberty and freedom of speech might be restricted in Rome itself – everywhere else there was peace and prosperity. Failure to nominate a successor to the emperor by some constitutional arrangement might have brought a new civil war, as it was to do often in the future; but before he died Augustus had adopted Tiberius, his wife's son by a former marriage, as his own, and shared with him all his own official positions, so that the transfer of power was smooth and unchallenged.

> At Rome consuls, senators and equites rushed headlong into servility. The more distinguished a man was, the greater his haste and insincerity. To avoid any appearance of joy at the departure of one emperor, or sorrow at the arrival of another, their expressions were carefully arranged in a mixture of tears and smiles, condolence and flattery.

> (Tacitus, *Annals* I, vii)

As for the People, one of Tiberius' first acts was to deprive them of their vote – elections were transferred from the popular assembly to the Senate. An army rebellion was quickly suppressed, and since Tiberius was an able administrator life in the provinces was just as settled and prosperous as under Augustus.

> Never have the Romans and their allies enjoyed such peace and prosperity as was given to them by Augustus from the moment he assumed absolute power, and is now being provided for them by his son and successor Tiberius, who is basing his own administration and laws on those of Augustus.

> (Strabo, IV, iv 2)

But Tiberius was temperamentally unsuited to a position of supreme power: in constant fear of conspiracy he withdrew for the last 11 years of his reign to the island of Capri, leaving Sejanus, the Prefect of the Praetorian Guard, to preside over affairs in Rome. These Praetorian guards and their commanders were from this time to have great influence on politics in Rome. Originally Augustus had formed nine cohorts, each of 500 men, to act as a sort of bodyguard for the emperor and his family. The fact that they served for only 16 years, and were paid three times as highly as the legionaries gives some idea of the importance attached to them by the emperor; but to avoid any impression of a military dictatorship they were stationed outside Rome and in various depots within the city, under the command of two prefects from the equestrian order. Sejanus, however, in AD 23 had been appointed sole prefect, and had concentrated the cohorts in a single camp just outside the city.

The Senate, alarmed by Sejanus' power, and afraid to take any decision without first writing to consult Tiberius on Capri, lost self-confidence and authority. Sejanus plotted to seize the throne himself, but was discovered and executed. When Tiberius learnt that his own son had been poisoned by Sejanus his fears and suspicions turned into a malevolent cruelty. Prominent men whom Tiberius feared for any reason were accused of treason, often on the flimsiest evidence: a casual gesture, or a few ill-chosen words were enough to send a man to his death. A race of *delatores*, or informers, sprang up, for, by the laws, in a successful prosecution part of the convicted man's property went to the informant.

When Tiberius died in AD 37 after six miserable years, every soul in Rome breathed a sigh of relief. His successor was his great-nephew, Gaius. The new emperor, now aged 26, had as a little boy accompanied his enormously popular father Germanicus on his military campaigns: dressed in miniature soldier's boots (*caligae*) he had been given the nickname Caligula, a name he kept all his life. At once he banished informers, reduced taxation, and pardoned political prisoners. Not unnaturally he was hailed as a hero. But soon he was intoxicated by limitless power: he claimed that he was a god, and proposed that his horse be elected consul. His extravagance exhausted the treasury, and rich men were compelled to bequeath their wealth to the state. His cruelty and near-insanity became intolerable and in AD 41, only four years after his accession, he was assassinated by some officers of the Praetorian Guard.

No successor had been indicated: the Senate began discussing the possibility of restoring the Republic and personal freedom. But while the Senate discussed, Praetorians rioting through the palace found Claudius, Caligula's 50-year-old uncle, skulking behind a curtain. As a child he had been crippled by polio, and was otherwise so ill-favoured that his grandfather Augustus, though admitting that the boy had brains, had banished him from his presence, unwilling for him to be seen in public. For all that he *was* a member of the imperial family, so now he was carried off to the Praetorian camp, and hailed as emperor: his promise of 15,000 sesterces a head for the Guard may have had something to do with it. But despite such an exotic and unpromising beginning, he ruled for 13 years with considerable success.

The emperor Claudius wearing an oak-leaf crown, the highest honour that could be awarded to a Roman

Claudius

Both Tiberius and Gaius had followed the advice left them by Augustus, that the Empire should not be extended beyond the existing frontiers. But Claudius added new provinces: the kingdoms of Mauretania in Africa, and Thrace, south of the Danube, whose kings had ruled by permission of Rome, were now taken over and became full provinces of the Empire. And in AD 43 a full-scale invasion was successfully launched across the Channel to Britain.

Claudius was determined that the greater size and complexity of the Empire should not mean that it was less well governed. The 'civil service' was reorganized, and a number of ex-slaves promoted to positions of unprecedented power. They became Claudius' personal advisers, and acted as ministers of separate state departments in a sort of inner cabinet. Although Augustus had used his own slaves in some degree to manage the Empire, the official position of the freedmen of Claudius was new. Such roles should perhaps have been taken by senators or equites: but they regarded anything which smacked of personal service as far beneath their dignity. At the same time they deeply resented the influence the freedmen wielded, and were incensed at the bribes they demanded: Tacitus' anecdote about the arrogance of Pallas, one of Claudius' most important freedmen, makes it clear that their unpopularity was not undeserved. A law was proposed in the Senate determining the punishment of freeborn women who married slaves:

> When the emperor revealed that it was Pallas who had suggested the proposal, an honorary praetorship and fifteen million sesterces were decreed as a reward: in addition, because he put the interests of the state before his ancient nobility – they pretended he was descended from the kings of Arcady – and allowed himself to be regarded as a servant of the emperor, it was suggested that he be offered the nation's thanks. Claudius declared that Pallas accepted the honour, but declined the money, content with his former poverty. The Senate's decree was put up publicly on tablets of bronze, loading praise for old-fashioned self-denial on an ex-slave who owned 300,000,000 sesterces.

(Tacitus, *Annals*, XII, 53)

One of Claudius' successes was his return to Julius Caesar's policy of granting citizenship to leading provincials, and even encouraging them to aim at public office – some Gallic chieftains were actually admitted to the Senate in AD 48. His most significant failure was his inability to control his womenfolk. The ambition of his fourth wife, with support from the powerful Pallas, proved fatal. Agrippina, who was Claudius' niece as well as wife, poisoned him after she had persuaded him to adopt Nero, her son by a former marriage, as his heir in preference to his own son Britannicus.

Nero

For a few years the new administration won universal favour. The 16-year-old Nero was guided by his tutor, the philosopher Seneca, and Burrus the Prefect of the Praetorians. But unable to resist the temptations of absolute power, within six appalling years he had discarded all his advisers and contrived the murders of Britannicus, his mother, and his wife Octavia. He shocked the aristocracy by personally taking part in musical and theatrical contests, and by driving a chariot at the races. Yet these activities endeared him to the populace, already charmed by the lavish public entertainments and gifts of free corn which he arranged.

When a great fire devastated the centre of Rome, Nero bought up land to build a 'Golden House' – a huge combination of magnificent buildings adorned with gold plate and mother of pearl, a lake surrounded by fine town houses, meadows, vineyards and

Nero

tilled fields. The main banqueting hall was circular, and constantly revolved, night and day. 'I have begun', he said, 'to be housed as a man ought to be.' When the Romans complained that there was no longer room for anyone else, and rumoured that Nero had started the fire himself, Nero put the blame on the Christians, and sent hundreds of them to death by horrible means (see p. 169). He next toured Greece, taking part in the various national festivals and, after winning first prize in every competition, brought home over 1,800 gold crowns. When his outrageous behaviour led to several conspiracies against him he reverted to the treason trials of his predecessors; but his days were numbered. The armies in Gaul and Spain revolted and marched towards Rome. Nero fled from the city in fear, and took his own life. As Tacitus said:

> Nero's death, caused an initial outburst of joy and relief; at the same time it evoked a variety of emotions, not only in Rome, among the senators, people and city garrisons, but also in all the legions and their generals – for one secret of imperial politics had been revealed – an emperor could be created elsewhere than in Rome.

(Tacitus, *Histories* I, iv)

Four Emperors

Tacitus is referring to a period of near-anarchy, known as 'The Year of the Four Emperors'. Powerful army commanders were saluted as emperor by their troops, and marched towards Rome. The first was Galba, governor of one of the provinces in Spain: but the Praetorian guard in Rome found him so tight-fisted that they lynched him, and proclaimed in his place Otho, commander of the other Spanish provinces, who had been one of Nero's favourites. Then Vitellius, commander of the Rhine armies, sent his troops into Italy. Otho marched north, was defeated and committed suicide. Once on the throne Vitellius devoted himself to unrestrained gluttony.

But the army of the east was not to be outdone. The troops hailed their commander, Vespasian, now crushing the Jewish insurrection of AD 66–70, as emperor. Sending part of his army towards Italy, to link up on the way with the Danube legions, who had also declared for him, he seized Egypt to cut off the corn supply on which Rome depended. By the time Vespasian himself had reached Rome, the fighting in Italy was over, and Vitellius was dead. Vespasian's first act was to ask the Senate formally to confirm his imperial authority, for he saw clearly that a constitutional basis to the power he had usurped was vital.

Vespasian

Vespasian and His Sons

It was obvious that the imperial dynasty founded by Augustus had come to an end, and equally obvious that there was room for a new one. Moreover, though Augustus had put an end to the civil wars, as peace stretched beyond his lifetime for another 55 years, it had become evident that there would be a return to unending civil strife unless good relations were established between the Senate and an able emperor. It was this relationship that Vespasian and the Senate succeeded in restoring. There has survived part of the bronze tablet containing the decree of the Senate which conferred the imperial power on Vespasian, and regularized for him all the rights variously acquired by previous emperors. Perhaps its survival is not due to chance alone: a document which gave explicit constitutional authority for the principate, an authority based on civil law rather than military force, must have seemed of the utmost value to all subsequent rulers, and worth preserving at all costs.

Vespasian governed with wisdom, economy and benevolence. He renewed Claudius' policy of extending citizenship to provincials, and carried it further by granting citizenship to all men who completed their term of service in the army *auxilia*. Moreover, he saw that the high offices of state were too important to be entrusted to ex-slaves. These posts were now held by leading members of the equestrian order, and senators too began to take over some of the higher posts in the administration. Even the noblest were ready to accept a share in the task of government.

The blessings of imperial rule, it seemed, were too valuable to be challenged. Here is a justification of Rome's Empire, put by Tacitus into the mouth of a Roman general addressing an assembly of Gauls after suppressing their revolt in AD 70:

> Roman generals invaded your land and that of the other Gauls not through their own greed, but at the invitation of your forefathers . . . We have taken up positions on the Rhine not to protect Italy, but to prevent any other German princeling like Ariovistus seizing power in Gaul. . . . All Gaul was plagued by civil wars amongst its kings up to the time you accepted our domination. Though we have been continually provoked, we have relied on our right of conquest only to ask for such taxation as would pay to preserve the peace. Harmony between nations cannot be secured without armies; armies cannot be secured without pay, and pay cannot be secured without taxation. That is the only difference between us: you Gauls very often command our legions, and govern this and other provinces – there is no discrimination against you. Good emperors are no less good because they rule a long way off: the cruel ones are most vicious to those that live near them. You must put up with the extravagance and greed of your masters with the same fortitude you show towards natural disasters like bad crops or floods. There will be faults as long as there are men, but they don't last for ever, and the good times between them make up for them.
>
> (Tacitus, *Histories* IV, lxxiv)

Vespasian was succeeded in AD 79 by his son Titus, who reigned for only two years: his name is probably best remembered by the Arch of Titus, set up to commemorate his capture of Jerusalem. He also completed the Colosseum, the enormous amphitheatre begun by his father. It was during his reign that Pompeii and Herculaneum were buried in the ashes of Vesuvius' eruption.

The seven branched candlestick from the Temple at Jerusalem, depicted on the Arch of Titus in the Roman Forum. The placards carried either side of the candlestick give details of victories, towns captured and booty taken

Pompeii

Though a letter from the Younger Pliny survives describing the eruption in some detail, the site of Pompeii was not discovered until AD 1748. Since then the excavation of this small seaside town, with some 20,000 inhabitants, has gone on more or less continually, especially in the last hundred years. It has revealed a wealth of detail of the lives of its citizens. Many of them were overcome by fumes or ash before they were able to escape, and their bodies, encased in a hard shell of compacted ash and pumice, gradually decomposed. The hollows which were left have been filled with plaster by modern archaeologists, and these plaster casts tell a horrifying story (see p. 155). Two gladiators died, chained in their cells and unable to escape. The corpse of a woman, wearing magnificent jewels, found in the same gladiatorial barracks, seems to confirm that gladiators were permitted visits from admirers of all sorts. A woman, with her baby clasped to her breast, was found, cowering at the base of a wall. The priests of the temple of Isis were just beginning a meal of eggs and fish, most of which was found intact. Carbonized loaves of bread, found in a baker's shop, can still be seen in the Naples museum.

The walls of many houses survive to a considerable height, still showing inside the brightly coloured paintings of mythological scenes or religious ceremonies with which they were decorated. The outer walls still bear the *graffiti* ranging from political slogans to blunt obscenities: old habits die hard! The amphitheatre, for gladiatorial and other shows, seated nearly 15,000, though the two theatres are much smaller. Shops and offices still line many of the well-paved streets.

Most of the evidence for the plans and descriptions of houses and *insulae* in Chapter 3 comes from Pompeii; nowhere else do the buildings of the Romans, with all the

105

furniture and revealing trivia of daily life which filled them, survive so completely and so undamaged. But for the eruption of AD 79 our knowledge of the everyday lives of the Romans would be much less than it is. Perhaps the overwhelming impression left on a modern visitor is of the vitality and general prosperity of this small Italian port. If we can rely on its evidence, it is clear that the reigns of Vespasian and Titus were not a bad time to be alive.

A view over the excavated ruins of Pompeii

Domitian

Domitian, Vespasian's second son, who came to the throne next, was calamitously different from his father. He was a ruthlessly efficient administrator, but impossibly arrogant. He ordered that he be addressed as 'Lord and God'; he openly despised the Senate, never consulted it, and only summoned it to declare what he wanted done. As a result, he was hated by the senators more than any previous princeps, and the opposition that naturally arose could not be kept secret. Treason trials and professional informers appeared again, introducing another reign of terror. Some books were published in praise of two philosophers who had been critical of the régime: the authors were executed and the books publicly burnt in the forum by the emperor's agents:

> They believed that this fire was exterminating the voice of the People, the liberty of the Senate, and the conscience of mankind. Teachers of philosophy were banished, together with every honourable study in case anything decent might offend the emperor's eyes. And we senators gave a remarkable example of subservience. Our ancestors saw the heights of liberty, we the depths of slavery: fear of spies made us deaf and dumb, and we would have lost our memories if it had been as easy to forget as to keep silent.

(Tacitus, *Agricola*, 2)

Domitian was assassinated in AD 96 without naming a successor. Now for the first time in over a century it was left to the Senate to determine the future. The best thing, they decided, was not a return to republican liberties, but to select another emperor, for they were convinced that the vast complexity of the Empire needed the certainty of one authoritative voice, not the deliberations of committees. Rome had never tried democracy: now it gave up the chance for ever.

CHAPTER TWELVE

Imperial City

The enormous scale of public building and restoration undertaken by the emperor Augustus has already been discussed. Although building and re-building went on continuously, just as it does in modern cities, Augustus had erected and restored so many buildings that there was much less left for his immediate successors to do, at least in the centre of Rome.

Augustus' concern for the city did not end with the 'show-pieces' he had built. He organised a corps of 7,000 freedmen, called *vigiles*, and put them in seven brigades each of 1,000 men. The city was divided into 14 regions, and each brigade of vigiles was responsible for the security of two regions, primarily as firemen, but probably to some extent acting as a police force as well. Their fire-fighting equipment was elementary: simple hand-pumps could cope with a small fire, but were unable to deliver very great volumes of water: leather buckets and sponges were also used to dampen undamaged walls to prevent fire spreading. A major blaze could only be controlled by demolishing the buildings in the path of the fire to create a space across which the flames could not reach.

The Great Fire

But in AD 64 all the efforts of the fire-brigades were in vain when the city suffered an appalling disaster: the 'Great Fire' in which Nero was rumoured 'to have fiddled while Rome burned', raged for nine days. Tacitus has this to say of it:

Rome is divided into 14 districts: four escaped unharmed, and three were levelled to the ground: in the other seven there remained only a few ruined, half burnt remnants of houses. . . . Nero took advantage of the national disaster to build his Golden House. . . . But the areas of the city which his house did not cover were not rebuilt haphazardly, as after the sack of the city by the Gauls [in 390 BC]: there was order, and planning, with the rows of streets regularly measured out, and wide avenues: a limit was imposed on the height of the buildings: open court-yards were left in the insulae, and porticoes were added to give protection to their fronts. Nero promised to erect these at his own expense and to clear the debris before handing the sites over to their owners. Financial grants were given, in proportion to the rank and wealth of the owners, provided that the houses and the insulae were finished within a specified time. Corn-ships returning down the Tiber were to dump the rubbish in the Ostian marshes. Special parts of the buildings were to be erected without timber, in fireproof stone from Gabii or Alba. He appointed water conservators to make sure that a larger public water supply should be more readily available, for private house-holders had been 'borrowing' it: everyone was to have fire-fighting equipment where it could be easily reached. Semi-detached houses were forbidden: each must have its own walls. These practical measures also made the new city more beautiful, though some people thought that the old form of the city had been better: high houses and narrow streets had offered protection against the heat of the sun, while the wide-open and shade-less spaces now burnt with an even greater heat.

(Tacitus, Annals XV, 40-3)

The new plans must have been welcome, for Rome had always been a rabbit-warren of narrow streets, with houses of highly inflammable material packed tightly together. Parts of Rome at least now came to resemble the many towns of Italy and the provinces which were built on the right-angle chess-board pattern (borrowed from the Greeks and Etruscans) that is also familiar in the camps of the legions. Other towns too, that had 'just grown' in unplanned muddle were redeveloped on more regular lines in the centuries after their foundation.

The town of Timgad, in North Africa, is an excellent example of logical Roman planning: the right-angled grid, the forum, the theatre and the insulae are quite clear. But the road leading away to the neighbouring town naturally could not maintain the same alignment: when a suburb was developed in later years the rows of new houses were built along this road, and the photograph shows how the original pattern was broken. Timgad illustrates another feature of most Mediterranean towns of the Roman Empire: the streets are still lined with hundreds of columns. Since a great part of the day was spent out of doors, roofed colonnades were provided for the main thoroughfares to offer shelter from the fierce heat of the sun as well as from sudden downpours. These are the porticoes mentioned in the extract from Tacitus on p. 107.

An aerial view of Timgad, in modern Algeria

A view over the remains of Timgad

But in some important respects Rome was unique. In the first place it was bigger than other cities: a survey of the 14 regions was carried out in the reign of Constantine; a few extracts from it will give some idea of how large the city was. There were 28 libraries, 8 bridges, 8 parks, 11 fora, 10 basilicas, 11 thermae (great public baths), 19 aqueducts, 29 main roads, 2 circuses, 2 amphitheatres, 3 theatres, 36 marble triumphal arches, 37 city gates, 290 warehouses, 856 baths, 1,352 fountains, 254 cornmills, 144 public lavatories; of the private houses of the rich there were 1,790, but of insulae the staggering total was 46,602.

There was, in addition to this list, a great plan of the city, known as the Forma Urbis, inscribed on marble which used to amaze ancient tourists in the capital, but unfortunately only fragments of it have survived.

There were, it is true, other great cities. Alexandria, the largest city of Egypt, had about 1,000,000 inhabitants; Antioch in Syria had a main street over four and a half miles long, and was the only city in the ancient world that could boast of street lighting at night. But Rome was set apart from these, for it was the centre of an empire. It was the great wealth of the capital, the unrivalled power of the emperors and the vast population which offered opportunities to be found nowhere else. The best architects, the best engineers and the best craftsmen flocked to Rome from the rest of the Empire. Their talents produced a great number of structures of breathtaking size and complexity. These were so strong that enough of them remains even today for our architects to be able to reconstruct them with considerable certainty.

There were great palaces built on the Palatine by a succession of emperors for their private use, official public buildings such as the basilicas and fora that served as law-courts, state ministries and business centres, and the great amphitheatres, theatres and thermae built for the entertainment of the populace. All these were made possible not only by the riches of Rome but by the development of building techniques and materials that other ancient civilisations either failed to discover, or ignored.

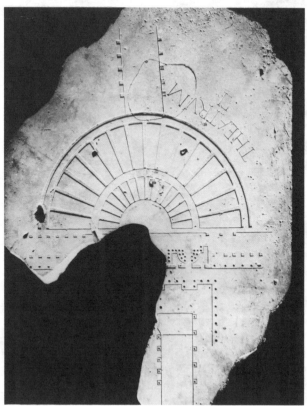

A fragment of the Forma Urbis, showing Pompey's theatre

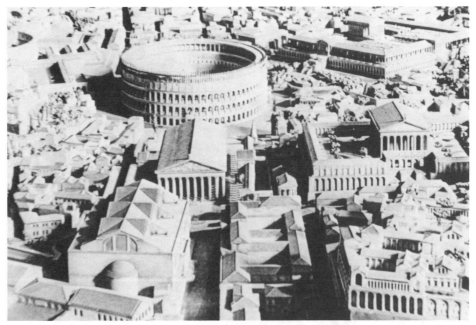

A view of the eastern end of the Roman Forum from a modern model reconstruction of the city. You can see temples and (front left) a basilica roof. The temple to the Divine Claudius stands to the right, behind the Colosseum

A modern model reconstruction of the Circus Maximus at Rome. The imperial palaces, high up on the left, overlook the stadium

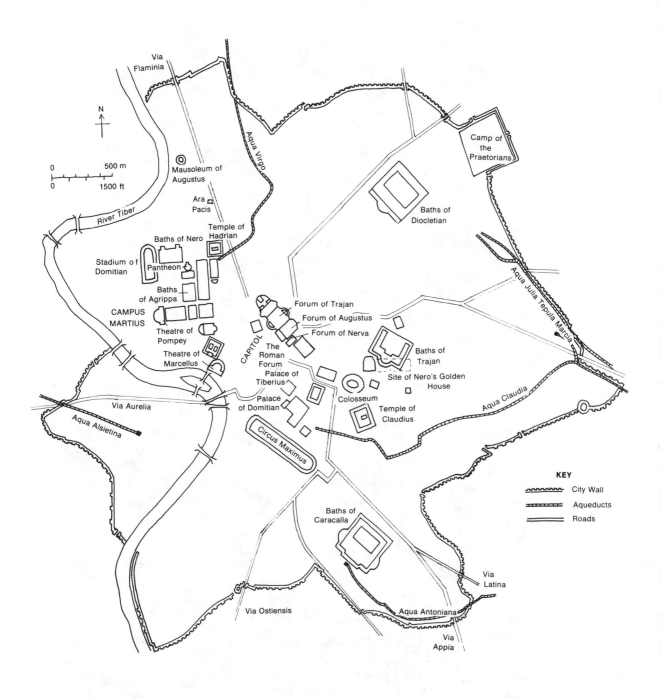

Imperial Rome in the first three centuries AD

Labels visible on the map:

Via Flaminia

N

0 500 m
0 1500 ft

Mausoleum of Augustus

Aqua Virgo

River Tiber

Ara Pacis

Temple of Hadrian

Baths of Nero

Stadium of Domitian

Pantheon

Baths of Agrippa

CAMPUS MARTIUS

Theatre of Pompey

Theatre of Marcellus

CAPITOL

The Roman Forum

Palace of Tiberius

Palace of Domitian

Via Aurelia

Aqua Alsietina

Circus Maximus

Forum of Trajan

Forum of Augustus

Forum of Nerva

Baths of Trajan

Site of Nero's Golden House

Colosseum

Temple of Claudius

Baths of Diocletian

Camp of the Praetorians

Aqua Julia Tepula Marcia

Aqua Claudia

Baths of Caracalla

Via Ostiensis

Aqua Antoniana

Via Latina

Via Appia

KEY
City Wall
Aqueducts
Roads

112

Building Techniques

Roman engineers made great use of the arch: a semi-circular wooden frame was made; on this were set wedge-shaped blocks of stone (voussoirs). When the last block, or 'keystone' was inserted, the wooden frame could be removed, as the voussoirs held each other in place. It was soon realised that a series of arches set side by side formed a vault, that a number of arches crossing a circular space in different directions and intersecting at the centre made a dome, and that two arches intersecting at right angles produced a cross-vault.

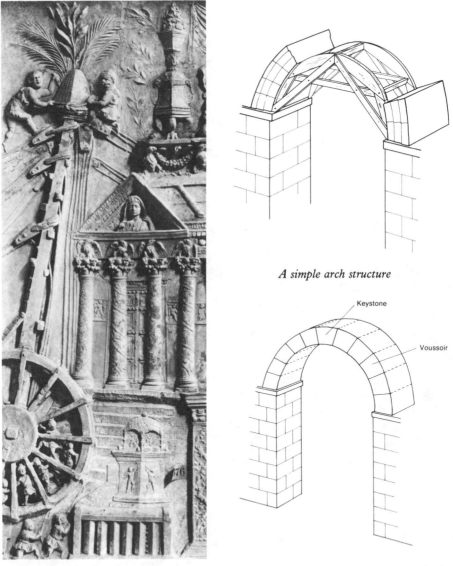

A simple arch structure

A Roman crane at work. This relief comes from the funeral monument of the Haterii, a family of building contractors who worked on the Arch of Titus and the Colosseum

Huge areas could be covered or spanned by combinations of these arches. The pillars of Trajan's bridge across the Danube, for example, are 43 metres (141 feet) apart: the dome of the Pantheon in Rome is 44 metres (144 feet) in both height and diameter; the central hall of the Basilica of Maxentius, also in Rome, the largest hall of ancient times, measured 80 by 50 metres (262 by 164 feet), and despite its immense size, was divided by only four pillars to support its lofty vaults.

Most of these great arch-structures, however, were not built from stone: Roman engineers used concrete. It was found that volcanic dust, *pozzolana*, mixed with the standard lime mortar produced a cement of great strength. Marble chippings, stones and even pieces of lava were mixed into this cement; the resulting liquid concrete was poured into moulds made from wooden planks. When set it formed one homogeneous mass that was almost indestructible. The final surface of the concrete was rough and unattractive, so a facing of marble, stone slabs, or baked brick was added. Over the centuries most of these facing materials have disappeared, and all that we see today is the unlovely concrete core. But without this core it would not have been possible to construct these buildings. The use of huge arches and concrete was a remarkable building revolution. Roman brickwork, too, was superb: these techniques were unsurpassed until last century when iron and steel were introduced into our buildings.

Massive fragments of the Baths of Caracalla: you can see, in the foreground, remains of the concrete core of the wall, and brickwork either side of the entrance, and where the two arches meet, some marble facing slabs

The interior of the Trier basilica

The exterior of the basilica at Trier in West Germany. It was once (c.AD 315) part of the imperial residence of the Emperor Constantine

Buildings of Genius

It is not difficult to find examples of the arch-structures the Romans built: the great aqueduct at Segovia in Spain, the Pont du Gard in France (see p. 66), and the Aqua Claudia leading into Rome itself show how elegant the simplest use of the arch can be. When the Romans built the theatre of Pompey, the first stone theatre, they could not copy the Greeks and line a natural hollow of the ground with seats; instead they raised the successive tiers of seats on a series of arches superimposed one upon the other. And amphitheatres, theatres-in-the-round as the name implies, used the same methods of construction. In the Colosseum the outer façade presents three storeys of arches, and arches were used throughout the whole structure to support the various levels. There were hosts of ingenious technical devices, as well, to fascinate the spectators. Lifts or elevators brought animals from the lower floors to the surface of the arena to be slaughtered in thousands: the arena could be flooded for naval displays, and quickly drained: a great awning, suspended by cables from hundreds of wooden masts rising from the top storey and manipulated by two corps of marines, provided shade from the heat of a summer day for spectators and emperor alike; and the 50,000 spectators could reach their numbered seats with little delay by means of broad passages and stairways that ran through the structure.

The Colosseum

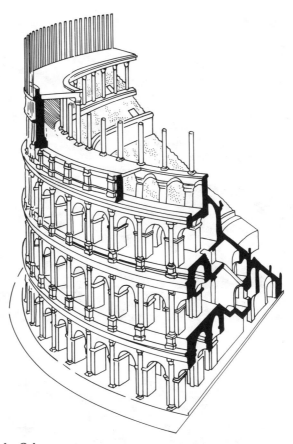

A cross-section of the Colosseum

Perhaps the buildings that the ordinary people of Rome knew best were the great *thermae*, or baths. They had been specifically designed to please and occupy the common people, and to stop them from thinking about the political realities of the imperial dictatorships. The remains of the Thermae of Diocletian are still considerable, and house one of Rome's national museums, while the three great vaulted bays of the central hall were converted into the Church of S. Maria degli Angeli by Michelangelo. There were huge dressing rooms, from which the bathers could go to the cold plunge or swimming pools, or through a series of heated rooms, progressively hotter, to the *caldarium*, finally to be rubbed down and massaged as in a modern Turkish bath. Ranged alongside the central block were exercise courts, *palaestrae*. There were also libraries, lecture rooms and restaurants. These buildings were surrounded by gardens and colonnaded walks, all decorated with statues and works of art of various kinds.

The emperor Caracalla built the largest set of thermae: they took five years to complete, and accommodated thousands. The central building covered 25,000 square metres, over 6 acres (this is about the same size as the Capitol Building, Washington DC, while St Paul's Cathedral, London, covers $1\frac{1}{2}$ acres), and the whole complex occupied over 32 acres.

117

The Baths of Caracalla

The interior of the church of Santa Maria delgi Angeli

Trajan's Market

But to the minds of the contemporary Romans the greatest of all these masterly buildings was the Forum and Market of Trajan. As business had increased in the metropolis, and the original Forum Romanum became too small, Julius Caesar had bought up a section of land adjoining it, cleared away the existing buildings, and built a new forum, with offices and law-courts. Augustus, Vespasian and Nerva all built new fora as business activity continued to increase. Finally the emperor Trajan employed Apollodorus, an architect from Damascus, to design the greatest of them all, larger than all the others put together, with a forum 122 metres (400 feet) square, two libraries, a great temple to the emperor, and, overlooking the forum, a semi-circular market, with shops in two tiers, of two and three storeys, which still survives. Apollodorus had to carve deep into the Quirinal hill to make room for this structure; the inscription on Trajan's Column, which records the episodes of his campaign in Dacia, also states that it is 30 metres (98 feet) high, and that the hill was also cut away to the same depth.

When the emperor Constantius II was shown around Rome for the first time, he was lost in admiration, as Ammianus Marcellinus, a historian of the fourth century, records:

> But when he entered the Forum of Trajan, a structure unequalled, I believe, anywhere on earth, and as all the gods as well admit, then he stood still in amazement: he gazed around at the mighty complex surrounding him, impossible to describe, impossible ever again for men to equal. Giving up all hopes of attempting anything like it, he simply said that all he could and would imitate was the equestrian statue of Trajan standing in the centre of the court.

(Ammianus Marcellinus, XVI, 15)

The semicircle of shops and offices in Trajan's market

119

People came from all over the world to see and marvel at these great buildings: they were copied in every province:

> The whole world is on holiday, so to speak, and has turned from warfare, the burden of past ages, to adorning itself with all sorts of happy schemes which it now has the power to make come true. Cities have ceased fighting each other, except in their rivalry to appear as beautiful and attractive as possible. Every quarter is full of gymnasia, fountains, ceremonial gateways, temples, workshops and schools.

> (Aelius Aristides, *To Rome*, 98–101)

These fulsome words may seem strange to us, but there is a good deal of truth in them: Roman styles and structures *were* copied in every city of the Empire, and the influence of them on modern architecture in Europe, the Americas and Australasia is still very marked.

CHAPTER THIRTEEN

Work and Slaves

When we look at the magnificent buildings, the ostentatious affluence and the extravagant spectacles of the city of Rome itself, it is easy to forget that in the ancient world it was on the land that most work was done, and most livings earned. For centuries Romans had been, and were happy to be, an agricultural people. Cincinnatus had been called from the plough to command Rome's armies as dictator. 'The bravest men and the hardiest soldiers come from the farming class', wrote M. Cato in the second century BC, 'and they are respected for the work they do.'

Even Cicero, who was no countryman, was prepared to admit that

> Of all the occupations by which money is made, none is better than farming, none is more profitable, none more pleasant, none more fitting for a free Roman.

> (Cicero, *de Off*. I, 42)

Stooping farmer drives an ox to market, past roadside shrines. The ox carries a sheep, slung over its back

121

Work on the Land

But not many farmers would have recognized Cicero's picture of them. Life on the land was never easy. At best the agricultural worker could earn enough to support a family: at worst, when the harvest was bad, he could expect hunger, insecurity, debt, even slavery, and the drift to the towns to find work. Things were very different for Cicero's senator-friends. Many of them had country estates, which were large and efficiently run by the resident bailiff. The farming techniques they used were scientific, and the profits they made more than adequate. Land was, after all, the safest investment, and the landowner expected to derive both profit and pleasure from his estate. Farming manuals gave detailed instructions about the running of a farm, how to raise flocks or herds, how to plant vines and olives and to harvest crops, how to keep bees, how to maintain equipment and supervise staff. Cato the Elder tells the landowner how to conduct a spot check on his estate.

> When you have found out what state the farm is in, what work has and has not been finished, send for the overseer and ask him what has been done and what still needs doing; whether the various jobs have been completed on time, and whether he can finish off those that are left. Then ask how the vines and the grain crop and all the other produce is doing.
>
> When you have got this information, calculate the various jobs and the time they took. If the amount of work seems unsatisfactory, and the overseer says that he worked his men hard, but that various snags occurred, draw his attention again to your estimate of the jobs to be done, and the time they should take.
>
> If the weather has been wet, remind him of the jobs that can be done on rainy days. Storage jars can be scrubbed and tarred, farm buildings cleaned, grain shifted, manure carried out and made into a pile, seed cleaned, ropes mended and new ones made. Tell him that on festival days they should have cleaned out old ditches, repaired the public road, cut back the brambles, dug the garden, cleared the pasture, and tied up bundles of twigs . . .
>
> Then give instructions, verbally and in writing, about what you want done. Look over your livestock and hold an auction. If the price is right, sell your olive crop and your surplus wine and grain. Also sell the old oxen, the diseased cattle and sheep, wool, skins, an odd wagon for instance, worn out tools, an old slave, a sickly slave, and whatever else you do not need. A landowner should be a seller, not a buyer.

> (Cato, *de Agricultura* II, 2.1–17)

Farms provided the neighbouring towns and cities with food, though Rome had to rely on Sicily, Egypt and Africa to supply its massive demand for corn. In return the towns and cities of a particular area were the centres of local industry, and supplied the other everyday needs of town and country people. Pompeii, the town smothered in the ash of Vesuvius' eruption in AD 79, gives us some idea of the trades and crafts which were carried on in a prosperous community.

Work in the Towns

From the ruins themselves, and the articles found among the ruins, archaeologists can piece together an account of the busy daily life of the citizens of Pompeii. So we find bakers, millers, dyers, fullers, smiths and metal workers, furniture makers, tanners and leather workers, shoemakers, jewellers and a surgeon, some with large and impressive premises, and beautifully decorated homes to match, others with a single room doing double duty as workshop and saleroom. From election posters, and lists of the supporters of particular candidates we learn of goldsmiths, fruitsellers, perfume and ointment sellers, woodworkers, fishermen, harvest hands, porters, muledrivers and many others. We can be sure, too, that Pompeii also had its butchers, builders, stonemasons, interior decorators, plumbers, potters, bartenders, innkeepers, undertakers and its professional men. From the articles themselves, especially those that bear trade marks and inscriptions, it is often possible to discover details of local industries. Pompeians used imported tableware, from Arretium, and as far as Gaul, as well as from neighbouring towns. On the other hand, the fish sauces (*garum, liquamen* see p. 138), from the factories of Umbricius Scaurus in Pompeii, were not only popular locally, but were exported to Rome itself.

Tombstone of Tiberius Julius Vitalis, butcher

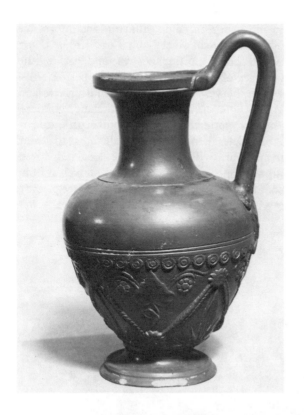

Arretine pottery

Woman game dealer serves a customer

Trade and Profit

Pompeii was a prosperous town ('Hurrah for profit' was found scratched on one of its walls), but there were many communities in Italy which did not enjoy a comparable standard of living. However the peace and prosperity of the early Empire helped the development of local industry everywhere, and the increase of wealth produced a greater demand for luxury goods. Regions became famous for the excellence of their specialized products – Campania for its glass, metalwork and luxury items, Apulia for its wool, Aquileia for its dyeworks. Rome itself became the centre for every imaginable kind of product, because the city could guarantee a market. Artists and craftsmen of every description displayed and sold their wares to Roman families. Imports too flooded in from all over the known world, now that the seas were clear of pirates, and the land routes safe and well maintained. A well-to-do Roman had unlimited choice, as an admiring Greek orator of the second century AD pointed out:

> From neighbouring continents far and wide a ceaseless flow of goods pours into Rome. From every land and every sea come each season's crops, the produce of countryside, rivers, and lakes, and articles skilfully made by Greeks and foreigners. So anyone who wishes to see these goods must either travel all over the world, or come here, to Rome. Anything grown or manufactured by any people can always be found here in abundance. So many merchants arrive from all points of the compass with their cargoes throughout the year, and with each return of harvest, that the city is like the common warehouse of the world. There are so many cargoes from India and Arabia Felix that you might guess that the trees there have been stripped permanently bare, and that Indians and Arabs must come here to beg for their own goods, whenever they need anything. Clothing from Babylonia, luxuries from barbarian lands beyond . . . Egypt, Sicily and Africa are your farms. . . . Everything converges here – trade, shipping, agriculture, metallurgy, all the skills that exist and have existed, everything that is bred or grown. Anything that cannot be seen in Rome does not exist.

(Aelius Aristides, *To Rome*, 11–13)

It cost less to transport a consignment by sea than by land, though most traders tried to avoid winter voyages. Some merchants sailed from port to port like tramp steamers, buying and selling whatever seemed profitable. Others were organized into companies, with offices and warehouses in the major ports. Sea journeys were slow by modern standards, for although a merchant ship could make three knots in a favourable wind, the captain used to keep the coastline in sight, in case clouds blotted out the sky and made navigation difficult. Shipwreck was common, and it is still possible to see the cargoes of ancient vessels on the sea bed. But the risks were worth taking, as a successful merchant, Trimalchio, tells his listeners.

> Make yourselves at home everyone. I was once in your position, but I've made the grade by my ability . . . I buy well. I sell well – anything else is nonsense. Good management brought me to my present good fortune – I was only as big as this candlestick when I came here as a slave from Asia . . . and for 14 years I was my master's favourite (and my mistress's, too, but that's another story). Then, by heaven's help, I became master of the house . . . my master made me joint heir to his estate, and I was worth more than a million sesterces. But no one has ever got enough, and I wanted to go into business. So I built five ships, loaded them with a cargo of wine – which was worth its weight in gold at the time – and sent it to Rome. But my luck couldn't have been worse! Every ship was wrecked. Neptune drank 30 million sesterces'

worth in one day! Do you think that stopped me? Not a bit of it – the loss only whetted my appetite . . . I built more ships, larger, better, luckier ones . . . and loaded them again with wine, bacon, fat, beans, perfume and slaves. . . . On one voyage I cleared 10 million sesterces, and I immediately bought back all the estates that had belonged to my patron, built a mansion, bought up young slaves to sell, and baggage animals too. Everything I touched grew like a honeycomb.

(Petronius, Cena Trimalchionis 75.8. ff.)

With profits like these to be made, trade routes to faraway places were pioneered. A Roman knight crossed the Danube at Carnutum and made his way north to the Baltic coast. Here he found large quantities of amber, a gem-like resin prized at Rome, and was able to establish a trade route to the source of supply, 600 miles away. Even more dramatic was the discovery by Hippalus of a direct sea route from Southern Arabia to India, making use of the summer monsoon to take the ship safely to the west coast of India. Pliny gives the details:

> The best way to sail to India is to set out from Ocelis. The first port in India, Muziris, is 40 days sail from there if Hippalus' wind is blowing. Muziris is not a desirable port of call, however. There are pirates in the neighbourhood, and the merchandise is not noteworthy. . . . A more serviceable port is called Becare. . . . Travellers set sail from India on the return voyage in December, or at any rate before 13 January, and so can make the round trip within the year.

(Pliny, Nat. Hist. 6, 26, 104, 105, 106 with omissions)

Arrival of a merchant ship in Trajan's harbour at Ostia, where a smaller craft is already unloading its wine jars. Neptune, the sea god, presides. Behind is seen the flame of the emperor Claudius' lighthouse. The large eye (right) is a charm against the Evil Eye

126

The merchant bound for India knew what to carry in his cargo, for he had taken the advice of a trader's guide book, written in Greek by an Egyptian merchant:

> Becare imports coin, topaz, thin clothing, figured linens, antimony, coral, crude glass, copper, tin, lead, wine (in no great quantities) realgar and orpiment; and sufficient wheat for the sailors as this is not dealt in by merchants there. Becare's exports are pepper, and in addition large quantities of pearls, ivory, silk, cloth, spikenard from the Ganges, malabathrum from the interior, transparent stones of all kinds, diamonds, sapphires and tortoiseshell.

(*Periplus of Erythraean Sea*, Anon, 46)

Loaded with luxury articles like these, the merchant sailed west, to the market at Alexandria, and a handsome profit. Through India too ran the Silk Route from China, along which plodded great caravans, carrying silk, drugs and precious stones. From Arabia came frankincense, from East Africa ivory, palm oil and tortoiseshell, from Syria fine glassware, expensive clothes and purple dye. Egypt produced fine cloth and paper as well as grain. To the west lay Spain's vast mineral wealth. 'Nearly all Spain abounds in mines of lead, iron, copper, silver and gold' wrote Pliny, while Gaul became famous for its pottery and foodstuffs.

Towing a wine barge along a river: a carved relief from Roman Gaul

Slaves

One other important cargo reached Rome's harbour at Ostia, though trade in this commodity grew smaller as the Empire ceased to expand. Slave traders operated profitably from the east Mediterranean and African coasts, and brought their human cargo to be sold in the slave markets of Italy. Here the slaves were exhibited, naked, with a placard round their necks to indicate their nationality, special skills and defects. Bidding for a skilled slave was fiercely competitive, and huge prices were paid for a craftsman, an educated person or an attractive youth or girl.

Like every other nation in the ancient world, Rome accepted slavery as the natural order of things. As the Empire grew, the vast influx of slaves to Italy began and every military triumph increased the numbers. 150,000 slaves were brought from Epirus in

167 BC after Rome's victory there. Victims of kidnapping by pirates, children who had been left in the open to die at birth, debtors and criminals all became slaves and passed through the great slave markets at Delos, Capua and Rome. At its peak Delos was said to be able to handle 20,000 slaves per day.

Rome and Italy and the lives of those who lived there were transformed by the influx. Industries, like the world-famous Arretine pottery (see p. 124) were based entirely on slave labour, while teams of slaves staffed the large estates which threatened the livelihood of the small farmer. Many of the craftsmen of Pompeii would either be slaves who had won their freedom, or descended from freedmen. More important for its effect on Roman society was the number of slaves in the households. Today we find it difficult to visualize life in a modest Victorian family with two or three servants. For the Roman citizen, to own only three slaves was to admit poverty.

Treatment of Slaves

A well-run home required slaves to clean, to cook and serve food, to look after clothes, to help with dressing and toilet, to keep the accounts, to copy and deliver letters, to supervise the lighting and fires, to watch the doors and tend the garden. A senator in Nero's time had 400 slaves in his town house alone, and some Romans, according to one writer, owned 10–20,000 in all. The emperor's staff, of course, was larger still.

Negro slave, cleaning a boot

Life for a country slave was harder. He could expect little or no relaxation, and the conditions in which he lived, in the primitive barracks, were vile, and not unlike those in the chain gangs in the southern United States. Even a comparatively humane scholar like M. Terentius Varro could talk of three types of farm equipment:

> The kind that speaks [i.e. slaves], the kind that cannot speak [i.e. cattle] and the voiceless [i.e. farm implements].

Varro's advice to prospective farmers shows how Romans were coming to terms with the problems of ownership. Incentives replace the whip, not because they are more humane, but more efficient:

> The slave foreman must not be allowed to use a whip to control his men, provided that he can achieve the same result with words alone. An estate owner should make his foreman more enthusiastic by giving him rewards, and taking care to allow him to have some property of his own, and a wife from among the other slaves, to bear him children. In this way a slave foreman becomes more reliable, and more closely tied to the farm . . . Those of the slaves whose work is best should be consulted about what needs to be done, for they will be less likely to think they are being looked down on. . . . Slaves will be made more eager to work by more generous treatment: more food, more clothes, longer breaks, permission to graze their own cattle on the estate and other concessions.

> (Varro, *Rerum Rusticarum* I, 17.1, 5–7)

Life for those slaves who were compelled to work in the mines or in an estate chain gang was savagely hard. Mercifully it was also short.

The number of slaves in Italy can only be guessed at. Perhaps for every five free men there were three slaves. This was a dangerously high proportion, as Seneca pointed out:

> On one occasion a proposal was made by the Senate to distinguish slaves from free men by insisting that they wore different clothes, but it became clear how dangerous it would be if slaves could actually *see* how few free men there really were.

> (Seneca, *de Clementia* I, 24.1)

Rome dared not underestimate the potential strength of her slave population. She had done so once, to her cost. In 73–71 BC, Spartacus, a slave trained as a gladiator, and a talented leader, had destroyed seven Roman armies and ravaged much of Italy with his slave army. Cheap slave labour on a vast scale had produced callousness and cruelty in the masters, resentment, hostility and finally rebellion in the slaves. From the earliest times a slave had no redress against his master's brutality. By law he was a piece of equipment which his master could use as he pleased. The slave could be bought, sold, hired out, used for breeding, punished or even killed at his master's will. A child born to a slave was the master's property. All a slave's earnings belonged to his master, and a master could whip, torture, brand, mutilate or crucify his slave, all within the law.

There was, however, some relief from his intolerable situation. Increasingly Roman masters discovered that fair treatment and rewards would encourage a slave to work better. For this reason a slave was often allowed to keep any money he earned (his *peculium*) and so, eventually, buy his freedom. He was allowed to take a wife from among the slaves of the household, and raise children. Finally, and most important, he might so impress his master with his hard work and good character, that he gained a position of responsibility, and ultimately his freedom. This hope of freedom, either by the master's will when he died, or by a ceremony before a magistrate, was undoubtedly an incentive for hard work and obedience, and very many slaves gained their freedom in this way.

As more and more slaves were born in Italy, spoke Latin, wore Roman dress and accepted Roman traditions, and the supply from overseas dwindled, their treatment gradually became more humane. Under the Empire, some of the harshest laws against slaves were changed, and this reflects a change in the attitude of society to the situation. Stoicism, too (see p. 167) with its emphasis on the brotherhood of man, influenced the better educated Romans, so that Seneca could write to a friend:

> I was pleased to hear those who had come from you saying that you live on friendly terms with your slaves, for this is what a sensible, well-educated person like yourself should do. People say, 'They are slaves', but I say that they are men, like us. 'Slaves' they say. No, they are humble friends. . . . Remember this, that the man you call your slave comes from the same species, enjoys the same sky, and breathes, lives and dies exactly as you do. You can imagine him to be a free man, he can imagine you a slave. . . . But this is my advice, in a nutshell. Treat your inferiors as you would wish to be treated by your betters.

> (Seneca, *Epist. Mor.*, 47.1, 10, 11)

Clearly, it was better to be a slave in Seneca's house than to be a free man in the poorest parts of Rome and Italy. A slave with a humane master had security, some comfort, and reasonable prospects. If he could gain his freedom there was plenty of scope for the talented ex-slave (like Trimalchio) even though Roman society treated him as an upstart. But it is doubtful how many Romans followed Seneca's lead, and it is worth remembering that a slave had to be tortured before he was allowed to give evidence in court, otherwise Romans believed him to be incapable of telling the truth, and that if a master was murdered by a slave, every slave in the household could be tortured and killed. 'In the law of Nature', wrote one Roman legal expert, 'all men are equal.' But of more concern to the slaves in the fields, the quarries and the mines was the same expert's view. 'As far as Roman law is concerned, slaves are considered as nothing.'

CHAPTER FOURTEEN

Every Day

The Shape of the Day

We have read of great generals and statesmen and poets, of their wives and their slaves. However different their lives may have been, some things were the same for them all: they were born and died; they slept at night and woke in the morning; they ate and drank; they shaved or combed their hair, and wore clothes or made them. We shall look in this chapter at the everyday things common to men and women in their daily routine.

The course of the Roman day was simple enough: the poet Martial described it like this:

> The first and second hours wear out the
>   clients at their morning salutation.
> The third hour puts the hoarse barristers
>   through their paces:
> Rome's varied businesses last right
>   through the fifth hour:
> The sixth hour gives the exhausted time
>   to rest, until
> The seventh hour wakes them up again.
> From the eighth to the ninth is enough
>   for the well-greased wrestlers:
> The ninth hour invites us to dent the
>   cushions on the dinner-couches,
> But the tenth – that is the time for my
>   poems.

(Martial, *Epigrams*, 4.8)

Getting Up and Dressed

From long habit the man of the house woke at dawn and got up: there was little of comfort to detain him in the bedroom, merely the bed (*cubile*), a chest for blankets or clothes (*arca*), and the chamber-pot (*lasanum*). He probably slept in his underwear, a simple loin-cloth, and his tunic, so it did not take him very long to dress. If he washed at all he simply bathed his eyes, mouth and hands in cold water, for he knew he would be attending a bath-house, whether public or private, later in the day. The mother of the emperor Augustus had started the fashion of the nobility attending public bath-houses, and from that day all classes, from the emperor himself to the humblest manual worker went to them, for many were free, and the charge at most was only the smallest coin.

Then he straightened his hair with a simple comb. From the second century before Christ to the time of Hadrian it was the fashion for men to be clean-shaven, but Roman shaving was such a painful operation that it was left to the expert. A visit to the barber was a regular duty, and barbers were so busy that many made a fortune, and their shops were always crowded with gossiping customers. The Roman barber had a razor of iron carefully sharpened and honed; but since he used no oil or soap to soften the bristles, but only damped them with water, shaving was painful, and few were skilful enough to avoid cutting the poor victim as well. Martial compared the barber Antiochus to a surgeon lopping away broken bones, and warned his friends against him:

> Those scars you see on my chin, like the marks on some old boxer's face, were not made by my angry wife in one of her tempers, but by the cursed hand and blade of Antiochus. The he-goat is the only beast with any sense – he wears a beard to escape Antiochus.

(Martial, *Epigrams*, 11.84)

And Pliny preserves the recipe for a plaster to staunch the blood – spiders' webs, soaked in vinegar and oil. When Hadrian grew a beard – either to cover an ugly scar, or merely because he could not see why an emperor should be tortured by a barber – the new fashion was thankfully adopted by everyone.

It is unlikely that the Roman cleaned his teeth as we do, though Pliny does say that to take away an unpleasant taste in the mouth one should 'rub the teeth with the ashes of a burnt mouse mixed in honey', and advises that they be picked with a porcupine's quill to make them stronger! After completing his sketchy toilet the man slipped on his tunic, if he was not already wearing it: sometimes he slipped one off, for it was usual to wear two tunics at night if it was cold, and even, if we can believe Suetonius on the chilly Augustus, four at a time. A senator's tunic was adorned with a broad purple stripe – the *laticlavium* – running from neck to waist, the knight's with two narrower stripes. The tunic was worn with a belt, and reached down to the knees – it was considered very effeminate to wear it longer. Then, before leaving the bedroom, he drew on his slippers or sandals (*soleae, sandalia*). It was not proper to wear these out-of-doors: the heavier

A toolmaker's shop; notice the simple tunic of the proprietor and the toga of the customer. This relief comes from an altar set up by the proprietor; his name was L. Cornelius Atimetus (first century AD)

calcei, with a leather tongue and four thongs, were then the proper footwear: if you went out to dinner you took your soleae with you – it was as bad to wear calcei indoors as to wear soleae outside.

Breakfast (*ientaculum*) was very simple, a cup of water and perhaps a morsel of bread and honey, or something cold left over from the day before; it was not necessary to sit down to eat it. Then work could begin. Even an emperor's day began no more elaborately: Suetonius says of Vespasian:

> When he was emperor he always got up very early, and was awake before dawn. Then he read through his letters and official reports; next his friends came in, and while exchanging greetings he put on his shoes and tunic. After finishing all the business that came up he went out for a drive, and then had a nap.

(Suetonius, *Vespasian*, 21)

Women's Dress

The lady of the house, like her husband, probably slept in her underwear: she wore a simple loin-cloth, and a brassiere or corset (though it is difficult to imagine anyone sleeping in whalebone), and a tunic. This was made of two rectangles of material fastened at sides and shoulders, to form short sleeves: it was of linen or wool, and usually finer and less thick than her husband's. Washing just as sketchily, she too drew on her slippers and chose her dress for the day. But then for the well-to-do, and the lady of fashion, the serious matter of the toilet began, and a maid to help was almost essential. First her hair was dressed. In the days of the Republic the hair was evenly parted and drawn back into a chignon, a fashion revived by Claudius. But the rest of the emperors saw their wives and ladies of court with hair piled high, tier upon tier. Juvenal describes such a lady:

> She crimps her hair into rows of curls, and builds it high, storey after storey. Look at her from the front, and you'll think she is an Andromache from the age of heroes: but from the back she's a different person altogether.

(Juvenal, VI, 505–7)

Some Roman hair styles

Sometimes her hair was dyed, and if it was scanty there were hair-pieces and wigs for sale, black from India, blonde from Germany. Then with tweezers she plucked out all superfluous hair, and turned to her make-up.

Her brow and arms were powdered white with chalk, her lips and cheeks rouged with *fucus*, a red rock-lichen, or wine-lees: her eye-brows and lids were darkened with ashes or antimony. All these powders, lotions and creams were kept in a variety of precious boxes and phials, many of which have survived. When the lady set out for the bathhouse, then all these pots and jars went with her in a special little case divided into compartments. Next came jewels – a diadem for her hair, if she was rich, and ear-rings and necklaces, bracelets and rings, which everyone wore. Roman and Greek jewellers were as skilled as ours, and many superb pieces of the craft still delight us today.

Three maids dressing a lady's hair. This relief comes from the lady's tomb

She was now almost ready to go out. The last garment to be put on was the *stola*, an elegant version of the tunic, fuller and flowing, reaching to the ankles. The material was fine linen or wool, and in summer light cottons from India, or the sheerest silks from the East, all in dazzling colours and adorned with splendid embroidery. Then with a light scarf, perhaps, to protect her elaborate coiffure from the wind, and a parasol to shade her from the sun, she would be off. Most women could not, of course, afford such fashions, but their love of bright colours would persuade most to wear such cheerful clothes whenever they could.

134

A simple parasol and comb. You can still see the chisel marks, just below the comb

A matron wearing a stola

Typical Roman jewellery

The Toga

For formal occasions a man by tradition wore a toga. This distinctive Roman garment was made of fine wool: it was in shape a segment of a circle, about 16 feet from point to point, and seven feet deep. It was slung under the right arm, and draped round the body, with both ends finishing on the right shoulder. Despite many statues of men wearing it, and a long but perplexing account in Quintilian, we cannot be absolutely certain of the details of the fastenings and folds. We do know, though, that even the Romans found it extremely difficult to drape it elegantly, and it was awkward to keep in place when walking, that it was very hot and heavy, that it was easy to make dirty and difficult to clean. Nevertheless, it was so distinctly the Roman garment (see quote on p. 175–6) that great efforts were made by the emperors to preserve its use. However the wishes of the ordinary people won, and they wore simpler cloaks or tunics over trunks, or even trousers. Most citizens of the Empire wore the toga only once – on their last bed on the day of their funeral.

Some elaborate togas, worn by priests and senators. The relief comes from the Ara Pacis

Work and Food

Even though only the poor would be without a slave to do the worst of the house-work, there was still the cleaning – they used feather dusters, cloths, dustpans and brushes, just as we do – the shopping and cooking to be done, and gossiping, too, when the chance came. (Most of the evidence seems to show, however, that men spent more time in idle chatter than their wives.)

For both men and women most of the day's work was over soon after midday. Their *prandium*, lunch, was very light, usually something cold left over from the previous night's dinner. How they spent the afternoon will be discussed in the next chapter: by about four in the afternoon everyone began to think of the *cena*, or dinner, the main meal of the day. In the early Republic this had been taken at midday, and most people sat at table to eat it. But the fashion changed, and by the early Empire most people dined in the late afternoon – their first solid meal of the day – and did so reclining on a couch propped by pillows on their left side.

Cushions for sale

The meal itself had three courses: each course, however, might have several dishes. The first course, or 'hors d'oeuvres', included shellfish, oysters and other tempting delicacies from the sea, as well as dressed vegetables, sliced eggs and even snails. The main course, which often comprised several meat dishes like hare, boar, pork, beef, kid, lamb, fish and fowl, was accompanied by vegetables and a great variety of sauces. (A Roman cook boasted that his sauces were so good that one could not tell what was being eaten underneath!) Finally dessert, which was usually fruit, nuts and figs. Wine was drunk both during and after the meal.

A beautiful drinking cup

We are lucky to have the fullest information of various dishes and how they were prepared, for we have a collection of Roman recipes, made in the fourth or fifth century after Christ, and ascribed to Apicius, which was intended for rich and poor alike. Apicius' recipes are increasingly being translated and used by modern writers on cookery, and an English version by Barbara Flower and Elisabeth Rosenbaum, *The Roman Cookery Book*, is a mine of fascinating information. There are of course some difficulties: most Roman dishes were covered with elaborate sauces, and the preparation of these is not easy. *Defrutum*, a common ingredient, was unfermented fruit-juice, boiled till it was reduced to a third – the translators used tinned grape juice, and boiled that down with great success. But the most common of all flavourings – it was used as we use salt – was *garum* or *liquamen*. Here is one recipe:

> The best *garum*, called *haimation*, is made as follows: take the entrails of tunny fish and its gills, juice and blood, and add sufficient salt. And leave it in a vessel for two months at most. Then pierce the vessel, and the *garum* called *haimation* will flow out.

In this kitchen the pots and pans were supported over a bed of burning charcoal: fuel and pots were stored beneath the oven

This unsavoury recipe was for large-scale use in factories, for *liquamen* was bought ready made, as we buy Worcestershire Sauce or tomato ketchup. A 'quick' recipe for the home – the one used by the English translators – is as follows:

If you wish to make the *garum* at once – i.e. not expose it to the sun, but boil it – make it in the following manner. Take brine and test its strength by throwing an egg into it to try if it floats: if it sinks the brine does not contain enough salt. Put the fish into the brine in a new earthenware pot, add origan, put it on a good fire till it boils – i.e. till it begins to reduce. Some people also add *defrutum*. Let it cool and strain it two or three times, until it is clear. Seal and store away.

Some of the recipes might be hard to stomach – stuffed dormice, for example, do not sound very appetising – but this chicken dish might still appeal.

Chicken with Milk and Pastry Sauce.

Braise the chicken in liquamen, oil and wine, to which you add a bouquet of fresh coriander and onions. Then, when done, lift it from its stock, and put into a new saucepan milk and a little salt, honey and a very little water. Set by a slow fire to warm, crumble pastry, and add gradually, stirring continually to prevent burning. Put in the chicken whole or in pieces, turn out on a serving dish, and pour over the following sauce: pepper, lovage, origan, add honey and a little *defrutum* and cooking-liquor. Mix well. Bring to the boil in a saucepan. When it boils thicken with cornflour and serve.

Roman dinners lasted a long time – Pliny regarded three hours as very moderate indeed – but it must be remembered that little else had been eaten in the day. Moreover, this was the main social occasion: work started very early and was followed by exercise and the visit to the baths, and men and women were apart for most of these activities. It was at dinner that the members of the family would expect to talk and exchange the day's news, and to entertain their friends. And when dinner was over, the very poor quality of Roman artificial lighting meant that most people went to bed early – to be up again at dawn the next day.

CHAPTER FIFTEEN

Entertainment

Exercise

As Martial's poem (see p. 131) made clear, the working-day was over by midday for many Romans – in summer time a man could have completed more than seven hours' work by then. The rest of the day was spent by a Roman of reasonable means in exercise and entertainment, after his siesta. From the eighth hour (about 1.30 p.m.) on into the ninth the energetic person would take strenuous exercise either on the Campus Martius, or, more likely, at the baths. The Campus Martius had traditionally been the area for young men to practise their athletic skills, running, boxing, wrestling, discus and javelin throwing, as well as riding and chariot driving and a variety of games. Later, when a succession of emperors built spacious baths (*thermae*) there were areas specially provided for athletic exercises, wrestling, and ball games.

Naturally, some Romans were more energetic than others. While the athletes went through their paces, men of all ages played a variety of ball games. In one called *trigon*, three players, positioned on three points of a triangle, flicked a small solid ball to each other with feints and dummies, just as cricketers today practise slip-catching in small groups. A gentler game of hand-ball was played with a larger inflated ball, while a ball stuffed with feathers may have served the same purpose as a medicine ball today. Meanwhile the wrestlers would oil themselves carefully, and work up a sweat in a series of bouts. There were exercises to everyone's taste, but a few preferred to play no part, like the intellectual addressed by Martial:

> Atticus ... every philosopher thinks the world of you. Other young men are carefully coached by boxing teachers with cauliflower ears, or are rubbed by grubby anointers at the Baths. But you don't prepare for the warm plunge with a ball of any description – small, air-or-feather-filled – or by practising harmless sword strokes on an unarmed stump. And you don't take up a wrestler's stance, well-greased with oil, or dart about to snatch the dusty handball.

> (Martial, *Ep.* 7.32)

To which his intelligent friend may have replied as Seneca once did to an athletic friend:

> What a foolish way to spend one's time, my dear friend, and most unsuitable for a cultured man, to exercise one's biceps, make oneself bull-necked and increase one's lung-power. However successful your training-diet is, and however magnificent your muscular development, you will never be as strong or as heavy as a respectable bull. What's more, the more weight you put on, the more limited and sluggish your mind becomes!

> (Seneca, *Ep. Mor.* 15.2)

The Baths

After exercise, the bath. First the bather undressed in a changing room. Then, carrying his towel, a flask of oil and a strigil he began to move through the rooms which contained baths of varying temperatures, heated by a hypocaust system. First, the *tepidarium*, or warm room, to prepare the bather for the hot water in the following room, the *caldarium*. Here the bather soaked himself, and, if he could not afford a slave to do it for him, he rubbed himself with oil. This he scraped off after a while, using the strigil, and made his way back through the warm room to the *frigidarium*, or cold room, where he plunged into the cold water. From there, after a brisk towelling, through the warm room again to the changing room.

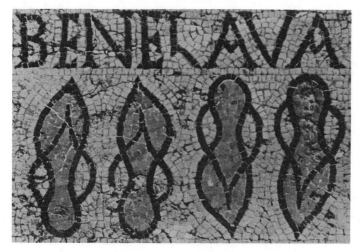

Mosaic at the entrance of a bath-house in Timgad, North Africa, reads 'Have a good bath'

An oil flask and strigils. Oil was rubbed on the skin after the bath, and the strigil was used to scrape off the mixture of sweat and oil

Under the emperors, baths ceased to be merely places where a Roman could bathe. They became more and more magnificent, and came to be luxurious recreation centres, fully equipped with gymnasia, libraries, reading rooms, gardens, art galleries, covered walks, terraces and shops. When Augustus became emperor there were 170 baths in Rome, but by the fourth century AD, with emperors like Nero, Trajan, Caracalla and Diocletian giving the lead, there were nearly one thousand. Diocletian's Baths could cater for 3,000 at the same time and the din must have been terrific – quite unbearable for those who lived nearby, or, in the case of Seneca, in a flat above one of Rome's smaller bath houses:

> Sounds of all sorts echo round me: I live over a bath house! Imagine the assortment of voices, whose noise makes me absolutely furious. When the stronger bathers take exercise, and swing heavy lead weights in their hands, and are working hard at it, or at least pretending to, I can hear their groans. And whenever they hold their breath, and then let it out, I hear the sharp whistling sound it makes. Then there's the oaf who is happy with a cheap oil rub – I can hear

141

Athletes and a trainer from the Baths of Caracalla

the slap of the masseur's hand on his shoulders: I can even tell by the sound whether the hand is flat or cupped. If, on top of this, the professional ball-player comes along and begins to keep score, that's the end. Then there's the arrest of a brawler or a thief, and the man who likes the sound of his own voice in the bath, as well as those who leap into the pool with a resounding splash. . . . Then the hair plucker, chattering to attract attention in his thin shrill voice, which rises and falls, and is never quiet unless he's actually plucking hairs, and then he makes the customer yell for him! And I cannot begin to count the various cries of the sausage sellers, confectioners and all the cook-shop peddlers, hawking their wares, each with his own peculiar pitch!

(Seneca, Ep. Mor. 56, 1–2)

Those who did not go to the baths found it pleasant to stroll in the gardens which emperors and wealthy citizens gave or threw open to the public, or to relax and gossip in the shade of one of the city's many porticoes. Some would scratch a simple criss-cross pattern on the ground, and play a game resembling draughts, or checkers, while others would sneak into a tavern to gamble with dice.

At the end of the ninth hour it was time for the one substantial meal of the day, dinner (*cena*). For the majority of the population, the meal was simple, but for the well-to-do, the evening meal was the day's main social event, and gave the opportunity to entertain friends and to eat and drink well. Such a meal was often punctuated by entertainment – recitations of poetry and prose, musical items, dancers, short plays, or acrobats. After the meal, the guests and host drank, talked and were entertained in various ways until the time came for the party to break up.

A small dinner party: the men recline on couches, the women sit. Two slaves (left) fetch and pour the wine, while two more (right) cook and serve the food

In the kitchen two slaves stoke the furnace (right), another scoops flour from a sack (centre) while another makes dough with water brought from outside. Scenes from a funeral monument in Trier, West Germany

Working Days and Holidays

On normal working days, therefore, there was plenty of time to relax, for those who could afford to do so. But Romans did not have, as we do, a standard working week. The nearest approach was the 'nundinum': every eighth day was a market day (*nundinum*) for country people, and this was a time for merrymaking and enjoyment, as it still is in many country towns. But although the names of the days in the modern week were already in use under the early emperors (Saturn, Sun, Moon, Mars, Mercury, Jupiter, Venus; compare the English and French weekday names), there was no regular weekend in the cities. Instead, every day had its particular significance, which was specified on the calendar. A mark on the calendar showed whether or not public business could be done on a particular day. Festival days were specified too, some permanent, some irregular. These were public holidays, on which public entertainments could be held. Under the emperor Claudius 159 days of the year were public holidays, and on 93 of these there were entertainments at public expense. Under later emperors this number increased, though the poorer citizens, who could not afford to stop work every public holiday, would make their days-off coincide with the more spectacular games.

The main games included a variety of entertainment, which was paid for at vast expense by the emperor, or the magistrates. As a general rule, the games began with a series of performances at the theatre, continued with gladiatorial displays, and ended with the chariot races.

Theatre

Romans had been an enthusiastic audience for drama ever since Livius Andronicus presented the first plays with continuous plots on the stage in 249 BC. The last 200 years of the Republic had seen great developments in the skills of writing and of production, with Ennius (239-169 BC), Pacuvius (220-130 BC) and Accius (d. 86 BC) writing tragedies, and Naevius (270-220 BC), Plautus (251-184 BC) and Terence (195-159 BC) the writers of comedies. In 55 BC Pompey had built the first stone theatre in Rome, and the primitive scenery and equipment of earlier theatres was replaced by elaborate machinery to produce realistic effects. The introduction of the curtain (pulled up from below, not dropped from above like modern curtains) – allowed a variety of scene changes. But the skills of the technicians, and the magnificence of the spectacles led to the decline and disappearance of the plays themselves. The first performance in Pompey's theatre – a tragedy by Accius – contained a procession of 600 mules as part of the booty from the Trojan wars. In tragedy, pageantry replaced plots, and attention was focused on the leading actor, and his extravagant display of singing and dancing skills. Comedy, on the other hand, was succeeded by knock-about farce and mime, slapstick and acrobatics.

The Amphitheatre and Gladiators

The theatrical performances came to be little more than an introduction to the main events of the games, the gladiatorial contests (*ludi circenses*) in the amphitheatre, and the chariot races in the various circuses. Rome has become notorious throughout history for the extravagance and brutality of its gladiatorial displays and the

144

bloodthirsty enthusiasm of the spectators. Few of these shows, however, were regular Roman festivals; in general they formed part of special celebrations (*munera*) given occasionally by individuals to commemorate an important event – a victory or the death of a famous man. Such public shows became increasingly spectacular, lavish and costly – an exceptional display given by the emperor Trajan lasted 117 days and involved almost 10,000 gladiators. But only a fraction of the city population could squeeze into the Colosseum which seated 50,000, and tickets for the displays will have been as hard to get as tickets for the Olympic Games today.

A bestiarius *(beast-fighter) spears a panther*

There were many kinds of gladiatorial games, ranging from the skilful contests between highly trained gladiators to the slaughter of helpless criminals by ravenous wild animals. These 'munera', held in the amphitheatre, began with a procession and an inspection of the gladiators' weapons. The rest of the morning was usually devoted to displays of wild animals, brought from all parts of the known world. The rarer species were merely exhibited, but beast fights were more usual. Sometimes one animal was matched against another, sometimes criminals were exposed, unarmed, to the starved beasts, sometimes trained hunters tracked and killed their quarry. Even an emperor could demonstrate his skill as an archer before an admiring audience: the great historian, Edward Gibbon (1737–94) describes the scene:

On the appointed day the various motives of flattery, fear and curiosity attracted to the amphitheatre an innumerable multitude of spectators: and some degree of applause was deservedly bestowed on the uncommon skill of the Imperial performer. Whether he aimed at the head or the heart of the animal, the wound was alike certain and mortal. With arrows, whose point was shaped in the form of a crescent, Commodus often intercepted the rapid career and cut asunder the long bony neck of the ostrich. A panther was let loose: and the archer waited till he had leaped upon a trembling malefactor. In the same instant, the shaft flew, the beast dropped dead, and the man remained unhurt. The dens of the amphitheatre disgorged at once a hundred lions: a hundred darts from the unerring hand of Commodus laid them dead as they ran raging round the arena. Neither the huge bulk of the elephant nor the scaly hide of the rhinoceros could defend them from his stroke.

Ostriches being transported to Rome

After the morning's entertainment, the midday period was more relaxed and light-hearted, with comic turns, novelty items, and mock contests with dummy weapons. But the spectacle was not always so harmless, as Seneca discovered, when he found himself watching the execution of defenceless criminals:

> By chance I attended the lunch-time entertainment at the games, expecting to see some amusing or witty turns, and some pleasant relief to give the spectators a rest from the slaughter of the morning. But the opposite happened. In the morning fighting, some compassion had been shown, but now it was murder pure and simple. The men had no defensive armour: their bodies are exposed to every stroke, and not one failed to make contact. . . . What is the need for armour, or for fighting skill, when these only delay the death blow? In the morning prisoners are thrown to the lions and the bears: during the lunch-break, they throw them to the spectators . . . every fight ends in death, and this all happens while most of the audience has left for its midday meal.
>
> 'But this prisoner was a highway robber, that one a murderer', you may say. So what? I agree that he deserved to suffer because of his crime. But what crime have the spectators committed to deserve to see his punishment? All day the crowd cries:
>
> 'Kill him, whip him, burn him! Why does he receive the sword thrust like a coward? Why does he strike so feebly? Why is he so squeamish about dying?' And when the show stops for an interval, the spectators cry:
>
> 'Let's have some throats cut in the meantime, to keep things interesting.'

(Seneca, *Ep. Mor.*, 7, 3–5)

After lunch the gladiatorial fighting began in earnest, and the highly trained gladiators pitted their various skills against one another. Gladiators were recruited from among prisoners of war, slaves and lesser criminals: even free men might enter

Gladiatorial combat. A Thracian has killed a Retiarius (lower left), while a Murmillo (upper left) is poised to deliver a death blow. A heavily armed Samnite (top right) advances menacingly

gladiatorial training school. As they enrolled, each swore this oath: 'I undertake to be burnt by fire, to be chained, to be beaten, to die by the sword.'

Under expert supervision a gladiator-under-training would learn the essential combat skills, and then specialize in a particular mode of fighting. A nimble-footed man might become a Retiarius, whose weapons were a net, trident, dagger and his own agility. Another lightly-armed fighter was a Thraex, who carried a small shield and a curved sword, while the stronger but slower gladiators became the heavily-armed Samnites, Secutores and Murmillones.

In the munera gladiators rarely fought an opponent from the same category – the contrast of styles and fighting skills made a contest more intriguing. Usually contestants fought to the death, but a beaten and wounded gladiator could appeal for mercy to the games' President (*munerarius*), who was often the emperor himself. The President in turn would follow the expressed wishes of the spectators, who might demand mercy for a brave fighter, but death for a weak one.

The successful gladiator received prize money and a crown, and, if he scored a run of victories, he earned at last the wooden sword, signifying freedom and an end to his fighting career – unless his lust for the fight drove him back.

Gladiators also took part in representations of naval battles – unusual and spectacular events involving thousands of contestants. Artificial lakes were constructed, but most impressive of all was the Colosseum, whose arena could be flooded when a mock sea battle was to take place. The poet Martial imagines the reaction of a visitor to Rome who can hardly believe his eyes at the scene:

> Don't be misled, visitor from distant lands, whoever you are, who have arrived late to watch the spectacle of this your first day at the sacred games. Don't let this naval battle and its ships deceive you, or the water which looks like the sea. For only a moment ago this was dry land. Don't you believe me? Watch while the fight rages over the waters: then, wait for a moment, and you will say, 'This was sea just now'.

(Martial, *de Spectaculis*, 24)

147

The Circus and Chariot Races

The climax to the games was the chariot racing. No spectacle was more brilliant, and no contest more exciting or more popular. The Circus Maximus itself, beautified and extended by various emperors, held 250,000 spectators, who watched up to 24 races a day, and sometimes more, interspersed with acrobatic displays. A race was usually seven laps of the 550 metre (600 yard) track, and was started by the presiding magistrate, who threw a white cloth from his raised platform. At this signal the chariots burst from their barriers (*carceres*) and hurtled into the first lap, while the charioteer, with the reins tightly bound round his body, fought to control the light chariot as it bounced along, jostling for a place on the inside, close to the central partition (*spina*). The turn was crucial. The driver had to graze the stone turning-post to achieve the best line round the sharp bend. Too sharp a collision would overturn the chariot, and the charioteer would be dragged behind his horses, trying desperately to cut the reins with his knife. At the end of each lap, one lap-marker (in the shape of an egg or a dolphin) was taken down from the spina, and the tension was maintained until the sprint off the final turn. A storm of applause greeted the winner, who was overwhelmed by the congratulations of the winning faction.

A chariot race in progress, shown on a mosaic from Britain, fourth century AD

The Romans supported a faction as people today support a football team. The factions were known by their colours as Whites, Greens, Reds and Blues. Each maintained stables and a huge staff of grooms, trainers, saddlers and the like. The best charioteers sold their services to the faction which paid the highest fee, and the successful driver was idolized by the people. Here is an extract from a commemorative inscription to one remarkable charioteer:

Gaius Appuleius Diocles, charioteer of the Red Faction, a Lusitanian Spaniard by birth, aged 42 years, 7 months, 23 days. He drove his first chariot in the White stable, when Acilius Avida and Corellius Pansa were consuls [AD 122]. He won his first victory in the same Faction, when Manius Acilius Glabrio and Gaius Bellicius Torquatus were consuls. . . . He won his

148

first victory in the Red Faction in the consulship of Laenas Pontianus and Antonius Rufinus [AD 131].

Grand totals: He drove chariots for 24 years, started in 4,257 races and won 1,462 victories. . . . In single-entry races (one team per faction) he won 1,064 victories, and 92 major money prizes, 32 of them (including 3 with 6-horse teams) of 30,000 sesterces, 28 (including 2 with six-horse teams) of 40,000 sesterces, 29 (including 1 with a seven-horse team) at 50,000 sesterces, and 3 at 60,000 sesterces. . . . He won, or was placed 2,900 times, and took 861 second places, 576 third places and 1 fourth. He tied with a Blue for first place 10 times, and a White 91 times. . . . In all he won a total of 35,863,120 sesterces.

(C.I.L. vol. VI, no. 16,048)

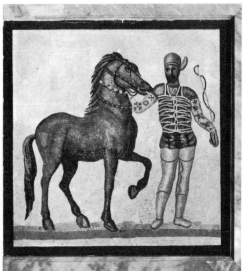

Charioteers of the factions from a mosaic in Rome

CHAPTER SIXTEEN

Literary Legacy

Roman prose and poetry had reached their greatest heights during the social and political disorder of the late Republic, and this Golden Age of Roman literature continued under the more settled years when Augustus was emperor. Of the major writers whose works were reviewed in Chapter 10 only Sallust and Cicero lived on after Julius Caesar's assassination in 44 BC and Cicero himself was murdered the following year on the instructions of Marcus Antonius.

Virgil and Horace

That same year a young poet, Publius Virgilius Maro, began work on a series of pastoral poems, the *Eclogues*, which were finally published in 37 BC. Virgil had spent some of his youth on his father's farm in north Italy, and his early poems reveal his love for the countryside and its people. The *Eclogues* depicted country scenes and imaginary country characters – goatherds, shepherds, country girls, their life, pastimes and love affairs. But though many of the poems create a world which is charming, carefree and rather unreal, the harsher realities of the troubled times in which Virgil was living often show through.

The countryside also formed the background for Virgil's next poem, published just after the Civil War had ended. The *Georgics* is a poem about farming and its four books deal with crops, tree cultivation (the olive and vine especially), animals and bees. But the *Georgics* is not a farming manual. 'Virgil did not wish to give instructions to farmers', wrote Seneca, 'but to give pleasure to his readers.' With a wealth of feeling, colour and imagery, the poet reveals the wonders of nature and the countryside, and the dignity of hard-working country people. Here he contrasts the simple life of the countryman with the gaudy affluence of the city dweller:

Oh too lucky for words, if only he knew his luck
Is the countryman who far from the clash of armaments
Lives, and rewarding earth is lavish of all he needs!
True, no mansion tall with a swanky gate throws up
In the morning a mob of callers to crowd him out and gape at
Doorposts inlaid with beautiful tortoiseshell, attire
Of gold brocade, connoisseur's bronzes.
No foreign dyes may stain his white fleeces, no exotic
Spice like cinnamon spoil his olive oil for use.
But calm security, and a life that will not cheat you,
Rich in its own rewards, are here. The broad ease of the farmlands,
Caves, living lakes, and combes that are cool even at midsummer,

Mooing of herds, and slumber mild in the trees' shade.
Here are the glades game-haunted,
Lads hardened to labour, inured to simple ways,
Reverence for God, respect for the family. When Justice
Left earth, her latest footprints were stamped on folk like these!

(Virgil, *Georgics* II, 458–74)

A goatherd milking; a commonplace scene, for the ancient world depended on goats for its milk

Virgil's greatest work, the *Aeneid*, was barely finished when the poet died in 19 BC. This patriotic epic, in 12 books of incomparable poetry, tells the story of Aeneas, a Trojan prince who escapes from the Greek sack of Troy, and of his many adventures and battles until he was able to found the kingdom which became Rome. But the Aeneid is not merely an adventure story. Through its description of the hardships, setbacks and final triumph of a good man, Aeneas, Virgil's poem underlines the struggle and achievement of Rome itself, and the great promise of her Empire, now at peace under Augustus.

Loyalty, integrity, moral seriousness, a sense of duty and obedience to the Divine Will are all qualities to be found in Aeneas, and, Virgil implies, in Roman civilization at its best. Underlying everything is the poet's belief in Rome's destiny – as Aeneas discovers when he visits the underworld, and learns Rome's future from his dead father:

Now bend your gaze this way, look at that people there!
They are YOUR Romans. Caesar is there and all Ascanius'
Posterity, who shall pass beneath the arch of day.
And here, here is the man, the promised one you know of –
Caesar Augustus, son of a god, destined to rule
Where Saturn ruled of old in Latium, and there
Bring back the age of gold: his Empire shall expand
Past Garamants and Indians to a land beyond the Zodiac
And the sun's yearly path, where Atlas the sky-bearer pivots
The wheeling heavens, embossed with fiery stars, on his shoulders.
Even now the Caspian realm, the Crimean country
Tremble at oracles of the gods predicting his advent,
And the seven mouths of the Nile are in a sweat of fear.

(Virgil, *Aeneid* VI, 788–800)

Critics in the ancient world recognised Virgil's greatness as a poet, and his reputation through the centuries has been massive, as has his influence on other poets. Quintilian, writing at the end of the first century AD compares him with Homer:

Of all epic poets, Greek or Roman, it is Virgil whose achievement comes nearest to Homer's. A distinguished orator, when asked which poet he thought came closest to Homer, replied, 'Virgil comes second, but is nearer first than third!' Indeed, though we Romans must bow before the superhuman genius of Homer, Virgil's poetry is more painstaking and thorough, because his task was harder. Homer is the greater poet in his outstanding passages, but the evenness of Virgil's poetry balances this.

(Quintilian, *Inst. Or.*, X, 1.85–7)

Literature owed one more debt to Virgil. It was he who introduced to Maecenas, his patron, the young clerk Q. Horatius Flaccus, whose poetry showed such promise. Maecenas, the friend and adviser of Augustus, and foremost literary patron of his day, made Horace's future secure by giving him some property and enabling him to devote himself to poetry.

Horace wrote poems of many kinds in a variety of metres, on many subjects. His poetry had a range of moods. He could be solemn, witty, pensive, flippant, bitter and gentle. He wrote about love, wine, money, idleness, courage, loyalty, integrity and death. With superb poetic skill he fitted the Latin language to Greek lyric metres, and his poems, especially his Odes, have been admired in literary circles ever since. Because of their variety, the poems cannot be described in general terms, and Horace's own personality is equally difficult to define. But Dryden's paraphrase of one of his Odes comes close to the spirit of his Roman predecessor:

Happy the Man, and happy he alone,
He, who can call today his own:
He, who secure within, can say,
Tomorrow do thy worst, for I have lived today.
Be fair, or foul, or rain or shine,
The joys I have possest, in spight of fate, are mine.
Not heaven itself upon the past has power;
But what has been, has been, and I have had my hour.

(Horace, *Odes* III, 29.41)

152

But neither Horace nor those poets who followed him during the early years of the Empire could match the inspiration and poetic genius of Virgil, in Quintilian's view:

> Rome's other poets trail a long way behind Virgil. Ovid is rather frivolous, even when writing epic poetry, and has too high an opinion of his own gifts. But some of what he writes deserves praise . . . Lucan's poetry is fiery and full of passion, and some of the views he expresses make it remarkable. Among Roman elegiac poets Tibullus, in my opinion, is the most terse and refined, though some people prefer Propertius. Among the writers of satire, Horace is neater and purer in style, and Persius, though he wrote only one book, achieved and deserved a good reputation. As for the writers of lyric poetry, Horace is very nearly the only poet worth reading. At times his poems reach the heights, and are lively and full of grace. His figures of speech are varied, and he is imaginative and successful in his choice of words.

> (Quintilian, *Inst. Or.*, X, 1.93, 94, 96)

Livy, Tacitus and the Prose Writers

As Virgil towered above his contemporaries in poetry, so Titus Livius over-shadowed his fellow historians. Livy's *History of Rome* (in 142 books) can be seen as the prose continuation of Virgil's verse epic, and traces the growth and development of Rome from its earliest days to the great Empire under Augustus. Like the Aeneid, Livy's history was patriotic in tone, and set out to describe and draw lessons from Rome's glorious but troubled past. Though Livy's judgement as a historian sometimes wavers, his achievement was colossal, both for its imaginative scope and its literary artistry. As Quintilian says:

> In history writing we Romans can stand comparison with the Greeks. Livy's historical narrative has great charm and outstanding brilliance, and the speeches which he puts into the mouths of his historical characters are eloquent beyond description, and perfectly suited to the person and the situation. As to the emotions, no writer has ever described them so accurately.

> (Quintilian, *Inst. Or.*, X, 1.101)

Livy died shortly after Augustus, and no historian of comparable ability emerged to take his place for almost a century. Perhaps this was not surprising. It needed a delicate touch to write history under the early emperors, some of whom were anxious that future generations should not be misled by ungenerous accounts of their reigns. Another historian, Tacitus, explains:

> Distinguished historians have already described the triumphs and disasters of early Rome, and the Augustan Age too had its talented writers. But historians of ability were frightened from their subject by the increasing tendency to flattery. When the early emperors were alive, fear prevented the publication of a true account of their reigns. When they were dead, history was distorted by the hatred their rule generated.

> (Tacitus, *Annals* I, 1)

But although no major history was published until Tacitus' own, poetry and prose writing continued to flourish into the second century AD. The best known works of

Ancient manuscript of Livy's History, *copied AD 400–50. In places the parchment is very thin, so that the writing from the other side shows through*

L. Annaeus Seneca are his letters and essays on moral subjects, but his plays too have had a great influence on European drama. Seneca's nephew, Lucan, already mentioned by Quintilian, wrote an epic poem on the Civil War. It is usually called 'Pharsalia' after the great battle between Caesar and Pompey. Uncle and nephew died at Nero's request in AD 65 for their suspected part in a plot on the emperor's life, together with Gaius Petronius Arbiter, author of an amusing and colourful satirical novel. Following them, M. Fabius Quintilianus, whose major work on the training of an orator has already been quoted, is one of the foremost educational theorists in history, while C. Plinius Secundus, the Elder Pliny, wrote a massive 102-volume *Natural History*, which dealt with a variety of topics, including the physical world, geography, zoology, botany, metals and minerals. He died in AD 79 during the eruption of Vesuvius, which was vividly described by his nephew, the younger Pliny, in a memorable letter to Tacitus:

> Vesuvius was alight in many places, with broad sheets of fire and towering flames, whose bright glare was intensified by the blackness of the night. To reassure his companions my uncle continued to tell them that these were fires which the anxious countryfolk had left, or that they were empty houses burning in an evacuated area. . . . Then he went to bed, and slept soundly . . . By now the courtyard next to his room was deep in a mixture of ash and pumice stone: the level of the debris had risen, so that if he had delayed any longer, he would have been completely shut in. So someone woke my uncle, and he came out and joined Pomponianus and the others, who had been watching the eruption all night. Together they debated whether to stay indoors or to keep clear of all buildings, which were now shaking under the intense, jarring shocks, and seemed to sway this way and that as if wrenched from their foundations. In the open, on the other hand, there was the danger of falling pumice stones, although these were light and burnt out. Finally they chose to stay outside . . . and tied pillows on to their heads with cloths for protection against the falling objects.

(Pliny, *Epist.* 6.16.6)

Unlike Cicero, Pliny wrote his letters for publication, but though this may make them seem a little artificial, their contents give a colourful and varied picture of life in Pliny's times.

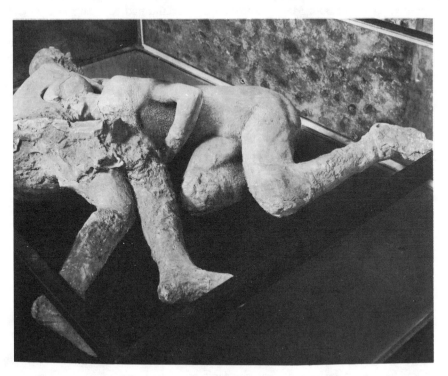

Victims of Vesuvius' eruption. The shape of the corpses was preserved by the layers of ash which covered them

155

The Satirists

Another of Pliny's letters concerns the death of the poet Martial, some of whose poems have been quoted on pages 131 and 132. Pliny writes:

> I am grieved to hear of Valerius Martial's death. He was a very gifted person whose mind was sensitive and perceptive. His poems were remarkable for the way they combined sincerity with wit.

(Pliny, Epist., 3.21.1)

Pliny was a friend and patron of Martial, whose short poems, the *Epigrams*, 'reflected life like a mirror', as the poet himself put it. Martial was chiefly interested in his fellow human beings, and his poems range from the most sensitive, sympathetic expression of feeling to biting satires, ridiculing men's weaknesses.

Through Martial's verse we can learn how precarious life in Rome could be for a poet who depended on the favours of the rich. For the successful, like Papirius Statius, poetry brought fame and prosperity:

> The city is all agog when Statius agrees
> to fix a recital-date. He's a sell-out: no one
> can resist that mellifluous voice, that ever-popular
> Theban epic of his. The audience sits there spellbound
> by such fabulous charm . . .

This description of a public poetry reading was written by Decimus Junius Juvenalis, a contemporary of both Martial and Statius. Juvenal had Martial's sharp eye for the vices and follies of his times but neither his sympathy nor his desire to please. One of the world's greatest satirists, Juvenal was a brilliant poet, and his bitterness and resentment combined with his inventive genius to produce the most powerful poetic attacks on society and individuals. Living conditions, patronage, pride, extravagance and many other aspects of city life came under Juvenal's lash. Here he writes a cruel caricature of a rich society woman:

> There's nothing a woman
> Baulks at, no action that gives her a twinge of conscience,
> Once she's put on her emerald choker, weighted down her ear-lobes
> With vast pearl pendants. What's more insufferable
> Than your well-heeled female? But earlier in the process
> She presents a sight as funny as it's appalling,
> Her features lost under a damp bread face-pack,
> Or greasy with vanishing cream that clings to her husband's
> Lips when the poor man kisses her – though it's all
> Wiped off for her lover. She takes no trouble about
> The way she looks at home: those imported Indian
> Scents and lotions she buys with a lover in mind.
> First one layer, then the next: at last the contours emerge
> Till she's almost recognisable. Now she freshens
> Her complexion with asses' milk. (If her husband's posted
> To the godforsaken North, a herd of she-asses
> Will travel with them.) But all these medicaments
> And various treatments – not least the damp bread-poultice –
> Make you wonder what's underneath, a face or a boil.

(Juvenal, VI, 460–73)

Tacitus

Some of Juvenal's bitterness can be found in the last great author of this period, the historian Cornelius Tacitus, to whom Pliny addressed his description of the eruption of Vesuvius. Tacitus, a senator, had lived through the purges of the emperor Domitian, and his resentment colours his magnificent descriptions of the personalities and events of the early Empire. Tacitus' *Histories* covering the period AD 68–96 were followed by the *Annals*, dealing with AD 14–68. Both works, with their undertone of pessimism, are in complete contrast to the patriotic, almost idealistic, approach of Livy to his country's past. In style, too, there is a marked difference; Livy's 'milky richness', as Quintilian described it, is replaced by an intense, compressed narrative style, full of striking phrases and memorable epigrams. Here is part of Tacitus' introduction to the *Histories*:

> We enter a period rich in disasters, scarred with hideous battles and torn by treason. Even peace was cruel. Four emperors died violently; there were three civil wars, and more fighting against foreigners –some conflicts combined the two. Success in the East was matched by failure in the West: there was chaos in Illyricum, the loyalty of the Gallic provinces wavered, Britain was conquered, and immediately abandoned. . . . Finally Italy too was overwhelmed by disasters which were unprecedented, or without parallel for centuries. The fertile coastal region of Campania was engulfed and entombed (by Vesuvius). Rome was ravaged by fire, which destroyed the city's most famous temples. Even the Capitol was set alight – by Roman hands. There was sacrilege in holy places, adultery among the great. The Mediterranean teemed with exiles, and its rocky islands ran with the blood of condemned men. In the city, the reign of terror was even more savage. The accuser's finger pointed at noble birth, wealth and high office (whether held or surrendered) and virtue's reward was death. The prizes for playing the informer were as odious as the act itself: successful accusers won priesthoods and consulships, others obtained imperial posts and gained influence at court. Hatred and terror held sway.

> (Tacitus, *Histories* I, 2)

Pliny had no doubt that Tacitus' writings would never perish.

> It is my belief that your histories will be immortal, and I am sure that my prediction will be borne out by the facts. And I confess that this is the reason why I am anxious to be mentioned in them.

> (Pliny, *Epist.* 7.33.1)

Events almost proved Pliny wrong. Twelve hundred years later Tacitus' name was known by only a handful of scholars, and only single copies of some of the parts of his histories survived – other parts had already disappeared for ever. How had this come about?

Books, Libraries and the Survival of Literature

In Pliny's time there were a great many copies of all the authors we have mentioned readily available to the literary-minded. Bookshops flourished, and private and public libraries were well stocked. The best Roman authors became school textbooks, and this led to a further increase in the number of copies. One other important development, from the second century onwards, was the gradual replacement of the awkward scrolls (*volumina* – see Chapter 10) by parchment books (*codices*) which were more convenient, easier to consult and longer lasting. So far, then, Pliny's expectations were fulfilled, and the works of accomplished new authors continued to be published, even though they did not match the literary distinction of the late republican and early imperial periods. C. Suetonius Tranquillus (AD 69–135) wrote a series of lively portraits of the early emperors entitled *The Lives of the Caesars*, which were followed by Aulus Gellius' *Attic Nights*, a collection of essays on a wide range of topics, and the *Golden Ass* by Apuleius – the only complete Latin novel to survive from ancient times. Finally, during the revival of literature in the fourth century, Ammianus Marcellinus wrote a fine history of Rome from the death of Domitian to his own times, and two poets, Ausonius and Claudian, recaptured some of the brilliance of the poetry of the Golden Age in their fine verse.

With the collapse of the Western Empire, however, and the wave of invasions by alien peoples (see Chapter 20) Roman society crumbled, and education and the care of books passed increasingly into the hands of the Christian Church. Monasteries (helped by cathedrals and church schools) began to collect and hoard books, and the monks were kept occupied in copying classical texts.

Another manuscript written about AD 800 of the same page of Livy as that shown on page 154.

As the Dark Ages proceeded, however, even this lifeline was cut, and with a few exceptions, texts were not copied for almost two hundred years (AD 550–750). This was not the only threat. Even those parchment books of classical literature already in existence were often required for re-use – parchment was valuable – and the original text was washed off to make way for a copy of some Christian writing.

A palimpsest, in which the earlier large lettering (c.AD 400) can be seen behind the smaller, more recent text of St Augustine, written about AD 650

But even in the darkest days, some interest in classical literature flickered, and monasteries in the furthest corners of Europe – in Ireland, and at York and Canterbury in England – kept the flame alight until the revival of learning under Charlemagne (AD 768–814). Now for the first time, old libraries and repositories were searched for books, and schools and monasteries restocked their shelves with copies of ancient masterpieces. But the fate of many authors and many works was still uncertain. The writings of Tacitus, Tibullus, Catullus and Propertius, the letters and some speeches of Cicero survived precariously in a few copies – sometimes only in one – and it was not until the great age of rediscovery, the Renaissance (AD 1300 onwards), that many of the texts now in print were brought into the light. Many had mouldered in attic rooms of monasteries, or gathered dust in cathedral outbuildings, and the scholars of the Renaissance, by rummaging, borrowing and even stealing, rescued many major works from oblivion. Inevitably, much was lost – of Livy's 142 books only 35 survive, two-thirds of Tacitus' *Histories* has perished and a third of his *Annals*. Nothing remains of the poetry of Gallus, much admired by Virgil. But by the end of the fifteenth century almost all the Latin literature we know today had been collected and was in print. Pliny's prediction was at last made good.

A medieval scribe copying. Scrolls and parchment codices are both in use

CHAPTER SEVENTEEN

Gods and Men

To understand the Roman's attitude to religion we must go back to the earliest days of the city and even earlier, to the primitive farming communities scattered over the plain of Latium. The farmer's life was hard and uncertain. Even when things went well he had to work long hours to make sure that his smallholding produced enough to provide for his family throughout the year. His constant fear was that there would be a drought, that floods would wash away his early crop, or gales smash down his full-grown corn. So it is not surprising that the peasant farmer, who depended on the seasons and the mysterious forces of nature for his livelihood, thought that everything in nature was controlled by spirits, or divine powers (*numina*). He believed that the growth of the seeds, the blight which might destroy the growing corn, and the harvest itself were all in the hands of supernatural powers, beyond man's understanding.

Lararium, *or chapel of the household gods, from a house at Pompeii. The family deity is in the centre, flanked by two other household gods. Beneath is a sacred serpent*

161

The Controlling Spirits

These '*numina*' were everywhere, in everything. Woods, rivers, sea, sky, even the boundaries to his farm all had controlling spirits, and commonplace activities like cooking and eating had a spirit presiding over them. Powerful spirits protected the home: Vesta watched over the hearth, Janus guarded the door, and the Penates looked after the store cupboard. The guardian spirit of the head of the family, his '*genius*', was given special attention, as were the spirits of the family's dead ancestors, the *Manes*, or Kindly Ones. Each day the head of the household (*paterfamilias*) made sure that prayers were offered to the various powers, and that the necessary ceremonies were performed. The main meal of the day was always accompanied by sacrifices and libations. In the home, as in the fields, the sacrifices and the ritual had to be correct in every detail, and performed at the right time. In this way the Roman hoped to establish good relations with the '*numina*', and so be 'at peace with the gods' (*pax deorum*). If the sacrifices were correctly performed, the spirits would be co-operative, and would even give warnings if disaster was approaching.

At first Romans did not think that the spirits had any particular form or shape. Only their power concerned the primitive farmers. But even in the early days of the community the Romans began to define the spirits and their functions more precisely, and to imagine that they looked like human beings. Gradually Janus and Vesta came to be thought of not as mysterious powers watching over the doorway and the hearth, but as gods, in human form, and with human characteristics. So too were Jupiter, the sky god, Quirinus, god of the assembled citizens, and Mars, the war god, who had once been god of the fields.

Gods from Abroad

As the city grew, and came into contact with more communities in Latium, and throughout Italy, more gods came to the notice of the Romans: Minerva, goddess of handicrafts and wisdom, Juno, wife of Jupiter and special goddess of women, Diana, goddess of fertility in women, Venus (who only later came to be thought of as the goddess of love), and Neptune, the god of water all came to be worshipped at Rome. Through the Etruscans and the Greeks, Romans discovered Ceres, goddess of the corn, Apollo, god of teaching and prophecy and Vulcan the fire god. Because of their dealings with the Greek cities of the south, Romans began to identify their gods with those of the Greeks: Jupiter was paired with Zeus, Juno with Hera, Minerva with Athena, and Mars with Ares. The Greeks believed that their gods had human shape, and they told countless stories about their exploits. The Romans came to accept these myths, and to apply them to their native gods, while at the same time they adopted many of the religious ceremonies of the Greeks.

It was Etruscan influence, however, which led to the building of the first temple at Rome, and to the first statues of the gods being made. From Etruria, too, came experts in the art of divination, who could tell whether the gods would be favourable towards a particular enterprise by examining the entrails of slaughtered animals, or watching the sky for lightning.

Inspection of the entrails of a sacrificial bull. The soothsayer (haruspex) believed that he could predict the future by carefully examining the colour, shape and position of the slaughtered animal's internal organs

Priests, and the State Religion

But Rome did not rely completely on imported cults. Every Roman historian who wrote about his city's early history agreed that Numa Pompilius (Rome's second king) established the official state religion. His Calendar fixed the festival days. His official decree laid down the ceremonies, rituals and every detail of the sacrifices, and he created the various priesthoods to supervise and regulate the state cults. He himself was the priest king, presiding over the state as the father presided over the family. Under him were the two most important 'colleges' of priests, the Pontiffs, with their leader the Pontifex Maximus, and the Augurs. The Pontiffs were responsible for administration and the Sacred Law, while the Augurs' duty was to make certain that everything undertaken by the state had the gods' approval. They did this by interpreting the signs given by the gods, in the flight of birds, for example, or in the feeding habits of the sacred chickens, and by using the skills taught by the Etruscan diviners. A third college of priests controlled the so-called Sybilline Books. Here again we see the influence of the Greeks on the Romans, for the books were a collection of oracles, brought to the city from Cumae by king Tarquin. In a crisis the Romans always asked the priests to consult the books and tell them what action must be taken to avert disaster.

An augur holding a lituus, *his special ceremonial wand. At his feet is a sacred chicken*

Next there were the individual priests, *flamines*, who were dedicated to the service of one particular god; Jupiter's priest, the Flamen Dialis, was the chief of these. Then came the groups of minor priests, the Salii, Fetiales, Luperci, and finally the Vestal Virgins, who watched over the fire of Vesta in her temple, and made sure that it never went out. In their personal life many priests had to obey strict rules. The Flamen Dialis for example:

> It is not customary for the Flamen Dialis to touch, or even mention by name a she-goat, raw flesh, ivy or beans. . . . He must not look on blood . . . the foot of the bed where he sleeps must be smeared with a thin coating of clay and he must not sleep away from his own bed for three nights in succession. . . . At the foot of his bed there should be a box full of sacrificial cakes. The clippings from his hair and nails must be buried under a fruitful tree . . . and he must not go outdoors unless he wears a cap.

> (Aulus Gellius, *Noct. Att.*, 10.15)

If a priest's private life could be complicated so were the rituals he performed. In the conduct of the sacrifices, every detail was vitally important, because the slightest mistake made the sacrifice void. The victim (a pig usually, but sometimes a sheep or an ox, or even all three for a special occasion) was slaughtered and its entrails inspected to make sure the omens were good, while the priest, wearing a veil on his head, said the correct prayers. Anyone watching had to maintain strict silence, and flute players played to drown any ill-omened noise.

164

Relief showing five Vestals attending the goddess. A girl of good family might become a Vestal when she was about seven. She then served the goddess for 30 years, and often longer

The Growth of Superstition

After the expulsion of the kings, the Pontifex Maximus finally became head of the state religion, and just as the early constitution was modelled on the family (see p. 18) so the state cults seemed to follow the pattern of the primitive family religion. But the differences were great, and became greater. The city priests with their temples, statues and complicated ceremonies could not achieve the reverence and awe which had characterized the simple country religion. Superstitious fears began to replace genuine religious feelings, and Romans became more concerned with omens and portents than with the gods themselves. Any disaster, like the defeats by Hannibal, sparked off a succession of prodigies, terrified the gullible people, and put the augurs into a frenzy of activity. Livy reports:

> Many strange things happened in and around Rome, that winter – at least they were said to have happened, and were believed too easily, as one expects when man's mind is confused by superstitious fears. A six-month old freeborn baby had shouted 'Victory' in the vegetable

market. In the cattle market an ox had walked up three flights of stairs and then, when the lodgers screamed, was so frightened that it jumped out of the window. . . . At Picenum it rained stones . . . and in Gaul a wolf pulled a sentry's sword out of its sheath, and ran off with it.

(Livy, XXI, 62)

The Influence of Greece

Two other developments served to weaken further the religious influence of the state cults. One was the influx of foreign religions (like those of Cybele and Bacchus) with which Rome's growing Empire came into contact. The other was the increasing scepticism among educated Romans, encouraged by the spread of Greek culture and philosophy to Rome and Italy. As early as 249 BC, P. Claudius Pulcher had revealed his contempt for the sacred chickens. Preparing to fight a battle at sea during the first war with Carthage, he was advised by his staff that the omens were not favourable – the sacred chickens would not eat. Unmoved, the consul dropped them overboard into the sea saying, 'At least they can drink'.

Two hundred years later, Cicero, writing about the skills of an augur, was equally critical:

Don't you see that choosing a victim for sacrifice is like throwing a dice, and the result proves my point. For when two sacrifices are examined, and the entrails of the first contain a liver with no top to it (the worst possible omen), it often happens that the next victim provides completely favourable entrails. What happens, then, to the warning given by the first entrails? Have the gods suddenly changed their minds?

(Cicero, *de Div.* II, 15.36)

Sacrifice of a bull, sheep and pig (suovetaurilia). *The priest* (right) *prepares the altar, while one of his attendants stands ready with a jug of wine to pour*

But Greek philosophy had a more positive influence. The teachings of Epicurus (see p. 93) showed that no one need fear death, while the Stoics preached a doctrine most attractive to educated Romans: a man must always aim at the highest moral standards, and must accept misfortune or accident calmly as a necessary part of living life in accordance with Nature. In this way he will come into harmony with God, the controlling force of the universe, and source of all life. Because all mankind have a share in this universal scheme all are 'brothers', and should treat each other well. Many intelligent Romans were attracted by Stoicism, and these teachings had a profound effect for hundreds of years.

But neither philosophy nor religion could prevent the disastrous civil wars which destroyed the Roman Republic. Ambition, greed and selfishness led to the disintegration of Roman society and the breakdown of its standards. Though the religions of the countryside and the home were still observed, the state religion decayed and its priesthoods began to have political associations. Even the temples were allowed to fall into disrepair. It was left to Augustus, who 'restored' the Republic after the Civil War, to revive the ancestral religion, and to make sure that Rome should once again be 'at peace with the gods'. Augustus himself became Chief Priest and, at great expense, brought back the old rituals and dignified ceremonies, and rebuilt the temples.

The emperor's supreme position soon made him the object of a cult. In the East, temples were dedicated to 'Rome and Augustus', and emperor-worship soon spread to the western provinces. After his death, Augustus was deified, as Julius Caesar before him had been. Later emperors were not always prepared to wait so long for divine honours.

The family of Augustus, and priests (left), *in solemn procession*

Foreign Gods Again

But it was easier to rebuild temples than to restore belief in the gods. More than a century of scepticism could not be brushed away. Romans did not lose their appetite for cults which required the worshipper to take part and involved him emotionally, in contrast to the state religion which required only passive spectators. New, non-Roman cults continued to pour into Rome, and many of them promised a new life and communion with the god which might continue after death. Following Cybele and Bacchus came Isis, Osiris and Serapis from Egypt, Ma from Cappadocia and Mithras from Persia. Mithraism became extremely popular in the army, and archaeologists continually find traces of the cult on the frontiers of the Empire which the armies protected.

Procession in honour of Isis, led by the priestess of the goddess, with her left hand bound by the sacred serpent, and carrying a sacred vessel. Next comes the holy scribe with the sacred book, followed by a prophet, carrying an urn of Nile water. Behind comes an attendant with a musical instrument and a ladle

All these cults made a strong appeal to the Roman's emotions which the state religion could not match. Astrology, too, the science of foretelling the future by the stars, grew in popularity and all classes consulted those expert in interpreting the signs of the heavens. Most astrologers were fakes, as intelligent people recognized, but this did not check their influence. Like most readers of popular newspapers today, Romans never missed an opportunity to learn their horoscope.

Jews and Christians

Finally, two other Eastern religions came to Rome, although no Roman would have guessed that they would survive and flourish long after the other cults, and the Empire itself, had disappeared. Communities of Jews, and the Jewish religion could be found in

Mithras slaying the bull, from which springs new life

almost all the major cities of the Mediterranean, especially in the East. Their worship seemed particularly strange to the Romans, because they had only one god. Jews did not eat pork, observed a Sabbath day every seven, and held exclusive services in their synagogues. Special rules had to be made whenever Jews were involved. No Jew could appear in court on the Sabbath, and Jewish soldiers would not parade on their Holy Day. As worship of the emperor became more widespread they were considered disloyal because they refused to attend the ceremonies. But though the Jews were often unpopular, and even victimized on occasions, Rome was tolerant towards them, in keeping with its usual policy.

In AD 64 Rome was ravaged by a fire which lasted nine days. Had the fire been started by an accident or deliberately? Was the emperor himself responsible?

> To dispel this rumour the emperor Nero produced scapegoats and inflicted every kind of torture on a group called Christians, whose depravity was well known. Their founder, Christus, had been executed during the reign of the emperor Tiberius by the governor of Judaea, Pontius Pilate. But though this deady superstition had been checked for a short time, it soon began to break out again, not only in Judaea (its starting point) but also in Rome itself. Those who confessed themselves Christians were arrested; they turned informers and great numbers were convicted, not so much for starting the fire as for being social misfits.
>
> In their deaths they were made objects of scorn. They were dressed in animal skins, and torn to pieces by dogs, or they were nailed to crosses, and made into torches to be lit at night when the daylight failed. . . . As a result, though they deserved the harshest penalties because they were Christians, the victims were pitied. For Romans felt that they were being sacrificed not for the public good, but to gratify the brutality of one man – the emperor.
>
> (Tacitus, *Annals* 15.44)

So Christianity came to the notice of the Romans, who so far had thought that there was no difference between Jews and Christians. The fact that only 30 years had elapsed between the crucifixion of Jesus Christ in Palestine and the first persecution at Rome shows how fast this latest cult spread. Inspired by the teaching of Paul (who as Saul of Tarsus had been one of the Christians' most enthusiastic persecutors before he, too, was converted), the new religion welcomed converts from all backgrounds, Romans included. Paul himself was a Roman citizen and was finally brought to Rome to answer a charge of treason. Very probably he died in Nero's purge. Most of the Christian converts came from the poorer sections of society, who were attracted especially by the belief in life after death, and the promise that Christ was soon to establish his kingdom on Earth.

From Nero's persecution onwards, the early Christian communities were treated with hatred and suspicion by the Roman authorities and by most of the population. Like the Jews, they appeared disloyal because they refused to worship the emperor, and their secret services increased public hostility towards them. The cult was forced to go underground, and to use secret codes, signs and passwords to avoid detection. Persecution was common, though it was usually limited to small areas. Except under Domitian and Marcus Aurelius there were no large scale attempts to wipe out the cult until AD 250 when a succession of emperors began systematic persecutions throughout the whole Empire. In these cruel and vicious purges, many Christians died as martyrs to their faith, but, remarkably, the number of worshippers continued to increase. At last in AD 311 an Act of Toleration was passed, and in AD 337 the emperor himself, Constantine, was baptised into the faith. From that time the Christian religion grew in strength and influence, until under Theodosius (AD 378–95) it was adopted as the official state religion.

The Chi-Rho symbol (derived from the Greek letters XP for Christ) combined with α and ω (first and last), as shown on the side of an early Christian sarcophagus

170

CHAPTER EIGHTEEN

Provinces

When Domitian died in AD 96, and the Senate chose Nerva to rule, the relief in Rome was immense. The news was carried at top speed to every province, and the governors shared in the rejoicing of the capital, for they no longer need fear their return to Italy. But the other inhabitants of the provinces were little affected: they welcomed the ceremonial celebrations, and groaned perhaps at their contribution to the official welcoming present, but nothing else: murder and intrigue at Rome made small difference to their lives.

It is not always easy to find out what life was like in the provinces, for most of the authors whose works have survived were Romans whose interests centred on the capital. But for life in the Middle East in the early Empire we have the fascinating evidence of the New Testament, and in particular the journeys through Greece and Asia Minor of St Paul and St Luke. In addition there is the invaluable series of letters between the Younger Pliny and the emperor Trajan when Pliny was sent on a special commission to the province of Bithynia. For a view of life in the western provinces – and there is a considerable difference between the two halves of the Empire as we shall see – we can look at Britannia: there is some literary evidence, and modern archaeologists have developed unrivalled skills in extracting information from the remains, few though they may be in comparison with the 'Roman ruins' of other countries.

Many cities in the eastern half of the Empire were old and famous long before Rome was founded, and most of the others were enjoying a high standard of civilization when Rome was still struggling for supremacy in Italy. These cities traded with each other for centuries, exchanging ideas and words as well as goods. They had seen empires rise and fall, as Babylon, Egypt and Persia had in turn dominated wide areas and many peoples. Then the Greeks, and in particular the Athenians, had collected and refined the wisdom of other peoples to develop a culture previously undreamt of. Alexander the Great had carried Greek ideas, and the Greek tongue, south to Arabia and the Sudan, east to India and Afghanistan, and north into Russia. When these lands in turn fell beneath the Roman sway, the change did not seem disastrous: indeed before long it was to prove an enormous blessing, for under the Romans they were to enjoy greater peace and prosperity than ever before or since. They could not, it is true, make war on their neighbours as they wished, nor govern themselves, nor decide the level of their own taxation. But these were liberties they had rarely if ever had. When the Macedonians were conquered they paid only half as much in taxation to Rome as they had to their own kings. And when 'it came to pass in those days that there went out a decree from Caesar Augustus that all the world should be taxed', Augustus' purpose in taking the census – for that is what the Greek in the New Testament really means – was to spread the burden of taxation as fairly as possible among all the provinces.

Provinces of the Roman Empire, c.AD 120

Benefits of Roman Rule

In return for paying taxes the benefits were many. First, with the elimination of the pirate fleets that had plagued the Mediterranean from the earliest times, sea-borne trade flourished greatly, and membership of the Empire meant a virtually unlimited new market for exports. Secondly, provincials could leave the defence of their lands to an army whose efficiency was unequalled, and for many years rarely challenged.

There was for the provincials, too, a considerable satisfaction in belonging to the Empire that dominated the known world. The citizenship, for which they all soon longed, meant a passport to travel, promotion in the imperial civil service if they wanted it, and personal safety. It is the imposition of a uniform system of law and order that was Rome's greatest gift to other countries. The corrupt governors of the republican era, mostly intent on lining their own pockets, gave place under Augustus and his successors to a series of honest and reliable administrators specially trained for their posts. Pontius Pilate may seem to us tactless, inefficient and corrupt: but the problems of religious and political riots, a problem which the world still faces today, are immensely difficult to

172

solve. When the magistrates of Philippi in Macedon, in fear of similar riots – 'these men, being Jews, do exceedingly trouble our city' – arrested and scourged St Paul and his companions, they hurriedly and fearfully let them go when they learnt that they were Roman citizens. The Antonius Felix who kept St Paul in prison in hope of a bribe (unsuccessfully) was an unhappy exception to the general rule: but he owed his appointment to his brother, the freedman Pallas, favourite of Nero. But when Paul appeared before Festus, in some vexation he 'appealed to Caesar' – and to Rome he went: it is ironic that he would have been freed without a charge to answer but for this appeal – for once he set the process of Roman justice in motion it could not be stopped.

In this carved relief from the Rhineland, near Trier, a rent or tax collector counts out a heap of coins, while the bearded tenant farmers, in Celtic hooded duffle-coats, wait to make their payments

In time of disaster the provinces could look to Rome for support: the following quotation about an earthquake in Asia Minor may well be compared with the fragmentary and often inadequate help that is supplied today in similar cases:

> In the same year [AD 17] twelve famous cities in the province of Asia were destroyed by an earthquake: it happened at night, and so the surprise and the effects of the disaster were all the worse. People fled to open ground, the usual course of action in such emergencies, but to no avail, for the ground opened and swallowed them up. There are reports of mountains subsiding, of flat ground rising into the air and of fires breaking out among the ruins. The worst suffering was at Sardis, and its people accordingly attracted the most sympathy: Tiberius promised it 10,000,000 sesterces, and remitted for five years all taxes due to be paid to the central treasury or his private one. Magnesia by Sipylus was next, both in damage and compensation. Ten other towns were excused taxation, and a senatorial commissioner was sent to inspect the damage and arrange reconstruction and rehabilitation.

(Tacitus, *Annals* II, 47)

173

A Provincial Governor in Action

The series of letters between the emperor Trajan and the younger Pliny, whom he sent specially to assist the cities of Bithynia which had got into financial difficulties, is too long to quote here, but a summary of some of the topics and their answers from Rome is instructive:

> Could you send out a land-surveyor: a lot of money could be recovered from the public works contractors if accurate surveys were made.
> I am afraid not: I need all those available here in Rome. Find a reliable one in your own province.
>
> The bath-house of Prusa is old: the people are prepared to finance the building of a new one if you give permission.
> Yes, provided that it won't strain the city's finances.
>
> A disastrous fire occurred because there was no fire-fighting equipment: this I have now remedied. But should I start a fire brigade, of about 150 men?
> No: any society of citizens turns into a political club, and you know what trouble these have caused.
>
> The citizens of Nicomedia have spent over 3,000,000 sesterces on two aqueducts, which have been abandoned before they were finished. The water supply is still inadequate: could you send out an engineer to prevent a third failure?
> Find out whose fault it was that so much money was wasted: someone has probably made a profit out of these mistakes.
>
> For how long are permits to use the official post valid after the date of expiry?
> Permits must not be used after the expiry-date: I make it a strict rule to send out new permits before the old ones have expired.
>
> I do not know what to do about the status, and cost of maintenance, of the people generally known as foundlings. The letters from previous emperors about this seem to me to be of doubtful authenticity: I have not sent them, because I am sure you have the genuine versions in your files.
> I can find no trace of such letters referring to Bithynia: any of these people should be able to establish his freedom without having to pay back the cost of his maintenance.
>
> I have given my wife permission to use the official courier service to get home quickly to console her aunt, whose father has just died. I hope you won't mind my breaking the rules on this occasion.
> You were quite right, my dear Pliny: it is your wife's duty to make her visit doubly welcome by arriving quickly.

(Pliny, *Epist.* 10 *passim*)

Roman Rule in Britain

In the eastern provinces the cities were old and had centuries of experience of municipal government which the Roman Empire could turn to its own ends. But in the west the situation was very different. Here, in Spain and Africa, Gaul and Britain, the societies were still tribal, and often nomadic. The new provincials did not welcome Roman rule at all, and often rebelled: many years of steady Romanization were needed before the people learnt the value of government and civilisation. The Romans occupied Britain, for example, to enlarge and strengthen the Empire in the west: they also hoped to find new markets in which their traders could sell the goods produced in Italy and other provinces, and also to find new sources of raw materials, minerals and foodstuffs. The geographer Strabo, writing in the time of Augustus, has this to say of Britain:

> Most of the island is level, and covered with forests: it produces corn, cattle, gold, silver, tin: these are all exported, together with leather, slaves, and excellent hunting dogs.

And again,

> The British are prepared to pay heavy duty, both on imports and exports – we send them ivory chains, and necklaces, amber, glassware, and other small stuff of this sort.

> (Strabo, 4.5.2–4)

But trade could not be conducted efficiently without market towns: nor could taxes be collected or law be administered without the proper offices and courts which are found in towns. The Romans decided that if no towns existed then they must be built. The first was the colony of discharged army veterans at Colchester, founded in AD 49: by AD 60 it already had a theatre, a senate house, and a temple to Claudius. This temple is important: it is an example of a deliberate policy, to encourage the worship of the emperor and the spirit of Rome, not only to overawe the natives with the majesty of the new ruler, but also to unify the myriad different peoples by making them share in a common worship.

Verulamium (St Albans) and London grew as quickly as Colchester. When all these were burnt down in the revolt of Boudicca in AD 60, over 70,000 Romans and their allies were butchered. The revolt was caused by the sharp practice of the procurator, the province's financial officer, who fled in terror at the disaster he had caused. With some difficulty Suetonius Paulinus, the governor, put the rebellion down: unfortunately he could think only of vengeance for the 70,000 who had died in the sack of the towns, and punished every tribe with fire and sword. But the new procurator, Julius Classicianus,

> disagreed with Suetonius' policy . . . he spread the word about that they [the Britons] should wait for a new governor, who would be free from anger or pride since he had not himself fought or conquered them, and would treat them mercifully if they surrendered. At the same time he sent a report to Rome: there would be no end to the fighting unless Suetonius were recalled: his present difficulties were only due to his vicious behaviour.

> (Tacitus, *Annals*, 14.36)

An imperial freedman was sent to investigate, and Suetonius was sent back to Rome. Classicianus stayed on to help rebuild the country, and died in office: his tombstone is in the British Museum. It is quite obvious that the government realised the importance of a quick settlement to the troubles, and was prepared to repair the wrongs that had been done, in order to restore peace.

Soon after the rebellion, rebuilding was in full swing. Tacitus, writing the biography of his father-in-law Cn. Julius Agricola, who was governor of Britain from AD 78–84 credits him with starting the work of rehabilitation, but we know from inscriptions that a start had been made by his predecessor.

> The following year [AD 78–9] was spent on very shrewd policies. People that are scattered and uncivilised are quick to fight. To make them ready to accept peace and leisure he had to prove how pleasant these are, so he encouraged individuals and communities alike, and gave

them official assistance, to build temples, town-centres and houses, praising all who co-operated, and rebuking anyone who was reluctant. There was keen competition to win his favour, and compulsion was unnecessary. He went on to make sure that the sons of the chieftains had a proper education: he declared that the intelligence of the British was worth more than the careful learning of the Gauls. Consequently men who had a short time before refused to learn Latin were now keen to speak it fluently. Roman fashions were adopted as well, and the toga was seen everywhere. Step by step the British descended to the demoralising pleasures which are found in porticoes, bath-houses and elegant dinner-parties. In their simplicity they called it 'civilisation' – it was in fact merely one method of keeping them quiet.

(Tacitus, *Agricola*, 21)

Tacitus' cynicism does not conceal the very real efforts being made to introduce the Roman way of life, or the readiness with which the British adopted their customs. We know of 14 major towns which became the capitals of tribal areas: they are distinguished by the impressive range of public buildings – law courts, council-chambers and tax offices which are an equally important part of county towns today – and by the regular rectangular grid of streets common in the towns of Italy and the legionary camps of the army. It is clear from the layout of these towns that Agricola lent the surveyors, architects and craftsmen of his legions for their initial development. They are Aldborough, Brough, Wroxeter, Caistor St Edmunds, Leicester, St Albans, Cirencester, Caerwent, Silchester, Canterbury, Winchester, Chichester, Exeter and Dorchester.

The grid of streets was soon filled with the bath-houses, shops, houses and temples common to Roman towns all over the Empire. Many towns were provided with amphitheatres outside their walls: the magistrates – these came from the local aristocracy, and many were granted citizenship at the end of their term of office – were expected to put on some of the shows in them – cockfighting, bear-baiting and

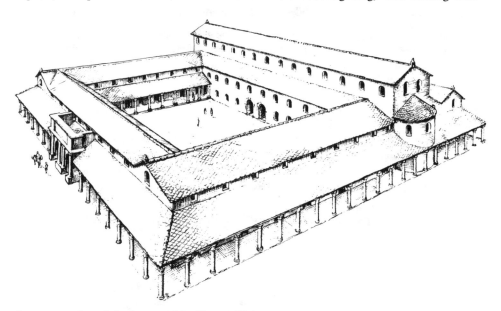

A reconstruction of the forum and basilica at Silchester

176

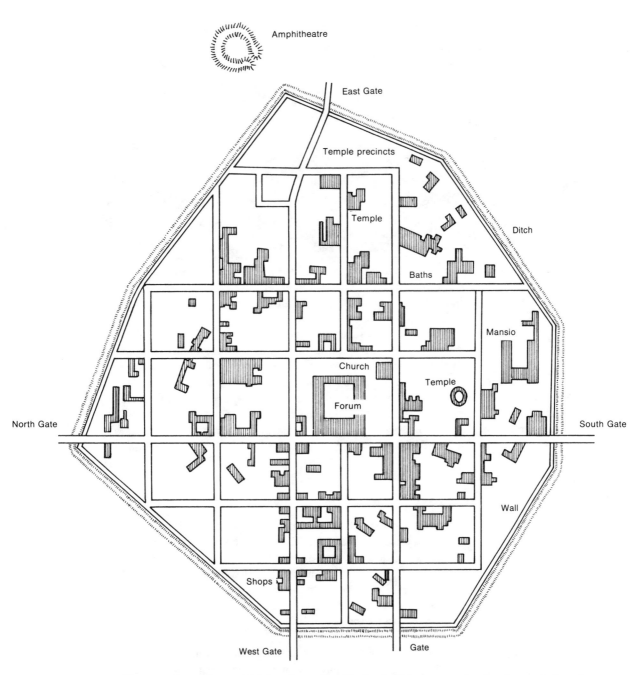

Amphitheatre

East Gate

Temple precincts

Temple

Ditch

Baths

Mansio

Church

Temple

North Gate

Forum

South Gate

Wall

Shops

West Gate

Gate

The town plan of Roman Silchester in southern England. Silchester was abandoned towards the end of the Roman period, and never built over: it was excavated at the end of the nineteenth century

177

An aerial view of the theatre at Verulamium: the banks of earth supported the rows of seats

gladiatorial combats for example, and perhaps wrestling and circus performances as well.

But probably the most important feature of the new towns was the market they provided for the people living in the surrounding countryside. Though some Britons continued to live in the primitive round thatched houses which they shared with their cattle, a great number built Roman-type villas. They cut down and sold their timber, planted more corn and bred more sheep and cattle. New tools, and foodstuffs were imported, such as apples, cherries, plums, carrots and cabbage, flax and rye. Wine from the Mediterranean, elegant tableware of fine pottery, pewter and silver from Gaul and Spain and silks from the East found their way into Yorkshire and Devon, even to Wales and Scotland.

Life in a Roman Province

The same policy of deliberate town planning – of bringing the scattered tribes into a closer area concentrated round a market and administrative centre – was also applied in Gaul, Spain and Africa. In these provinces, richer and nearer Rome, the towns were far larger and more sumptuous than the British ones. In Africa there were over six hundred towns, and the remains of many of them rise above the sands, though in their heyday they were surrounded by green fields and orchards, for the Romans had complicated irrigation schemes. In the south of France the amphitheatres of Nîmes and Arles still rise above the streets.

Life in the provinces became more and more concentrated in and around the towns which the Romans encouraged the inhabitants to build. The great villas in the countryside, with their mosaic floors (and, in Britain, hypocaust heating systems), were owned very often by rich men who also had homes in the towns: and since the villas were the centres of large agricultural estates producing food for sale, their dependence on the

The amphitheatre and theatre at Arles, southern France

The Roman theatre at Orange, southern France

towns is obvious. The same pattern is to be seen all over the Empire with little variation except that imposed by geography and climate. The citizens of the Empire travelled frequently from country to country exchanging ideas and customs, for there were no bars on travel, and no strong nationalistic feelings: it was more important to be a Roman citizen than a Gaul or a Cilician, a Briton or a Cretan.

The tombstones of 'foreigners' who settled and died in Britain are quite numerous: two deserve special mention. The first, found at Tyneside reads: 'To the memory of Barates of Palmyra, standard-maker, aged 68 years.'

Barates, it would seem, is an ex-soldier, perhaps originally from Syria, who had retired to live near Hadrian's Wall, where it is likely he had spent his service, and to make and sell flags and ensigns.

At South Shields is another: the Latin inscription reads: 'To the memory of Regina, of the Catuvellaunian tribe, who died aged 30, freedwoman and wife of Barates of Palmyra (who set this up)'.

Underneath in Palmyrene script is: 'Regina, freedwoman of Barates. Alas!'

Regina sits in a wicker chair, wearing bracelets and a necklace of similar pattern. She holds a distaff and spindle, and an open jewel box; by her left foot is her work basket with its balls of wool.

So here is a soldier from a Syrian oasis, and a slave girl of Belgic descent who had lived in East Anglia, married and living together in the north of England near a wall designed by a Roman emperor who had been born in Spain. The happy combination of races is typical of the Roman Empire, and of the cosmopolitan life of the men and women who peopled its provinces.

The tomb of Regina

CHAPTER NINETEEN

Army

Citizen Soldiers

The growth of Rome to greatness was not due to chance: every stage in its growth was a prize won by its armies. In the earliest days, when the state was threatened, the citizens were hastily summoned from their farms and assembled on the Campus Martius, the Field of Mars, god of war, in prearranged 'centuries'; these were groups of a hundred men, and even when the group was reduced to around 80 men, probably for tactical reasons, the name 'century' was retained. A man's wealth decided which century he should fight in: the richest citizens naturally served as the cavalry, and the poorest as the lightly armed troops who could not afford full armour as protection. The absence of the men from the land they farmed, when the scene of the war was a few miles away from Rome, did not matter very much when the war might last only a few days, and a battle an afternoon.

When the number of Roman citizens increased it was not necessary for all the citizen body to fight, and selective conscription from those owning land was organized. With the extension of Rome's power, soldiers had to fight far from their homes, and when campaigns might last a whole summer, or even for more than a year, pay was introduced so that men could feed, clothe and arm themselves. A settled army organization arose. There were four legions, each of between 4,000 and 5,000 men divided into companies known as *cohortes*. A force of similar size was conscripted from the 'allies', who over the years took the place of the legionary cavalry and the light-armed troops. In battle the companies were arranged into three lines with spaces between each company. The front lines consisted of young men, still to prove themselves, equipped with javelins and spears (*hastae*), known as *hastati*: the second line of *principes* was formed of older men with superior weapons, and cylindrical shields. In the third line were the *triarii*, veterans of proved courage.

Livy describes the manner in which these lines went into action:

When an army was drawn up in these lines, the first to engage were the hastati: if they could not drive off the enemy, they retreated slowly between the gaps in the line of principes, who took up the battle with the hastati following behind. The triarii knelt beneath their standards, with the left leg thrust forward, and with their shield propped on their shoulders; they held their spears slanting upward with the butt end firmly resting on the ground, like a bristling line of defence-works. If the principes also were unsuccessful they withdrew steadily to the triarii: this is the origin of the expression, when people are in difficulties, 'Now we're down to the triarii'.

When the hastati and principes had retreated through spaces in their line, the triarii stood up and immediately closed their ranks, blocking the lanes as it were, and since there were no more reserves fell on the enemy in one complete mass. The enemy, charging, as they thought, defeated men, were terrified by this as they saw a new army rise up in even greater numbers.

(Livy, VIII, 8)

In time of crisis, in the wars against Hannibal for example, the legions could be rapidly expanded, and even slaves were enrolled in the ranks. Polybius estimates that when Hannibal crossed the Alps the total numbers of Romans and allies able to bear arms were not less than 700,000 footsoldiers, and 70,000 horsemen. All these, of course were never engaged at one time, but there were huge armies: at the battle of Cannae, for instance, Livy estimates that 50,000 were killed, 4,500 were captured and 19,000 escaped, and other historians put the figures considerably higher. But the ease with which Hannibal's much smaller army defeated them, and the enormous casualty figures, indicate that the standard of training in these large, hastily conscripted, forces was pathetically low.

The Legionary Soldier – Marius' Mule

At the end of the next century, a war in Africa, and the threat of an invasion into Italy by half a million wandering Gauls and Germans, showed the need for such a rapid expansion in the size of the army that the ordinary methods of conscription were inadequate. The commander-in-chief, Marius, allowed all citizens, whether they had property or not, to enrol on a permanent basis, making the army their career. All men were issued with the same weapons, and underwent the same rigorous training, so that the distinction between the lines disappeared. The former part-time army of landholders had been replaced by an almost professional army. The Senate approved this new development in the hope of removing the large numbers of unemployed who thronged the city, but in doing so they had doomed the Republic. The propertyless volunteers signed on for 16, later 20, years in the hope of booty, and with the promise of grants of land at the end of their service. Since the Senate failed to devise a regular system of granting land, men due for discharge looked to their generals to provide it, and consequently owed their loyalty to a man and not to the state. Supported by their legions, army commanders like Sulla and Pompey could intervene decisively in government: the last in the line of ambitious generals were Julius Caesar and Augustus, who ended the Republic and founded the Principate.

The reforms of Marius and the extension of the citizenship to all free Italians by 89 BC brought to an end the difference between Roman and allied contingents. The cavalry and light-armed troops, called *auxilia*, were now recruited in the provinces. They were organized into cohorts of 500 or 1,000 men, divided like the legions into centuries of roughly 80 men. The cavalry cohorts were also known as *alae*, wings. The auxiliary infantry had specialized rôles: they were archers, with bows of steel and ivory, slingers firing roundshot with speed and accuracy, or swimmers who guided horses across rivers while holding their weapons clear of the water. The auxilia were paid less than legionary soldiers, but at the end of their service they were granted citizenship, which must have seemed reward enough.

The tombstone of Rufus Sita, an auxiliary cavalryman, was found just outside the colonia *at Gloucester, in England*

When Augustus emerged as sole ruler of the Empire there were over 60 legions under arms. The standing army, whose task from now on was to protect the frontiers of the Empire, was reduced to about 30 legions, each with between 5,000 and 6,000 men. Every legion had a name and number – the four that invaded Britain, for example, were the Second Augusta (The Emperor's Own), the Ninth Hispana (The Spaniards), the Fourteenth Gemina (Gemina, twin, indicates that this legion had been formed from the amalgamation of two others), and the Twentieth Valeria (The Valerians). Their senior officer was a *legatus*. In each legion were 60 centuries of about 80 men, commanded by a centurion: other officers were the *optio*, or second in command, the *signifer* or standard bearer, who was also the treasurer of the men's burial club, and the *tesserarius* who was responsible for the watchword.

Roman centurion's helmet with eagle decoration

The legionaries were highly trained men. As well as being the foot-soldiers of the line they were skilled engineers, road-makers and bridge-builders, surveyors, carpenters, masons and artillerymen. Many of the great roads and fine new towns in the provinces were planned and built by the men of the legions, as well as the forts and walls that defended the frontiers. In battle the auxiliaries used to fight in front of the legions, and on the flanks, to shield the legionaries, whose skills were so much harder to replace, and many battles were won by the auxiliaries before the legions went into action at all.

The photograph of the model of a legionary soldier from the Grosvenor Museum at Chester, England, shows his large shield and efficient body-armour. The metal strips were probably fitted loosely with thongs on a leather jerkin to allow freedom of movement; a scarf was worn round the neck to prevent the metal chafing it. On the march he carried two javelins: the shaft was of wood, the metal section of soft iron. Only the point, and the socket into which the wood fitted were hardened: the javelin was thrown at a range of about 30 yards, and the soft metal of the shank bent when it landed; if it hit the ground it would bend and be useless to throw back, and if it pierced the shield or armour, it would be difficult to pull out.

After hurling his javelins, the legionary followed up with his short stabbing sword (*gladius*): he did not waste time slashing, or raise his arm high and so expose his side, but stabbed at the face and stomach of the enemy. The sword was carried on his right side in a wooden or leather sheath, and hanging from the left of his belt was a dagger (*pugio*) or knife. His thick-soled heavy sandals were studded with hobnails: he wore a linen vest, on top of that a woollen tunic, and in cold weather a rough woollen cloak. In difficult country when his gear could not be carried on wagons he had to shoulder not only all his weapons but also rations for a fortnight, trenching tools, a couple of heavy stakes which were used in the camp fortifications and all his cooking pots as well. Little wonder legionaries were called *muli Mariani*, Marius' mules.

A model of a legionary soldier

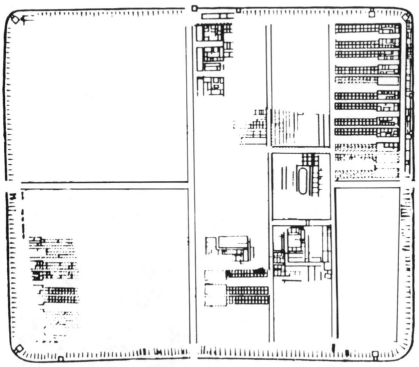

A reconstruction of the corner of the fortress at Caerleon in southern Wales

Pay and Conditions

In the time of the Empire a legionary signed on for 20, sometimes 25, years. His pay was quite small, and he had to pay for his own food and clothing. He ate simply – corn made into a gruel or porridge, bread, cheese and beans – and drank cheap vinegary wine. Since his food used up a third of his pay we can have some idea of the value of his earnings. His life was tough, and discipline hard. When the German legions mutinied in AD 15, their ringleaders incited them by recalling their sufferings: of course they exaggerated, but an extract from such a speech recorded by Tacitus probably contains a good deal of truth:

> Nothing has been done over the years to remove abuses: old men have been serving for 30 or 40 years, their bodies maimed by wounds. Discharge does not mean an end of service; we are kept in the reserve, still under canvas, enduring the same fatigues under another name. And if anyone lives through all these dangers, he is sent to the ends of the earth and given a water-logged marsh or unploughed mountain which they call a 'farm'. It's a hard life with nothing to show for it: body and soul are worth a couple of coins a day, and this has to provide clothes, weapons, tents and the bribes for the sergeant if we want to avoid a beating or non-stop fatigue duty. There's no rest from beatings or wounds: the winter is awful, we spend the summer working: war is dreadful and peace a profitless bore. There'll be no relief till terms of service are fixed: we want a rise in pay, a 16-year contract, with no service in the reserve, and a lump-sum at the end of it, paid in cash on the spot.

> (Tacitus, *Annals* II, 16)

Routine

Terms of service *were* gradually improved, but army life was always hard and busy. A Jewish priest, named Josephus, was captured by the Romans during the Jewish rebellion in Israel: in his account of the war, published in AD 75, he includes this admiring account of the victorious army:

> They seem to be born with swords in their hands: they never stop training, and their training is as hard as real war. Every day a soldier exercises as keenly as if he were in action. Consequently they don't regard fighting as very difficult, for they are never thrown out of their usual formation, never paralysed with fear or exhausted by hard work.
>
> They never let the enemy catch them unawares. When they invade an enemy's country, they always build a camp before they engage in battle. They don't build it in any random fashion, nor do they work in a muddle or get in each other's way. They level the ground if it is uneven, and mark out a square for the encampment, taking a mass of men and tools along with the army to build it. Inside, it is divided into rows for the tents, and from the outside the perimeter looks like a wall, with towers spaced out at regular intervals. Between the towers they set up various types of artillery, for firing stones or arrows. A gate is made in each side of this surrounding rampart: the baggage animals can get in easily, and the gates are wide enough for the troops to dash out on quick raids in an emergency. Streets divide the camp conveniently into quarters. The officers' quarters are in the middle, and the general's HQ, which is like a small temple, is in the exact centre. What emerges is something very like a city: there is a market place, a craftsmen's section, and offices where the centurions and officers settle disputes among the men. Both the outer wall and the buildings are finished in next to no time, because the workmen are so skilled and numerous. They dig a ditch round outside the wall, if necessary, two metres deep and two metres wide. When they have finished building the wall they go to

their quarters in the tents by companies, in a quiet and orderly manner. All their other fatigue duties are performed by companies in the same disciplined and reliable way, the collection of food, wood and water when they are needed. The time for breakfast and dinner is not left for the men to choose; they all have their meals at the same time. The times for sleeping, getting up or sentry-duty are all signalled by a trumpet-call: in fact nothing is done without the word of command.

At dawn the men report to their centurions, who then go together to salute the tribunes: all the officers then go to the commander-in-chief. He gives them the watchword, according to custom, and the other orders to be conveyed to the other ranks. In battle they maintain the same discipline: they advance, retreat or wheel round by units, as is necessary.

When it is time to break camp the trumpet sounds, and there is instant activity. They take down the tents, and pack everything for departure. The trumpet sounds again, for them to get ready; they quickly pile the baggage on the mules and pack animals, and stand ready waiting, like runners at the starting line. Then they set the camp on fire, so that it cannot be used by the enemy, for they can easily build another one for themselves. The trumpet for departure sounds a third time, to hurry on anyone who is slow, so that no one is left out of the ranks. Then the herald stands on the general's right hand, and calls out three times to ask if they are ready to fight. They shout out three times in reply, 'Yes, ready!', almost without waiting for the herald to ask, and filled with a martial enthusiasm they raise their right hands in the air as they shout. They then march forward quietly in good order, each man keeping his place in the ranks, as he would in battle.

(Josephus, *Wars of the Jews* III, 72–105)

In battle the steadiness of the legions, their discipline and fire-power were devastatingly effective, even against enemy forces far superior in number. On one occasion in Britain, for example, after Boudicca's rebellion a Roman force of perhaps 9,000 men faced a British host of unparalleled size, 'so confident that they had brought their wives to see their victory, placing them on carts pitched round the edge of the battlefield'. The general spoke to encourage his men; when the enemy approached he gave the signal.

At first the legion stood still, not moving a step; then, as the enemy moved closer, they launched their javelins with unerring aim, and charged in wedge formation. The auxiliary charge was as fierce, and the levelled lances of the cavalry broke any vestige of resistance. The rest of the enemy turned tail, but escape was difficult as the ring of carts blocked their path. Our men slaughtered their women as well, and their oxen, pierced with spears, added to the piles of dead.

(Tacitus, *Annals* XIV, 37)

Here the courage of the men and their limited hand-weapons had won the day: a later account of the legions in full array with all their equipment explains why they were irresistible:

The legion is victorious because of the number of the soldiers and the types of machines. First of all, it is equipped with hurling machines which no breastplate or shield can withstand. They have a *ballista* mounted on a carriage for every century: each of these has mules and a detail of 11 men for loading and firing. The larger these are, the greater the distance and penetration of the missiles. They are used not only to defend the camps, but firing from behind the heavy armed infantry in the field they provide covering fire. Neither the armoured cavalry of the enemy, nor his infantry with their shields, can hold their ground against their firepower.

There are usually 55 mounted ballistas like this in every legion. In the same way, each of the ten cohorts has an *onager*, drawn ready-loaded on carriages, so that if there is an attack on the ramparts the camp can be defended with arrows and stones.

(Vegetius, II, xxiii)

A Roman ballista bolt, shot at Maiden Castle in Dorset in England in AD 44, found during excavations lodged in the front of a British defender's spine, after passing right through his body

The system of training, and rigorous army discipline, which guaranteed this efficiency, remained unchanged for many years. But gradually, as provincials were admitted to the legions, the difference between legionaries and auxiliaries disappeared. The emperor Hadrian, in order to encourage the provincials to enter the army, introduced the policy of recruiting the legions from the provinces in which they were stationed: a German who enlisted, for instance, in one of the legions guarding the Rhine could expect to stay there for the rest of his life. The temporary camps, too, were converted into permanent fortresses with both walls and buildings of stone. It might be expected that such a policy would produce slackness, and Hadrian himself spent half his reign touring the provinces to inspect his troops and to ensure a high standard of discipline. But afterwards these high standards did deteriorate: soldiers 'married' local girls – though this was officially forbidden – and were more interested in cultivating their small-holdings, or in trading, than in the rigours of military discipline. In the anarchy of the third century the soldiers were granted continual increases of pay, and all sorts of special privileges, as emperors attempted to buy their loyalty. But as home recruitment continued to decline, barbarians from the wrong side of the imperial frontiers were enrolled into the army in ever larger numbers. Since these mercenaries owed allegiance to the paymaster rather than to any idea of patriotism, their loyalty was always suspect.

Roman soldiers building a wall. This scene comes from the huge relief spiralling round Trajan's column. Such scenes are invaluable evidence for the dress, weapons and activities of the Roman army on campaign at this time

By the time of Constantine the vigorous efficiency of the legions had gone, and the training programmes outlined by Josephus were old-fashioned. Leaving the troops on the frontiers as peasant soldiers, tied to the land, Constantine instituted mobile armies, composed almost entirely of armed cavalry, stationed behind the frontiers, but ready to ride wherever danger threatened. For a hundred years and more they kept the hosts of barbarians at bay, and even when the Roman armies disappeared, as the finances of the Empire collapsed and enormous hordes swept in, Constantine's military organisation, in which the cavalry replaced the infantry as the basic force of the army, persisted for centuries. The huge mounted armies of the Middle Ages stem from this final development of the Roman army.

CHAPTER TWENTY

From Order to Chaos

The 'Five Good Emperors'

When in AD 96 the Senate decided that the times needed another emperor, not liberty, their choice fell on one of their own number, a decent old lawyer named Nerva. He introduced many sensible ideas in his short reign. When the Praetorian Guard, indignant at having no voice in the election, threatened trouble, Nerva adopted as his son, partner and successor, an eminent soldier called Trajan. Thus at last a sensible answer to the problem of the imperial succession was found: the emperor, with the title of Augustus, chose carefully a younger and able colleague, with the title of Caesar, whom he could train. On the death of Augustus, the Caesar assumed his position and title, and chose his own Caesar, and so on.

In his relations with the Senate, too, Nerva set a pattern that was followed by the next four emperors. They consulted the Senate regularly, submitting legislation to it for approval, and keeping it fully informed. They swore on oath not to execute any senator unless he had previously been condemned by his fellow senators after a free trial.

More and more senators were now drawn from all areas of the Empire: especially important were those from Asia Minor and other eastern provinces, where the Greek-speaking population began increasingly to be involved in imperial administration. Large numbers of senators and equites took part in provincial and municipal government: it is not surprising that a greater interest in the provinces is shown by Trajan and his successor, Hadrian, for these were the first emperors to be of 'foreign', in this case Spanish, origin.

The emperor Trajan

191

Nerva also began a remarkable philanthropic practice that lasted over 200 years: large sums of money were set aside to provide loans for farmers at a low rate of interest, an action which guaranteed poor farmers their livelihood, and assured a steady agricultural labour force. More important, the interest on these loans was used to support and educate orphans and the children of the poor: an impressive record of such donations survives on the façade of the new speakers' platform he put up in the Forum.

During Trajan's reign (AD 98–117) the Empire reached its greatest extent. He overran a large part of the Parthian empire, occupying Armenia, Mesopotamia and Assyria. His campaigns over the Danube, which added Dacia as yet another province, are recorded in a series of sculptured pictures spiralling up the massive pillar known as Trajan's Column. The title conferred on him by a grateful Senate, *Optimus Princeps*, 'Best of Rulers', is a tribute both to his military prowess and to his benevolent concern for his subjects.

Trajan's column, commemorating his campaigns in Dacia

Hadrian

When Trajan died, the transfer of power to Hadrian was uneventful. He spent over half of his long reign (AD 117–38) outside Italy, touring the provinces. Believing that the Empire was too large, he withdrew from Trajan's new conquests in the Parthian empire; in Britain he set a limit to the province with his famous Wall, and in Germany the actual frontier of the Empire was marked with a great customs barrier of earthwork and palisade. Cities throughout the world were encouraged to aim, first at 'Latin status', which granted citizenship to their magistrates, then at the status of *municipia*, whereby citizenship was allowed to all.

In the past, provincial governors had controlled both soldiers and tax officials, and conducted a census or a campaign with equal authority. Now for the first time military and civil careers were separated, and senators and equites received specific training in the interests of the state. From this time onward a steadily increasing proportion of the inhabitants of the Empire was involved in the running of it, though the dangers of a system in which fewer people were engaged in production and more and more in record-keeping had not yet been seen.

The rule of Antoninus Pius (AD 138–61) was recognized even while he was alive as a 'Golden Age', so great were the blessings of international peace and unparalleled material prosperity. Edward Gibbon, the English historian, was no less certain:

> If a man were called to fix the period in the history of the world, during which the condition of the human race was most happy and prosperous, he would, without hesitation, name that which elapsed from the death of Domitian to the accession of Commodus.

But it is likely, in fact, that this was a dangerous complacency: the rich and the powerful were so content that they thought any change must be for the worse, and neglected the unhappiness of the poor within the Empire, and the envy of the barbarians outside it.

Under the last of the 'Five Good Emperors', Marcus Aurelius (AD 161–80), the first cracks in this happy state began to appear. He was forced to spend most of his reign in

193

frontier campaigns, as barbarians on the far banks of the Rhine, Danube and Euphrates attempted to migrate into the Empire. Taxes were raised, and thousands of men conscripted into the legions. Shockingly, plague spread from the east throughout the Empire. For the first time people began to wonder about the omnipotence of the Roman world, and looked with worried eyes at the vast sums of money poured out to defend it.

The End of the 'Golden Age'

Despite these difficulties, Aurelius was on the point of final victory when he died. Unhappily he had abandoned the principle of choosing the best man to succeed, and left the throne to his son, Commodus. According to Cassius Dio he turned out to be 'a greater curse to the Romans than any pestilence or crime'. He at once made peace with the barbarians and hurried back to a life of luxury and sadistic pleasure at Rome, which he decreed should be renamed Commodiana. He entrusted the government to a series of short-lived advisers, and used the threat of renewed treason trials to extort money from the rich.

In AD 192 assassins replaced him with Pertinax, who had been Aurelius' right-hand man. In three months of vigorous and honourable government he set out to undo the damage done by Commodus. But as his measures included stricter conditions of service for the Praetorian Guard, as if to show that the real power lay with them and not the Senate, the Praetorians murdered Pertinax, and put the throne up for auction. An aged and incompetent senator named Didius Julianus won with a promise of 25,000 sesterces per man. The Senate had no choice but to ratify his election.

But now three separate army groups on the frontiers, jealous of Praetorian arrogance, hailed its own commander as emperor. Septimius Severus, from Pannonia, easily won the race to Rome. Julianus was deposed, condemned by the Senate, and executed by the Guard that had sold him his throne. Severus had the good sense to replace the existing Praetorians with men chosen from his own legions. He overcame his rivals, Pescennius from Syria, and Albinus from Britain, in four years of ruinous war, maintaining the loyalty of his soldiers with lavish gifts.

Septimius Severus

Fourteen years of restless and successful campaigning followed as a series of attacks was made from lands outside the Empire: to pay for it he was forced to devalue the currency and double taxation. Italians now had to pay taxes as well, for Severus, who had been born in north Africa, saw no reason why they should be treated more generously than the provincials. When Severus, worn out by his ceaseless exertions, died at York, in Britain in AD 211, the principate, so happy under Antoninus, had turned into a ruthless military dictatorship. His dying words to his sons were recorded by Dio Cassius:

> Stick together, spend your money on the troops, and let everyone else go hang!

(Dio Cassius, LXXVI, 15)

Caracalla soon murdered his brother, but followed the rest of his father's advice, increasing army pay by 50 per cent. Equally expensive was his policy of *paying* the barbarians to stay away from the frontiers! It has been suggested that when he granted citizenship to every freeborn inhabitant of the Empire in AD 212 he did so to increase the number of people from whom he could collect taxes without raising too much antagonism, and not because he was prompted by a philanthropic desire to improve the lot of his people.

Women Behind the Throne

Caracalla was murdered in AD 217 by his Praetorian Prefect, Macrinus, who became the first emperor never to have been a senator. But within a year Macrinus was killed and replaced by a distant relative of Caracalla: Elagabalus was only 15, but was supported by his grandmother, Julia Maesa. His claim to the name Severus had been enough to win the support of the eastern armies, always mawkishly sentimental towards members of the 'royal family'. Elagabalus was a religious fanatic, devoted to spreading the worship of a Syrian sun-god. His behaviour was outlandish: in addition he completely neglected anything connected with the administration. The only surprise is that he lasted four years before the Praetorians murdered him. But the soldiers sentimentally clung to the Severan family, and chose Elagabalus' cousin Alexander. Since he was still only 13 the real power lay in the hands of his mother, Julia Mamaea. He was always content to be guided by her, so in reality the Romans were from AD 222–35 governed by an empress.

She realized that the attempts of her predecessor to secure the loyalty of the soldiers by increasing their pay had only made them greedy for more. Accordingly she did her best to magnify the prestige and apparent authority of the Senate, handing over the management of the Empire to a small council of senators drawn from the larger body. A distinguished lawyer, Ulpian, was then chosen to command the Praetorian Guard.

For 12 years the Empire enjoyed unaccustomed peace and stability. In order to diminish the importance and power of the armies Alexander and his mother avoided any frontier disturbance which might have required military intervention, and encouraged a wide range of civilian activities. Teachers and scholars were subsidised; landlords who improved their property were excused taxes; everybody engaged in a trade or industry that served the capital was enrolled in a specific guild and carefully supervised.

Sadly their efforts were in vain. A new and aggressive Persian king invaded the eastern provinces: a partial victory for Alexander was not enough to secure his troops' loyalty. When German tribes threatened the Rhine frontier Alexander attempted to bribe the mutinous legions. Before he could win enough time to arrange to replace them Alexander and his mother were butchered in a riot. The throne went to the Thracian Maximinus – a half-barbarian who could barely speak the Latin tongue, an ex-shepherd who had never been to Rome.

Julia Mamaea

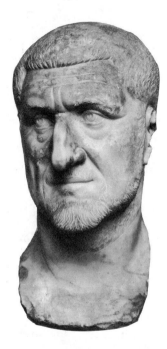

Maximinus Thrax

Breakdown

Chaos followed. Between AD 235 and 284 over 50 Augusti or Caesars were nominated by one army or another: one was captured by the Persians, another died of the plague: the rest all met a violent end. Two parts of the Empire broke away: for 15 years there was a separate 'Empire of the Gauls' which included Britain and Spain, and in the east Queen Zenobia of Palmyra for a few years set up an empire which stretched from Asia Minor to Egypt. Barbarians flooded over the frontiers, plague and famine devastated huge areas of the provinces. Grinding taxation ruined farmers and townspeople alike: thousands ran off to the woods and joined bands of outlaws swollen by deserters from the armies, and these ransacked the countryside, robbing and burning. The population fell disastrously, so barbarian mercenaries were hired to defend the frontiers. To find their pay the emperors had to devalue the coinage again and again – copper coins were coated with a wash of silver and issued as solid silver. Since the coinage could not be trusted a primitive system of barter took its place.

Order Restored

At last the civil wars slowly came to an end. With the accession of Diocletian in AD 284 political stability was restored, and the boundary lands were secured, but at enormous cost. The state was militarized, and the soldiers became the privileged class instead of the landed aristocracy. Retired centurions were given huge grants and promoted to the equestrian order; equestrians replaced senators as provincial governors and legionary commanders. The Senate was no longer asked to regularize the emperor's powers: after AD 280 it never issued a decree, and became nothing more than the city council of Rome.

Diocletian increased the size of the army, and also the number of generals, so that each had fewer men under his command, and would thus be less likely to risk revolt. In the same way the provinces were divided into a greater number of smaller provinces: groups of these were then formed into *dioceses*, each under a *vicarius*. As each province needed a certain number of officials, the civil service grew larger too. But there were more important changes: the Empire was split into two parts; Diocletian became Augustus of the East, Maximian, a fellow soldier, Augustus of the West. To each Augustus a Caesar was appointed heir, with his own province to govern: in effect the Empire was divided into four tetrarchies.

The greatest hardship in ordinary life was the continuing rise of prices. Diocletian, in a vain effort to control inflation, issued a list of maximum prices: some examples follow:

Pork	1 pound	12 denarii
Beef	1 pound	8 denarii
Chicken	1 brace	60 denarii
Butter	1 pound	16 denarii
Soldiers' boots		100 denarii
Shoes, patrician		150 denarii
Shoes, senatorial		100 denarii
Shoes, equestrian		70 denarii
Boots, women's		60 denarii

And wages, too, were fixed:

Farm labourer	per day	25 denarii
Carpenter	per day	50 denarii
Picture painter	per day	150 denarii
Barber	per head	2 denarii
Teacher of Greek or Latin	monthly per pupil	200 denarii

However, the increasing demands on the Empire's resources led to a shortage of money, and the price rises were not prevented. The vast army of soldiers was shadowed by another army of census-takers, as taxation was reassessed. The census was taken every five years: first, to enable it to be taken efficiently, the citizens had to stay on their land while they were counted: soon they were required to stay on the land where the census-takers had found them. In the end these compulsions led to a rigid control of labour: everyone now worked for the good of the state, as the state directed.

Perhaps the most surprising thing that Diocletian did was to resign in AD 305, persuading his fellow Augustus to abdicate at the same time. Diocletian intended that the two Caesars should succeed, but within months the system broke down as the soldiers again tried to dictate the succession to suit themselves. Four rival Augusti emerged. One was Constantine, who had fled for safety to Britain, and made claim to his share of the Empire from there. He believed that Diocletian's division of the Empire into four parts was mistaken, and over the years fought and defeated his rivals one by one, to become sole emperor in AD 323.

'The Tetrarchs' – a statue group thought to represent the two Augusti and their respective Caesars

Constantine

Eusebius, Bishop of Caesarea and a close friend of the emperor, who wrote a scholarly history of the Church, tells how Constantine, on the way to one battle, saw in a vision, a cross in the sky, and the inscription 'With this sign conquer!' Thereafter his troops carried the Chi-Rho monogram on their shield, a sign formed from the first two letters of the name Christ, in Greek (see p. 170). He guaranteed freedom of worship for the Christian Church, though he was not baptized himself until shortly before his death in AD 337.

The conversion of Constantine eventually led to the union of Church and state: imperial taxes went to the coffers of the Church, bishops became civil servants, and the titles, rules and regulations of the Empire invaded the Church.

But despite a more enlightened attitude to religious matters, every soul in the Empire was governed by a severe autocracy. From this time onward the survival of the state depended on the maintenance of vast armies of soldiers, and armies of civil servants nearly as large. The task of these civil servants was to wring enough money out of the rest of the population to pay for the armies and themselves. Constantine and his successors issued decrees by which craftsmen, peasants, civil servants, fishermen and soldiers alike were tied to their jobs for ever: a son was forced to enrol in his father's guild, and take up his father's occupation.

The bond of tenant farmer to the land was very strong: since he was forced to purchase his seed and stock, and hire his tools, from his landlord, a single poor harvest could lead to lifelong debt and bondage. From this state developed the feudal system that spread throughout Europe in the Middle Ages, for landlords were tied to the land they owned as much as the serfs who tilled it for them.

A massive head of the emperor Constantine, more than 2.6 metres (8 feet) high. The seated statue from which it came measured 12 metres (40 feet) and dominated Constantine's basilica in the Roman Forum

For all these harsh measures and frantic edicts the economic decline continued unchecked. The West was stripped bare and beggared by taxation. Huge resources remained in the East, however: so, in order to be nearer these resources, and to be better able to guard the Danube and Euphrates where the greatest perils lay, Constantine moved from Rome, and built a new capital on the site of the old Greek city of Byzantium, now renamed Constantinople – 'Constantine's city'. Here the Roman Empire was to last for a thousand years, right up to AD 1453, when weakened and impoverished it was at last overrun by the Turks.

Even in the West the end was slow to come: despite the countless scares and unceasing struggles on one frontier or another, millions of Roman citizens were born, worked, grew old and died under the protection of the state: no matter how grim the taxation, no matter how tedious their daily round, their lives were infinitely more secure and desirable than those of the poor creatures outside the Empire's boundaries. But thousands of miles away in Asia the savage Huns began to move westward, driving the Alani and Goths before them. At last in AD 367 the defences broke, and the great armies shredded away; the Visigoths, Suebi and Vandals set up their own kingdoms within the Empire.

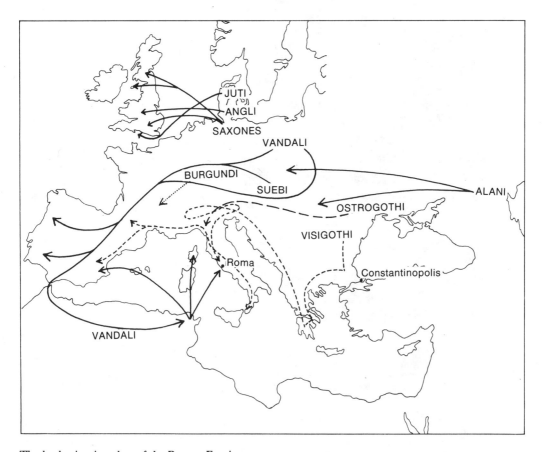

The barbarian invaders of the Roman Empire

200

For a short time the west was regained and the Empire re-united by the colossal exertions of the great Theodosius. But in AD 408 Alaric the Goth broke into Italy, and sacked Rome two years later. In that year, AD 410, the legions stationed in Britain were withdrawn to defend the shrinking Empire. When the towns of Britain appealed to Rome for help against the invading Saxons, the emperor Honorius could do nothing but encourage them to look to their own defence. But as the map shows, the troops could not succeed. Before long the Goths and Vandals had occupied Spain: east Gaul was held by the Burgundians, the north by the Franks.

In AD 429 the Vandals moved on to north Africa. Then in AD 451 the Roman general Aetius won the last great victory of Roman arms when he drove the terrible Attila the Hun out of central France. But only four years later Vandal pirates sailing over from Africa sacked the city of Rome so thoroughly that half of it was left derelict for ever, and its population sunk to around twenty thousand, for all the major administrative services distributing food and water had broken down. And in AD 476 the last emperor of the West, Romulus Augustulus, was deposed by a mutinous captain of mercenaries, the German Odoacer. There were no more: the Empire of the West was over.

CHAPTER TWENTY-ONE

Rome's Legacy

The last years of the Western Empire must have brought untold horrors for millions. But it must not be thought that there was a sudden change in AD 476 from cultured comfort to barbarous squalor. The real tragedy lay in the gradual breakdown of the law, order and efficiency of the Roman Empire. There was no one to order or pay for the repair of roads, aqueducts or public buildings: as coinage lost its value, and barter took its place, all the organized systems of food distribution disappeared. The peasants, who had been tied to the land, in desperation rose up and murdered their masters: they let cultivated lands revert to scrubland and forest, and so soon died of starvation in their thousands.

Yet not everything was lost. As the remaining citizens and the barbarian invaders settled down and learnt to live side by side, common languages developed out of the various provincial dialects. Their roots were Latin, but not the literary Latin of Cicero or Virgil. Even in Rome's greatest days there had been major differences between the Latin used in books and public speeches, and the everyday Latin of peasant farmers, soldiers and shopkeepers. Even greater were the differences between the Latin of Rome and the Latin of the provinces, where local languages and dialects combined or competed with the official language of the Empire. All spoken languages change gradually, and as the years passed these regional variations of Latin blended with the languages of the invaders and became the early forms of Spanish, Portuguese, Provençal, French, Italian and Romanian – the so-called Romance languages. Even in

	RABIES PREVENTION	**No animals from abroad may be landed**
	LA PREVENTION DE LA RAGE	**Défense de débarquer des animaux**
	TOLLWUT VERHÜTUNG	**Es ist verboten, Tiere an Land zu bringen**
	LA PREVENZIONE DELLA RABBIA	**É vietato portare animale dall'estero**
	LA PREVENCION DE LA RABIA	**Es prohibido desembarcar animales del extranjero**

Can you identify the languages used on this sign? Which words are Latin-based?

countries where other influences were stronger, as in Germany or the Celtic parts of Britain, clear traces of Latin can still be found, while English contains thousands of Latin-based words.

Centuries later, the explorers and empire-builders of Western Europe carried their languages to the ends of the earth – almost as Virgil had predicted – so that people as far apart as Chile, Tanzania, Hong Kong, India, the Philippines, the United States and Australia all speak languages which are based mainly, or in part, on Latin, while the Roman alphabet is used even more widely. English-speaking nations prove the durability of Latin every day: more than 60 of the words used so far in this chapter have Latin roots, and many commonplace words and abbreviations are taken directly from the ancient language – post mortem, et cetera, alibi, visa, habeas corpus, alma mater, AD, a.m., Q.E.D., e.g., and many others. The British pound (£) derives from the Latin letter L, which stood for *libra* which meant 'a pound-weight'. The American 'cent' comes from the Latin *centum*, meaning a hundred.

But much more survived the decay and collapse of the Western Empire in the fifth century. Constantine's new city at Constantinople (see p. 200) became the capital of the Empire of the East: we now call it the Byzantine Empire, after the Greek city Byzantium which first occupied the site. This Christian Empire of the East outlived Rome's Western Empire by almost a thousand years, and preserved much of the civilizations of Greece and Rome.

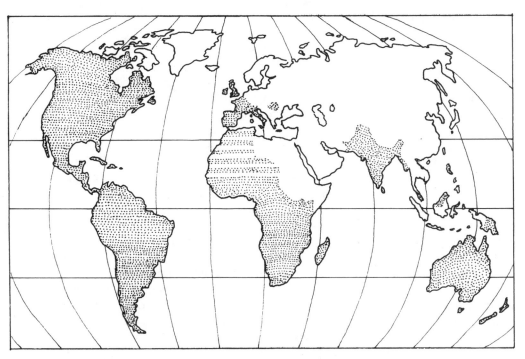

The shaded areas represent countries of the world where Romance languages or English are in everyday use, either as the main written and spoken language, or for official and commercial purposes

Interior of the cathedral of St Sophia at Constantinople. Built in the sixth century by Justinian, this remarkable church, with its soaring arches and mighty dome, surpassed the buildings of Rome itself in splendour

But the Christian Church of the West which had been able to grow from its small beginnings (pp. 169–70) because of the peaceful conditions and reliable communications which the Empire had created, also proved to be a surprisingly effective bridge between the Ancient World and the Middle Ages. After the disintegration of society and the decay of city life, the Church, with its fine buildings, its bishops and its well-ordered constitution, came to be seen as the last guardian of authority and good order. At its head, in Rome, was the Pope, a new Pontifex Maximus, adopting the title held by the chief priest of the old religion (see p. 163). Bishops and church leaders modelled their organization on the administrative machinery of the old Empire – an English archbishop still presides over a 'province'. A succession of Popes tried to create a single universal Christian community under their leadership, just as the Emperors of the second century aimed to establish the unity of the civilized Roman world. The Church's system of law (the so-called 'Canon Law'), administered in its courts, was closely related to the Roman law of the earlier Empire. Church services and ceremonies were all conducted in Latin, and Latin was the language of all religious writing and scholarship.

We have already seen (pp. 158-9) how the Church played a crucial role in preserving many major works of Latin literature and scholarship during the Dark Ages. The tradition they were keeping alive was, of course, 'classical' rather than merely Roman. For eight hundred years before the collapse of the West, almost every aspect of Rome's life and culture had been influenced by Greek civilization (see pp. 24, 36, 71ff., 93, 97, 152ff., 163, etc.). Roman literature, in particular, takes almost all its models from the writings of Greeks. Greek writers had created the main literary categories – including epic, tragedy, comedy, biography, history, lyric poetry and oratory – which their Roman successors like Cicero, Plautus, Lucretius, Virgil, Horace, Ovid, Livy, Seneca and Tacitus used so effectively. Without this 'classical' literature, in both languages, preserved by the Church in the West, and by scholars and libraries in the East, the history and civilization of later Europe would have been very different. In addition to the literary forms, Greek and Roman writers provided much of the subject matter, the stories, themes and plots for their successors throughout Western Europe and the English speaking world. The works of Dante, Chaucer, Milton, Shakespeare, Goethe, Molière, Corneille, Racine, Rousseau, Pope, Shelley, Dryden, Keats, Wordsworth, Byron, Joyce, Pound and Eliot, to name only a few of the most obvious, are influenced at every point by their predecessors in the Ancient World.

In their writings too, the Romans had set out (and the churchmen preserved) the ancients' ideas about government, empire and politics, as well as their moral and religious beliefs. Some of these, like the philosophy of the Stoics (see p. 167), influenced the thinking of the early Christian Fathers. But in the unsettled centuries before the Renaissance, the rulers of empires (like Charlemagne) or of smaller feudal kingdoms were less interested in the theory of government than in effective ways of preserving order (and their thrones). Roman laws provided them with a solid foundation for their power, and in doing so became one of the most important legacies of antiquity. Roman law had been codified, in detail, by the Eastern Roman Emperor Justinian in the sixth century. Many of its principles lie at the heart of modern legal systems, and are still studied in universities and colleges where lawyers are trained. Examples of Justinian's Code include 'no man shall be a judge in his own case', 'no appeal for mercy should be made while a case is being tried' and 'a man should have the right to face his accusers'. The word 'justice' itself derives from the Latin *jus* meaning law.

A mosaic in the church of San Vitale, Ravenna, showing Justinian, who briefly reunited Italy to the Eastern Empire. He is accompanied by guards (note the emblem on the shields), officials and priests, including Archbishop Maximinian

But when interest in the classical times was reawakened during the Renaissance, the other major political legacy of the Ancient World made its impact – the belief in individual freedom which the Greeks had been the first to express in writing, and in their way of life. The Greeks' ideal of freedom was reflected in their eagerness to question and criticize, to experiment and explore themselves and the world around them. One of its most potent results was the emergence of democracy as a method of government, and though imperial Rome gave no real political responsibility to the people, its scholars and writers preserved the ideas of democracy and individual freedom in their writings – ideas which have shaped our lives and communities ever since. Inevitably the emblems and titles of Rome's empire have been adopted by other states and leaders over the centuries: Napoleon I of France claimed the rank of 'Emperor' and 'first consul' in the early nineteenth century, and Mussolini paraded the 'fasces' in Italy during the 1920s and '30s. The imperial eagle, too, displayed by Rome's emperors as a symbol of their power and authority, has been used by nations since ancient times, and is still the national emblem of Germany, Poland and the United States. Russians no longer have Tzars, of course, and Germans have no Kaiser; both titles derive from Caesar. But most nations today incorporate democratic principles in their constitutions. Many call themselves 'Republics', as the Romans did, and, like the United States, name their 'Senate' after the Roman model.

Napoleon I (1769–1821) shown as a modern Roman Emperor in a portrait by Ingres

Poster from the Mussolini era, advertising a competition for grain production. Notice the two appearances of the fasces (in the main picture, and in the emblem, bottom right), symbolising the power of the Fascist state and recalling Rome's imperial heritage

The Capitol in Washington DC where Congress and the Senate meet

*Marcus Aurelius, Emperor
AD 161–80, addressing his
troops. Two standard-bearers
carry the legionary eagle,
the most prized possession of
each legion*

*Nazi storm troopers (SA) with their leader, Ernst Rohm. They carry standards which were clearly
modelled on Roman originals*

In other spheres too, Rome's Empire ensured the survival of many of the finest achievements of antiquity. In scientific and mathematical thinking, the Greeks were supreme. Archimedes discovered fundamental laws of hydrostatics, mechanics and ratios. Aristarchus concluded that the earth was a sphere, spinning in space as it orbited the sun, while Euclid's textbooks on geometry are still widely used by advanced students. Rome's contribution to scientific progress was more practical. By assimilating many of the principles of Greek geometry and trigonometry, Romans became expert surveyors, road builders and water engineers. As Rome's armies advanced, and the Empire grew, surveyors and route measurers went to work, charting distances and listing towns and resting places. All their researches were incorporated into a major geographical treatise by Claudius Ptolemaeus (Ptolemy) in the second century AD. Despite errors and inaccuracies, Ptolemy's writing and maps summarized Roman knowledge of the earth's surface, and remained in use until the Age of Discovery, 14 centuries later. By applying the principles of mechanics Rome's engineers learned to hoist and balance heavy weights, and to solve the problems of architectural stress. Julius Caesar used the skills and knowledge of Alexandrian astronomers to devise a calendar which remains the basis of the one we still use. Aristarchus' astronomical theories inspired Copernicus in the early sixteenth century.

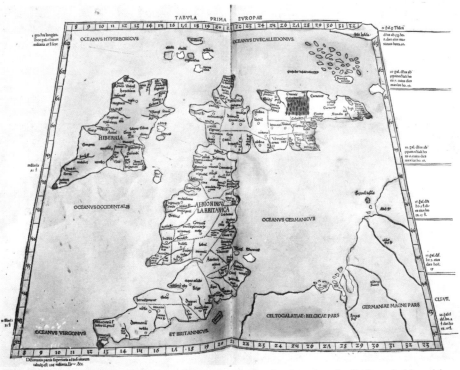

Map of Britain from the second century based on the fixed points given by Ptolemy in his writings. The position shown for Scotland is unusually inaccurate for Ptolemy

Rome's first 'hospital' was the site of the temple of the Greek healing god, Aesculapius. Sick slaves were abandoned here to save their masters the expense of treating them. The Tiber island, where the temple stood, has had a proper hospital since 1548. Notice the span of the Pons Fabricius on the right – the oldest bridge over the Tiber still in use, built in 61 BC. Engraving by the great eighteenth-century engraver, Piranesi

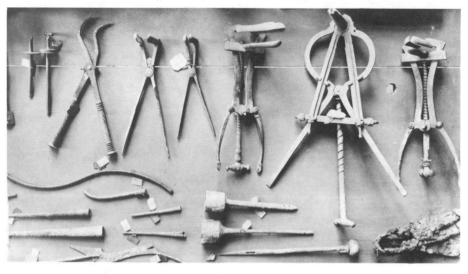

A collection of Roman surgical instruments

Medicine too remained almost unchanged in the years between the outstanding discoveries of the Greeks (Hippocrates in the fifth century BC followed by the Alexandrian anatomists) and the advances of William Harvey, for example, in the seventeenth century. The court physician of the emperor Marcus Aurelius, Galen, wrote extensively on anatomy, physiology, pathology and a wide range of medical subjects. His works remained the standard textbooks in medical schools until the seventeenth century. Roman organizational genius also led to the building of hospitals in communities and military camps: these became a regular feature in Christian times, and provided a model for the hospitals for the sick and outcast in the Middle Ages. Medical practice was also helped by the Romans' recognition of the importance of sanitation. By conveying fresh water into towns and cities along canals and aqueducts, by building underground sewerage systems to remove waste, and by providing public baths and lavatories, Rome achieved standards of hygiene unmatched until Victorian times.

A public lavatory in Ostia, near Rome. Privacy was not a priority for the ancient world

Metal covers for water services in modern Rome. The initials stand for Senatus Populusque Romanus – the Senate and the Roman People. The cover at the top of the picture gives access to a drain and the other one to a water main. The water, Acqua Marcia, comes from one of the sources used by the Romans in Imperial times

The last, and most easily visible, of Rome's major contributions to later history was in art and architecture. In art, as in so much else, Romans acknowledged their debt to the Greeks, and much of the wall painting and sculpture which has survived since ancient times reflects this dependence. Many Roman copies of lost Greek originals can be seen in our museums, and the few paintings which can still be viewed, particularly at Pompeii, or in Etruscan tombs, reveal Greek rather than Roman inspiration. But Roman artists achieved real distinction and originality in their portrait statues and tombstone carvings which still bring the ancient people to life (see, for example pp. 77, 79, 103, 193 and 196). Roman public monuments, too, broke new ground: their triumphal arches and memorial columns were often imitated by later rulers. In particular the finely carved figured friezes, like those on triumphal arches (p. 105), Trajan's column (p. 190), the Augustan Altar of Peace (p. 19) and on hundreds of stone coffins (sarcophagi pp. 78, 164) influenced the medieval craftsmen who carved the figures on the decorated doorways and pillars of their churches and cathedrals. Painters as well as sculptors in the Renaissance also drew inspiration from these relief carvings.

A portrait by the French artist David (1748–1825) of Madame Verninac, wearing an 'Empire' style dress, fashionable during the early nineteenth century

212

As for the architectural heritage of Rome, we learned in Chapters 4 and 12 how builders and designers adopted many of the principles and decorative features of the Greeks. But it was their own independent understanding of the arch, the vault and the dome (see. p. 113), together with their mastery of concrete, which enabled them to construct the imposing public buildings, private palaces, bridges and aqueducts which were such important symbols of Rome's imperial dominance. Some are still in use, particularly the early churches, whose design was closely based on the basilica (see p. 115). The transport systems of most European and Mediterranean countries follow the lines of the original Roman roads (see p. 63) and many historic cities retain the traditional grid pattern in their streets. Today, throughout the world, but particularly in Europe, the Americas and Australasia, we can see buildings, public and private, large and small, with features which originate in the architecture of Greece and Rome.

Chiswick House, near London, built in the classical style in the early eighteenth century

Monticello, Virginia, USA, designed by Thomas Jefferson, artist, linguist, scientist, town planner and author of the Declaration of Independence, in the late eighteenth century. Jefferson had seen Roman buildings in southern France and had become enthusiastic about the classical style

213

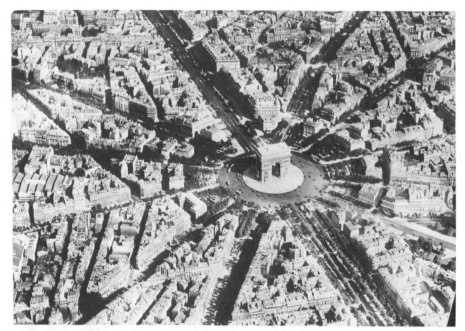

The Arc de Triomphe, Paris

The interior of one of Rome's great churches, St Paul's-outside-the-Walls, completed by the Emperor Honorius in the fifth century AD. Its beams were gilded, its columns made of marble and brightly coloured mosaics lined the nave. Engraving by Piranesi

'If you seek his memorial, look around you.' These words, originally in Latin, were a tribute and epitaph to Sir Christopher Wren. They can be found inscribed in his classical masterpiece, St Paul's Cathedral in London. But they apply equally well to the heritage of the classical world as a whole. The legacy of Rome, together with the achievements of the Greeks which Rome's Empire assimilated and passed on to us, helped to shape our society over the centuries, and still affects our daily lives in many different ways. If we look around us, we may start to discover just how much we owe to the Ancient World.

St Paul's Cathedral, London. Its magnificent classical dome remains one of the city's most famous landmarks

The Latin Language

The Alphabet

Latin is one of the family of Indo-European languages which also includes Greek, Persian, German and Celtic. Brought into Italy at some time before 900 BC, it developed in the plain of Latium, and so is called 'Latin' rather than 'Roman'. It was influenced by Greek, and by the non-Indo-European language of the Etruscans. Originally it had 21 letters, but two more, Y and Z, were added in Cicero's time; but these were only used for words taken into Latin from Greek. The alphabet is

A B C D E F G H I K L M N O P Q R S T V X Y Z

Small letters did not come into use until the Middle Ages. The small form of V was u. In early times C was pronounced like a 'g' in *get*; that is why C is used for the abbreviation of Gaius. Later, C was used for the 'k' sound; then the 'g' sound was represented by C with an added stroke, i.e. G, and K only survives in the word Kalendae and the *praenomen* Kaeso. The letters I and V were also used both as vowels and consonants; the Romans made no distinction *in writing* between vowel I and consonant I (pronounced like y in *yet*), or between vowel V and consonant V (pronounced like the English *w*); in modern Latin texts consonant V is usually printed as v, (e.g. *vultus*) but j is only rarely used for consonant I.

The following letters were used as abbreviations for the very few Latin forenames used by the Roman upper classes.

A	= Aulus	M	= Marcus	S(ex)	= Sextus		
C	= Gaius	M′	= Manius	Ser	= Servius		
Cn	= Gnaeus	Mam	= Mamercus	Sp	= Spurius		
D	= Decimus	P	= Publius	T	= Titus		
K	= Kaeso	Q	= Quintus	Ti	= Tiberius		
L	= Lucius						

The Language

If we look carefully at a page of Latin we shall recognise parts of many of the words: since a vast number of English words are derived from Latin this is hardly surprising. But if we look more closely, we may notice that the same word, if it occurs more than once, may have a different ending, or even two or three different endings. These endings have distinct purposes.

For example, the sentence

senex servos vidit = The old man saw the slaves

In sen*ex* the ending tells us that *senex*, the old man, is the subject of the sentence: in serv*os*, the letters *os* tell us that *servos*, (slaves), is the object and also is plural, and in vid*it* the ending indicates that the subject of this verb, which means 'see', is a singular noun. *servos senex vidit* also means 'The old man saw the slaves'; the order does not affect the meaning, but only gives a slightly different emphasis. Again.

   servi fortes senem viderunt = The brave slaves saw the old man

The different ending to serv*i* tells us that now that the slaves are the subject; the ending of *fortes* (brave) indicates that it agrees with the slaves and not the old man, sen*em* tells us that the old man is now the object, and *viderunt* is the plural form of *vidit*.

This is not the place for a Latin lesson, but you can see how greatly a language that does have different forms of a word, an *inflected* language, as it is called, differs from English though traces of inflexion do still survive in English – I saw him; he saw me; I am, you are, he is; I stand, they stood, and so on.

How complex Latin is may be judged from the following: an ordinary noun has 12 different forms; all nouns have a gender (as in French), either masculine, feminine or neuter (the Latin word for 'neither'): an adjective has 36 forms, and a verb over 150, and of these 150+ forms the three participles and the gerundive are like adjectives, and so each have 36 different endings!

APPENDIX B

Latin Numerals

All Latin numbers were written with seven signs:

   I = 1, V = 5, X = 10, L = 50, C = 100, D = 500, and CIƆ or M = 1,000.

Numbers were written side by side, in descending order, and were added together;
   e.g. III = 3, VII = 7, LXXVII = 77, MDCCCLXVI = 1,866

If a smaller number is placed before, i.e. to the left of, a larger number, then the smaller number is subtracted from the larger number which follows it:
   e.g. IV = 4, IX = 9, XIX = 19, XXIX = 29, XC = 90, MCMXCIV = 1,994

The Romans were not always consistent: IIII is often found, even XXXXXX for LX. For numbers above 1,000, when the additive method might be clumsy, special signs were designed for 5,000, D, and 10,000, ⊚ while a bar written above a number indicates that it is to be multiplied by 1,000 ($\overline{X}$ = 10,000) and a bar with tails above a number shows that it must be multiplied by 100,000 ($\overline{X}$ = 1,000,000).

It will be obvious that these numbers could not be used, as our Arabic numbers may be, to work through calculations. Calculations were worked out in the head or on an abacus, then the answer was written down with the numerical signs above, in just the same way that we use electronic calculators today.

Date-chart

Dates in Roman History		Contemporary Events and Writers
900 BC	First settlements on Palatine and Esquiline hills	*c.* 850 Homer writes *Iliad* and *Odyssey*
753	Foundation of Rome	Hesiod: *Works and Days*, *Theogeny*
	Kings: Romulus	
	Numa Pompilius	
	Tullus Hostilius	
	Ancus Martius	Sappho: love poetry
	Tarquinius Priscus	Solon reforms constitution of Athens
	Servius Tullius	Pisistratus, tyrant of Athens
	Tarquinius Superbus	
509	Republic formed	
506	Battle of Lake Regillus	
494	First plebeian secession	
493	First tribunes appointed	Wars between Greeks and Persians
458	War with Aequi: Cincinnatus	Aeschylus: 7 tragedies survive
450	Twelve Tables of law published	Sophocles: 7 tragedies survive
449	Tribunes increased to 10: sacrosanctity guaranteed by law	Euripides: 19 tragedies survive
		Pericles leads Athens
437	War with Etruscans, Cossus wins *spolia opima*	Parthenon built
421	First plebeian quaestor	Peloponnesian War, Athens *v.* Sparta
410	Rome overcomes Latin League	Aristophanes: 11 comedies survive
406–396	Siege and capture of Veii	Thucydides, historian of Peloponnesian War
390	Gallic tribe sacks Rome	Socrates dies 399
390–38	War with Latin neighbours	Xenophon, *Anabasis*, etc.
367	One consul must be plebeian	Plato, *Republic*, *Dialogues*, etc.
358–351	Successful wars in Etruria	
356	First plebeian dictator	
343–341	1st Samnite war	Demosthenes, orator and statesman
338	Victory over Latins: Latin League dissolved	
337	First plebeian praetor	Alexander the Great
327–311	2nd Samnite War	
321	Defeat at Caudine Forks	
312	Appian Way to Capua built	
311–303	War with Etruscans, Umbrians, Aequi and Marsi	
304	Aqua Claudia built	
298–290	3rd Samnite War	
287	Lex Hortensia: *plebiscita* become law	
280	Pyrrhus lands in Italy	
275	Pyrrhus leaves Italy	

Dates in Roman History		Contemporary Events and Writers
272	Tarentum surrenders	
264–241	1st Punic War	Livius Andronicus: translates Homer into Latin
241	Sicily becomes first Roman province	
220	Via Flaminia built	
218–202	Hannibal: 2nd Punic War. 204 Rome invades Africa	
200–194	War in Greece	Ennius: tragedies, and *Annales*
197	Spain organised as two provinces	Plautus: 20 comedies survive out of 130
179	First stone bridge over Tiber	
177	Sardinia pacified; 175 Corsica annexed	
171–168	War in Greece	
167	Sack of cities in Epirus; 150,000 enslaved	Terence: 6 comedies survive
163	Roman protectorate of Syria	
146	Rome destroys Corinth and Carthage	
144–140	Aqua Marcia built	
133	Pergamum becomes province of Asia Minor	Polybius, *Histories*
	Tiberius Gracchus tribune	
123–2	Gaius Gracchus tribune	
120	Province of Gallia Narbonensis added	
107	Marius consul, defeats Jugurtha	
104–100	Marius, consul again, defeats Cimbri and Teutones	
102	Annexation of Cilicia	
91–90	Social war against Latin allies	
88	Sulla marches on Rome	
87	Marius captures Rome, dies January 86	
82–80	Sulla dictator: dies in 78	
73–71	Spartacus' slave revolt	
70	Crassus and Pompey consuls	Cicero: *in Verrem*, etc.
63	Pompey adds Bithynia et Pontus, Syria, Cyrene and Crete as provinces	Lucretius: *de rerum natura*
	Cicero consul: Catilinarian conspiracy	
60	Alliance of Caesar, Pompey and Crassus	Catullus: love poetry, etc.
59	Caesar consul	Sallust: *bellum Catilinae, bellum Jugurthinum*
58–49	Caesar in Gaul: invades Britain 55 and 54	
53	Death of Crassus	Caesar: *de bello gallico, de bello civili*
49	Caesar crosses Rubicon	Cornelius Nepos: *de viris illustribus*
48	Death of Pompey after Pharsalus	
44	Death of Caesar	
42	Death of Brutus and Cassius at Philippi	
31	Octavian defeats Antony and Cleopatra	Horace: *Odes, Epodes, Satires*, etc.
		Virgil: *Eclogues, Georgics, Aeneid*
	EMPERORS	Livy: History of Rome
		Propertius, Tibullus: love poetry, etc.
27 BC–14 AD	Augustus (new name of Octavian)	Ovid: *Amores, Metamorphoses, Fasti*, etc.
14–37	Tiberius	Life and death of Jesus Christ
37–41	Caligula	
41–54	Claudius; AD 43 invades Britain	
54–68	Nero; AD 60 revolt of Boudicca	Lucan: *Pharsalia*

Dates in Roman History		Contemporary Events and Writers
69	Galba, Otho, Vitellius, Vespasian	Seneca, *Letters to a Stoic*
		Petronius, *Satyricon*
69–79	Vespasian	Pliny the Elder, *Natural History*
79–81	Titus	Pliny the Younger, *Letters*
81–96	Domitian	Statius: *Silvae*, etc.
96–8	Nerva	Tacitus: *Histories, Annals, Agricola*, etc.
98–117	Trajan	Quintilian, *The Education of an Orator*
117–38	Hadrian	Martial: *Epigrams*, Juvenal: *Satires*
138–61	Antoninus Pius	Plutarch, *Parallel Lives*, Suetonius: *Lives of the Caesars*
161–80	Marcus Aurelius (Verus 161–9)	
180–92	Commodus	
193	Pertinax; Didius Julianus	
193–211	Septimius Severus	
193–95	Pescennius Niger	
195–97	Clodius Albinus	
211–84	27 other emperors	
284–305	Diocletian, splits empire into East and West. Six other emperors	Christians persecuted AD 311: The Act of Toleration
306–37	Constantine	AD 337: Constantine baptised into Christian faith
337–78	12 other emperors	
379–95	Theodosius	Christianity becomes official state religion
395–475	24 other emperors	
475–6	Romulus Augustulus	Last Roman emperor in West

Questions

Chapter 1   *The Growth of Rome*

1. Make a list of the advantages of Rome's geographical position.

2. Do you know of any legends about the place you live in? Are legends 'just stories'? Which parts of them could be 'true'?

3. How much can the discoveries of archaeologists contribute to our knowledge of an ancient city? What problems does a modern archaeologist face in investigating a city like Rome or London?

4. How significant an influence did the Etruscans have on the development of early Rome? Try to find pictures of their wall-paintings, and their tombs.

5. Look up the word 'fascism' and find out why the 'fasces' were chosen as a symbol by Mussolini in 1926. Which other Roman emblems have been used by governments and individuals, over the centuries?

6. What are the distinctive features of a Republic?

7. What does the story of the Gauls' conquest of Rome tell you about the character of the early Romans?

8. Estimate the nature and extent of Greek influence on Rome from the city's foundation to 275 BC.

9. In your own words, what was a 'Pyrrhic' victory?

10. Look carefully at the map on p. 12. How do you think did the network of roads contribute to Rome's control of the Italian peninsula? Why were so many colonies on or near the coast?

Chapter 2   *Peoples of Italy*

1. How did the geography of Italy – its fertile plains, rivers, mountains, etc. – affect Roman history?

2. Why did the Romans, rather than the Greeks or the Etruscans, become the masters of Italy?

3. Is Livy's story of Cincinnatus likely to be historically true? Does it matter if it is or not? Why did Livy include such apparently irrelevant detail in it?

221

4. Is the modern family unit less close than the Roman one? Give reasons for your answer.

5. Why did Roman schoolboys learn the Twelve Tables of law by heart for so many centuries after they were published?

6. After 287 BC *plebiscita* – resolutions passed by the plebeian assembly – had the force of law over all the populace. Can you see anything wrong in this?

7. In ancient times the north of Italy was poor, the south prosperous. Why do you think the reverse is the case today?

Chapter 3   *Houses*

1. Why did the Romans adopt Greek architectural designs (and room names) for their houses?

2. Draw the plan of the ground floor of a modern house. How and why does it differ from the plans of Roman houses? Is it better or worse?

3. In what ways are modern apartment blocks likely to be better than Roman *insulae*?

4. Are there modern equivalents to Roman *thermae*? See also Chapter 15.

5. If the design of Roman houses was suitable for the Italian climate, why are modern Italian houses not built to the same design?

6. In what way is it possible that the houses and *insulae* excavated at Pompeii and Ostia may not have been typical of those in the rest of Italy?

7. Is 'mass-production' the only reason for the superiority of modern over Roman furniture?

Chapter 4   *City*

1. List the advantages and disadvantages of the 'grid-iron' pattern for city roads.

2. Why did the Romans copy first Etruscan and then Greek temples rather than develop their own style?

3. List the similarities between ancient Roman and modern cities. Is there any significant difference that has not been caused by railway trains or automobiles?

4. What are the modern equivalents of the Circus Maximus? Why was the Circus Maximus so large?

5. What differences are there between Augustus' rebuilding programme and the normal rebuilding that constantly goes on in our cities?

6. Look at the plan of Rome on page 17: why was there only one bridge over the Tiber until 179 BC?

7. What could have made it necessary for Julius Caesar to build a new forum (and for later emperors to build four more)?

8. Was it sensible for Julius Caesar to ban wheeled traffic, except for builders' wagons, from Rome in daylight? What was good or bad about this ban?

Chapter 5   *The History of the Success and Failure of the Republic*

1. Make a list of the powers and responsibilities of the Senate in the second century BC.

2. Imagine that you are a farmer, trying to make a living from your small farm in the years after Hannibal's defeat. What are the threats to your way of life?

3. You are a conservative senator, living at the time of Sulla (p. 49). Write a letter to the dictator urging him to restore full powers to the Senate, giving your reasons and identifying all the Senate's enemies.

4. Julius Caesar is the most famous of all Romans in the Republican period. Why is his name so well known, and what lasting achievements does he have to his credit?

5. The Ides of March: find out about the way that Romans organized the days of the month in their calendar (see also p. 144), and how they wrote the dates.

6. Read the inscription (p. 54) recording Augustus' achievements. Can you imagine a modern monarch, president or prime minister making similar claims? What changes would you make in the text if you were in power?

Chapter 6   *Imperium: How Rome Acquired and Governed Its Empire*

1. How could Rome acquire territory 'by accident' (p. 57)?

2. Trace any parallels you can find between the growth of Rome's Empire 270 BC–AD 180 and the development of the British Empire in the eighteenth and nineteenth centuries.

3. List any examples you know of cruelty by conquering nations. Have matters improved this century, and what rules exist to prevent such excesses?

4. Find a translation of Tacitus' *Agricola*, and read Chapter 21, and the speech of Calgacus in Chapters 30–4. Then compose a short speech by a leading provincial complaining about the corruption of Rome's rule. Next write an answer, from an honourable Roman governor, setting out the advantages of living in a province of Rome's Empire.

Chapter 7   *Roads*

1. Do you find anything surprising about the map of the roads in the Roman empire?

2. Who decides whether new roads should be built today?

3. Find out who pays for the construction and upkeep of modern roads and bridges.

4. Could the Romans have spread their civilization without building roads? Are good roads essential for modern civilization?

5. Do the motorways and roads of modern developed countries waste land that could be better used for other purposes?

6. What are modern equivalents of *cursus publici* and *mansiones*?

Chapter 8   *Growing Up*

1. Find out what you can about 'coming of age' in the modern world, and the form it takes in different societies. What are the main differences?

2. Compare the education of a young Roman boy or girl from a wealthy family with your own. List some similarities and differences.

3. How many of Quintilian's ideas about teaching do you agree with?

4. At every stage of Roman education, great emphasis was placed on speaking and oral exercises. Why?

5. Compare the attitudes of Romans towards marriage with those of modern societies throughout the world. What do the various wedding ceremonies have in common?

6. How restricted were women's lives in Roman times? What influence could women exert?

7. Compare Roman funeral rituals with their modern equivalents. Why do you think that the Romans attached so much importance to their ancestors at this time?

Chapter 9   *A Politician's Progress*

1. Why was the ability to speak well in public so important to an ambitious young Roman?

2. It was very hard to become a consul without having a consul among your ancestors. Why should this be, and what does it tell you about Roman society?

3. Re-read the advice Quintus Cicero gave to his brother Marcus. What does it tell you about Roman politics?

4. The early emperors allowed no one outside the imperial family to hold a triumph. Can you think of any reasons for this?

Chapter 10   *Writing and Writers*

1. What were the main differences between a Roman *volumen* and a modern book? What impact did this have on the design (and size) of libraries?

2. Make a list of other love-poets whose poems you know. Why have poems been used so often to express loving feeling?

3. What does Lucretius mean when he writes about 'being high up in Reason's calm temple, protected by the teaching of wise men . . .' (p. 93)?

4. Compare the security arrangements described by Cicero (p. 95) with their modern equivalents at a Summit meeting, for example.

5. Find out how fast the post travelled at the beginning of the last century, and compare the time a letter takes to reach a correspondent in Rome today.

6. Read what you can about Caesar's two invasions of Britain. How successful were they?

7. What reasons can you think of to explain the remarkable flourishing of Roman literature and culture, at the time of its greatest political crisis and civil war?

Chapter 11   *The First Emperors*

1. Re-write the quotation from Tacitus at the beginning of the chapter as you imagine Tacitus would have done if he had approved of Augustus.

2. Why did the Senate and people acquiesce in the transfer of power to Tiberius on Augustus' death, and not try to recover it for themselves?

3. List the good and bad points of the rule of the first four emperors: do the good points outweigh the bad?

4. Why was Nero's behaviour so outrageous, and why was he able to get away with it for so long?

5. Do you think the speech quoted by Tacitus (on p. 104) is a fair summary of Roman rule?

6. Find out as much as you can about Pompeii. How would life in it compare with life in your town or city today? Would the citizens of Pompeii be any less happy than we are? (Remember that they would not miss modern inventions they did not know about.)

7. The burning of books by Domitian's agents has had more than one parallel throughout history. How many can you discover? Can such repressive measures ever stamp out freedom of speech and thought for long?

Chapter 12   *Imperial City*

1. Why do you think no one before Augustus had set up a system of *vigiles?*

2. Do Nero's actions to promote the re-building of Rome after the Great Fire seem good or bad? Could he have done more?

3. What do you think would be good or bad about living in Timgad?

4. Write a letter to an imaginary Roman friend, describing a day spent in the *thermae* of Caracalla.

5. Is there anything surprising about the statistics of the survey carried out by Constantine (p. 109)? Think of a city of comparable size near you.

6. Try to find a translation of Seneca's Letters, e.g. Seneca: *Letters from a Stoic*, Penguin: read Letter 7, then either, write a similar letter to a friend, justifying, or condemning, the games in the Colosseum, or discuss: 'Can anything justify the performances put on in the Colosseum?' Bear in mind our own society's enjoyment of bloodsports like hunting and shooting, and the popularity of violent contact sports like boxing.

Chapter 13 *Work and Slaves*

1. What can we learn from Pompeii and other archaeological sites about the economic life of the Roman world?

2. Write a short extract from a speech, modelled on p. 125, commending a local store for the range of its foreign goods.

3. Find out about three explorers since ancient times who set out to discover new trade routes. Where did they travel?

4. Look up all the Indian commodities, mentioned on p. 127, whose names you do not know.

5. How might a person become a slave?

6. Find out about the conditions of slaves in the southern states of America, and the slave trade of the eighteenth and nineteenth centuries. What differences are there between these 'modern' slaves and their Roman predecessors? On what grounds do you consider slavery wrong?

7. Imagine that you are the literate slave of a kind master. Write a letter to a fellow slave defending the idea of slavery, in the light of your experience.

Chapter 14 *Every Day*

1. List the differences between the daily life of Roman men and women and men and women of today.

2. What are the advantages and disadvantages of shaving?

3. Does any part of a Roman lady's make-up and dress seem desirable today?

4. What can women and girls do today that was denied to their Roman counterparts?

5. If you were transported back to Roman times, what modern food would you miss? Is there any part of Roman diet which you would like?

6. Find out what you can about the daily routine of life last century, before the invention of gas-lighting or electricity. Was it significantly different from Roman daily life?

7. How far would Roman lifestyles have been possible without slaves?

8. Several emperors had to issue decrees to enforce the wearing of togas on public occasions. Why do you think they did so? Can you see any advantage in wearing the toga?

9. Would all Romans have had the long dinners – over three hours – that Pliny thought were essential?

Chapter 15   *Entertainment*

1. What are your views about the pattern of the Roman day?

2. Why did so many Emperors build baths, at great expense?

3. Compare Roman 'holidays' with our own. How many days per year does an average worker have as holidays? Should you count weekends?

4. What are advantages (and disadvantages) of the 'working week'?

5. What do you think is the difference between comedy and farce?

6. Imagine that you are a gladiator, who has fought successfully for many years in the *munera*. What are your thoughts as you prepare for the contest which may lead to the wooden sword?

7. What made the chariot races so popular?

Chapter 16   *Literary Legacy*

1. Why did the countryside and the lives of country people play such an important part in Virgil's *Eclogues* and *Georgics*?

2. Find out all you can about Homer. In what ways does Virgil's *Aeneid* adapt the stories and themes of Homer's epics? What do you understand by the word 'epic'?

3. What sort of debt did Rome's writers owe to the writers of ancient Greece?

4. 'It was difficult to write unbiased history under the first emperors.' Explain Tacitus' reasons for making this claim.

5. Read Pliny's description of Vesuvius' eruption again. Show how Pliny's writing fills in the gaps left by archaeologists.

6. What do you understand by the word 'satire'?

7. 'Books passed increasingly into the hands of the Christian Church.' Why did this happen?

8. What great fifteenth-century invention ensured that all the texts that had survived the Dark Ages and medieval period would remain until today?

Chapter 17 *Gods and Men*

1. Find out about the beliefs of St Francis of Assisi. How did his attitude to nature compare with that of the early Romans?

2. What is your opinion about sacrifices? Why was it important for every detail to be correct?

3. Mars, once god of the fields, eventually became god of war. Why did this change take place? (See also Chapter 1 and p. 18.)

4. What influence did Greeks have on the religious beliefs of the Romans?

5. Examine the Romans' superstitious belief in omens. Give some modern examples. Do you believe in them? If so, why?

6. P. Claudius Pulcher and Cicero, as reported on p. 166, had major reservations about traditional belief in augury and omens, but they would still attend sacrifices. Why?

7. In your own words explain the main differences between the philosophy of the Epicureans and that of the Stoics.

8. How much truth is there in astrology? Do you read *your* stars?

9. Rome was very open-minded about new cults. Why then were the early Christians often hated and even persecuted?

Chapter 18 *Provinces*

1. 'They enjoyed greater peace and prosperity than ever before or since.' Make two lists of the benefits and disadvantages of life in Rome's provinces during the second century AD.

2. Can you see any advantages for living in the Roman empire rather than in your own country now?

3. What do you think Pliny was like, judging from the series of letters quoted on p. 174 – 'a fussy old man, unable to make up his own mind', or 'a sensible administrator, properly seeking guidance from the central administration'?
(Book 10 of Pliny's letters, available in many translations, offers much more evidence.)

4. Do you think the Romans were right to encourage the building of towns in new provinces?

5. The move from the countryside into towns is still continuing in the modern world: is this inevitable? Is urban life in any way inferior to rural life?

Chapter 19   *Army*

1. Why do you think the Senate never organized the soldiers' pay and conditions of service so as to secure the loyalty of the legions to the state, rather than to their general?

2. How did Augustus encourage the *esprit de corps* of his legions?

3. Why was soldiers' pay so small?

4. Imagine you are a legionary soldier after one year's service in the legion based at Caerleon; write a letter – the first you have sent – to your father in Rome telling him of your experiences.

5. Find out how a *ballista* worked, and what provided its power.

6. What advantages and disadvantages do you think there were in having soldiers serve in the country of their birth?

Chapter 20   *From Order to Chaos*

1. Discuss the quotation from Edward Gibbon on p. 193, producing evidence from your reading to support or deny it.

2. Assess the importance of the Praetorian Guard in the history of the Empire.

3. Compare the different steps taken by Julia Mamaea and Diocletian to restore order to the Empire.

4. Diocletian's harsh measures worked: what disadvantages must have followed from them?

5. An ordinary soldier and a farm labourer earned much the same. In Domitian's day a soldier was paid 300 *denarii* a year, and a farm labourer's pay was fixed at 25 *denarii* a day by Diocletian. Work out what annual rate of inflation this represents.

Further Reading

1.   MORE DETAILED GENERAL BOOKS

R. Barrow, *The Romans*, Penguin
Cambridge Ancient History, vols VIII–XI, CUP
T. Cornell and J. Matthews, *Atlas of the Roman World*, Phaidon
M. Crawford, *Roman Republic*, Fontana
B. Cunliffe, *Rome and her Empire*, Bodley Head
D. Dudley, *Roman Society*, Penguin
             The Romans, Hutchinson
M. Grant, *History of Rome*, Weidenfeld & Nicolson
             World of Rome, Cardinal
N. Lewis and M. Reinhold, *Roman Civilization: A Sourcebook*, 2 vols, Harper and Row
   Torchbooks
Oxford Classical Dictionary, OUP
Oxford Companion to Classical Literature, OUP
Oxford History of the Classical World, OUP
H. Scullard, *History of the Roman World, 753–146 AD*, Methuen
             From the Gracchi to Nero, Methuen
R. Syme, *The Roman Revolution*, OUP
J. Wells, *The Roman Empire*, Fontana

2.   BOOKS ON SPECIFIC TOPICS

Early Rome:

P. Connolly, *Hannibal and the Enemies of Rome*, Macdonald
M. Grant, *The Etruscans*, Weidenfeld & Nicholson
R. Ogilvie, *Early Romans and the Etruscans*, Fontana

Towns and Cities:

P. Connolly, *Pompeii*, MacDonald
B. Cunliffe, *Fishbourne: A Roman Palace and its Gardens*, Thames & Hudson
D. Dudley, *Urbs Roma*, Phaidon
M. Grant, *Cities of Vesuvius*, Weidenfeld & Nicholson
             The Roman Forum, Thames & Hudson
M. Hadas, *Imperial Rome*, Time-Life
A. McKay, *Houses, Villas and Palaces in the Roman World*, Thames & Hudson
E. Nash (ed.) *Pictorial Dictionary of Ancient Rome*, Hacker

Daily Life:

J. Balsdon, *Life and Leisure in Ancient Rome*, Bodley Head
                Roman Women, Bodley Head
P. Brunt, *Social Conflicts in the Roman Republic*, Chatto
J. Carcopino, *Daily Life in Ancient Rome*, Penguin
F. Cowell, *Everyday Life in Ancient Rome*, Batsford/Carousel
L. Dell' Orto, *Ancient Rome, Life and Art*, Summerfield
B. Flower and E. Rosenbaum, *Apicius – The Roman Cookery Book*, Harrap
M. Massey, *Women in Ancient Greece and Rome*, CUP
U. Paoli, *Rome, its People, Life and Customs*, Longman

Literature:

R. Ogilvie, *Roman Literature and Society*, Penguin
The *Penguin Classics* in translation

Education:

R. Bonner, *Education in Ancient Rome*, Methuen
E. Castle, *Ancient Education and Today*, Penguin
H. Marrou, *History of Education in Antiquity*, University of Wisconsin Press

Technology:

P. Green, *Roman Technology and Crafts*, Longman
L. and J. Hamey, *Roman Engineers*, CUP
J. Landels, *Engineering in the Ancient World*, Chatto and Windus

Art and Architecture:

M. Henig, *Handbook of Roman Art*, Phaidon
D. Macauley, *City. A Story of Roman Planning and Construction*, Collins
M. Wheeler, *Roman Art and Architecture*, Thames & Hudson
S. Woodford, *History of Art, Greece and Rome*, CUP

Work and Travel:

R. Chevallier, *Roman Roads*, Batsford
C. Mossé, *The Ancient World at Work*, Chatto and Windus
M. Finley, *The Ancient Economy*, Chatto and Windus

Sports, Games and Entertainment:

M. Grant, *Gladiators*, Penguin
K. McLeish, *Roman Comedy*, Macmillan

Religion and Philosophy:

R. Ogilvie, *The Romans and Their Gods*, Chatto and Windus

The Army:

P. Connolly, *The Roman Army*, Macdonald
G. Webster, *The Roman Imperial Army*, A. & C. Black
J. Wilkes, *The Roman Army*, CUP

Roman Britain:

A. Birley, *Life in Roman Britain*, Batsford
R. Collingwood and R. Wright, *Roman Inscriptions of Britain*, OUP
S. Frere, *Britannia*, Routledge
I. Margary, *Roman Roads in Britain*, Baker
A. Rivet, *Town and Country in Roman Britain*, Hutchinson
P. Selway, *Roman Britain*, OUP
G. Tingay, *From Caesar to the Saxons*, Longman
J. Toynbee, *Art in Roman Britain*, Phaidon
R. Wilson, *Roman Remains in Britain*, Constable
Ordnance Survey Map of Roman Britain, HMSO

The following series contain useful information about many aspects of life in the Roman world.

Longman – *Aspects of Roman Life*
Allen & Unwin – *Greek and Roman Topics*
Macmillan – *Inside the Ancient World*
Shire Publications
British Museum Publications

3.   NOVELS

J. Arden, *Silence Among The Weapons*, Methuen
P. Bentley, *Freedom Farewell*, Victor Gollancz
L. Douglas, *The Robe*, P. Davies
R. Graves, *I, Claudius*, Penguin
          Claudius The God, Penguin
P. Green, *The Sword of Pleasure*, John Murray
M. Machado, *In Caesar's Shadow*
N. Mitchison, *The Conquered*, Jonathan Cape
R. Sutcliff, *The Eagle of the Ninth*, Puffin/Penguin
          The Lantern Bearers, Puffin/Penguin
          Outcast, OUP
          The Silver Branch, Puffin/Penguin
R. Warner, *Young Caesar*, Collins
          Imperial Caesar, Collins

INDEX

This index makes no pretence of being complete. Incidental references to names or places are not listed, and it is presumed that anyone seeking information about legionary organization or the *auxilia*, for example, will refer to the chapter on The Army.